From EDEN To PARADISE

Something Stronger Than Time

An Autobiography by
John Stuart Gilbert

A Father's Reflections by
Bruce Stuart Gilbert

From Eden To Paradise
Something Stronger Than Time
An Autobiography by John Stuart Gilbert A Father's Reflections by Bruce Stuart Gilbert

Printed in the United States of America

ISBN 9781624192869

Note: While the earliest biblical manuscripts, as well as most Bible translations, do not capitalize personal pronouns referencing God, some writers have chosen to do so in an effort to honor and express reverence for Father, Son, and Holy Spirit. Others have chosen not to do so in an effort to be consistent both with the original text and standards of English grammar. Because the authors of this effort, as well as quoted others, have individual preferences in this matter, the reader may notice an inconsistency in the use of such pronouns. We trust that these individual preferences will not be a distraction.

www.xulonpress.com

Contents

PART ONE

FROM EDEN TO PARADISE

Something Stronger Than Time

PART TWO

A FATHER'S REFLECTIONS

In The Middle of A Thousand Nights

Part One

From Eden to Paradise

Something Stronger Than Time

John Stuart Gilbert

This effort is dedicated to . . .

Alan Robert Gilbert

Who in John's words is . . .

"The only person who ever lit up my heart
just because you entered the room."

In a town called Paradise, California lived a young man named John Gilbert. I like to think of him as a friend of mine, though we've never met. When he was five years old, John was diagnosed with Duchenne muscular dystrophy. It is a genetic, progressive, and cruel disease. He was told it would eventually destroy every muscle and finally, in a space of ten more years or so, take his life.

John passed away a short while ago at the age of twenty-five. Toward the end of his life. . .he had only enough strength to move a computer mouse with his right hand. But he did that brilliantly. He sent me a manuscript of the story of his life that is one of the most moving pieces I have ever read.

~ John Ortberg
Pastor, Menlo Park Presbyterian Church

Foreword

"... and The Light shone in the darkness
and the darkness never overcame it."

This is one of my very favourite concepts. Darkness never overcomes light, but light always scatters darkness. The life of my dear friend John Gilbert was a constant illustration of this wonderfully liberating truth.

When I first saw him, John was sitting in his wheelchair in the aisle of a church in Paradise, California. His fifteen year old body was undersized and already seriously distorted as he had by then suffered for ten years with Duchenne muscular dystrophy. I went over to him with the intention of cheering him up. His radiant smile, quick humour and breadth of knowledge soon blew away any ideas I had that I might be the giver and he the receiver.

It was to be my delight to know John for ten years before he left his increasingly frail shell and moved on into real life. Much of this connection was by email, but I had the blessing of staying in his home for a week on three or four occasions.

Paul tells us that day by day our physical body decays but our "inward man" is renewed by the Holy Spirit. This was demonstrated in John at each opportunity I had to connect with him, but not only in John. Caring for him was a huge physical and emotional burden which was accepted with enormous grace by his parents, Bruce and Cathy. John's younger brother Alan completed the family and might have resented the attention John needed just to survive, yet such was the presence of God and the strengths which He gives to those who lean on Him that the overall impression was always one of love and faith showing brightly against a dark background with hope and joy breaking through any threatening gloom.

John's anticipation of his death is one of the most beautiful and exhilarating passages I have read. It makes great reading for anyone who has doubts about the character of God or about their own future.

It is a great privilege to be asked to write this foreword, and it is my sincere hope that many will read John's story and discover the hope and thrill of knowing John's Jesus.

~ Ken Needham
Ballymartin, County Down
Northern Ireland

Introduction

Wouldn't it be wonderful to generate an original thought—one that was destined to help someone; an idea, an invention, maybe a perspective that was novel and fresh and would solve old problems, or perhaps shed light on new ones?

New thoughts like that happen all the time. These days I suppose they're mostly about science and technology; good enough. However, I suspect there are precious few fresh thoughts relative to love, or kindness, or character. Those have been thought and said.

It's left for the rest of us to own them.

§

I have a son named John. And while he currently resides in the very real presence of God, I claim him with confidence in the present tense.

During the last year of his life, John wrote a manuscript—page after page of experience, insight, and wisdom was crafted into an autobiography with a constricted right hand whose only remaining function was to lightly grip a computer mouse one click, one letter at a time. With the exception of a bright mind and a knowing smile, that was all that was left of a twenty-five year old body that had withered and yielded to dystrophic devastation; a body that had progressively become uncooperative with the desires of a young boy's heart.

John presented his manuscript to Cathy and me in April of 2002. He died June 3, 2002 at a quarter past midnight.

John wrote beautifully, candidly, and inspiringly of his life. He nakedly shared his dreams and fears, his hope and desperation, his imagination and his reality. Neither John's effort, nor that which follows in the form of fatherly reflections, is the polished work of a seasoned author. We are not elite scholars with recognizable names and impeccable credentials from prestigious universities. Neither is there anything "cool" about this work (a young man named Paul Grant wrote a book titled *Blessed Are The Uncool* [1] ~ John would have liked that!). Rather, these are the personal reflections of a dying boy, often simple and imperfect, often profound and insightful.

§

John was diagnosed with Duchenne muscular dystrophy on his fifth birthday. We were told his life expectancy was sixteen years; he lived to be twenty-five. Well before the time came, and too long after it passed, I had convinced myself that I was both emotionally and theologically prepared for John's death.

Tomorrow it will have been ten years since John left this earth. I have proudly (and foolishly) maintained my "prepared" position . . . until recently.

I don't know when it began. Perhaps it was the day his heel cords were surgically severed to stop the grotesque contractions. Maybe it was the day his service dog Friedman died, or the accumulation of having watched helplessly as John suffered in too many ICU's. Most likely it's associated with the emotional abuse he suffered at the hands of cruel schoolmates, or the residual wounds left in the wake of family members who seemingly dismissed his passing. In any case, my long established surrender to God's sovereignty somehow began to morph into a silent, growing, and insidious resentment. Not against God; I've never questioned God. Yet somehow *in my own sin* I learned to associate the human imperfections of those around me with the hideous Satan-sponsored sufferings my son had born far too long.

For years now I have often been startled with sudden and uninvited images of John's physical and emotional torment. Without warning I've been seized with regret at missed opportunities to have loved him better, to have somehow better eased his loneliness, to have made him laugh just a little more. From out of nowhere I find myself waylaid by a sadness that he'd never been kissed by a special girl. Occasionally I am ambushed by the vision of his body bag being wheeled from our home in the middle of the night. The grace and peace offered by a kind and loving God must find a willing recipient. I have not always done that well.

It's a strange thing. A life of growing joy and contentment is too often undermined by a subtly festering sadness, bitterness, even anger—an insistent yet often imperceptible enemy in that it tempts with a false and inappropriate sense of power over that which I've had no hope of controlling or resolving. The antithesis of the calm and peace and stillness I've so desperately sought—an appropriation of the 'easy yoke'—the enemy has harmed my soul. But, in its addiction it has masked itself as a valued friend capable of keeping John near me so that I might continue to fight the unwinnable battle on his behalf. What father does not instinctually protect his child?

The thing is, calm and peace and stillness, while too often elusive, *really are* available, but never through sadness, bitterness, or anger; only through surrender. These conditions of the soul are Scripture's promise; but just like Jesus they must be received, appropriated, owned.

The irony, of course, is that our son no longer needs protection. John—his repentance genuine, his obedience faithful—is quite alive, living vibrantly in an extraordinarily mysterious reality in the very real presence of God. Now his faith has indeed become a conscious awareness of a heavenly reality. Though my humanness has so often denied it, John does not need me any longer.

I have never said, or thought, or written those words until this very moment. They are heart-breaking—and cathartic. *He doesn't need me...*

> What sadness that brings in its reality.
> What freedom and joy that brings in its reason.

§

John's manuscript was an effort to share his story and perspectives with those who might be called to a similar journey—and with those whose lives would be marked by the suffering of loved ones, particularly children. Not long before John died he informed me with a rather uncharacteristic firmness that he had not written his story for it to sit on a shelf; rather that others might benefit from his life and perspectives. He asked me to ensure that it would make its way into as many hands as might find it of value. I assured him I would do my best.

However, *I have not done my best.*

Rather, the best I can conclude is that I must have unconsciously believed that by hoarding his writings I could somehow keep him close—and continue to protect him, of course. And, by delaying the fulfillment of my promise I always had something to look forward to, like keeping your fork for the dessert that was yet to come—a project we could do *together*. Silly, I know; and not particularly healthy. Nevertheless, now a decade later I've come to understand the danger and selfishness in delaying the fulfillment of my commitment. It's time to release John's thoughts to as many as might find value in them, and in so doing better appropriate the hope, peace and grace that's been available all along.

As for me, my desire is that *Reflections* will compliment *Eden*; that the anecdotes shared and the perspectives offered might illuminate the integrity and character that marked John's life and gave him hope. My desire is that as you read John's story and my reflections that follow, you too will find confidence in anticipation of *something stronger than time*.

Proudly John's Dad
~ Bruce Gilbert

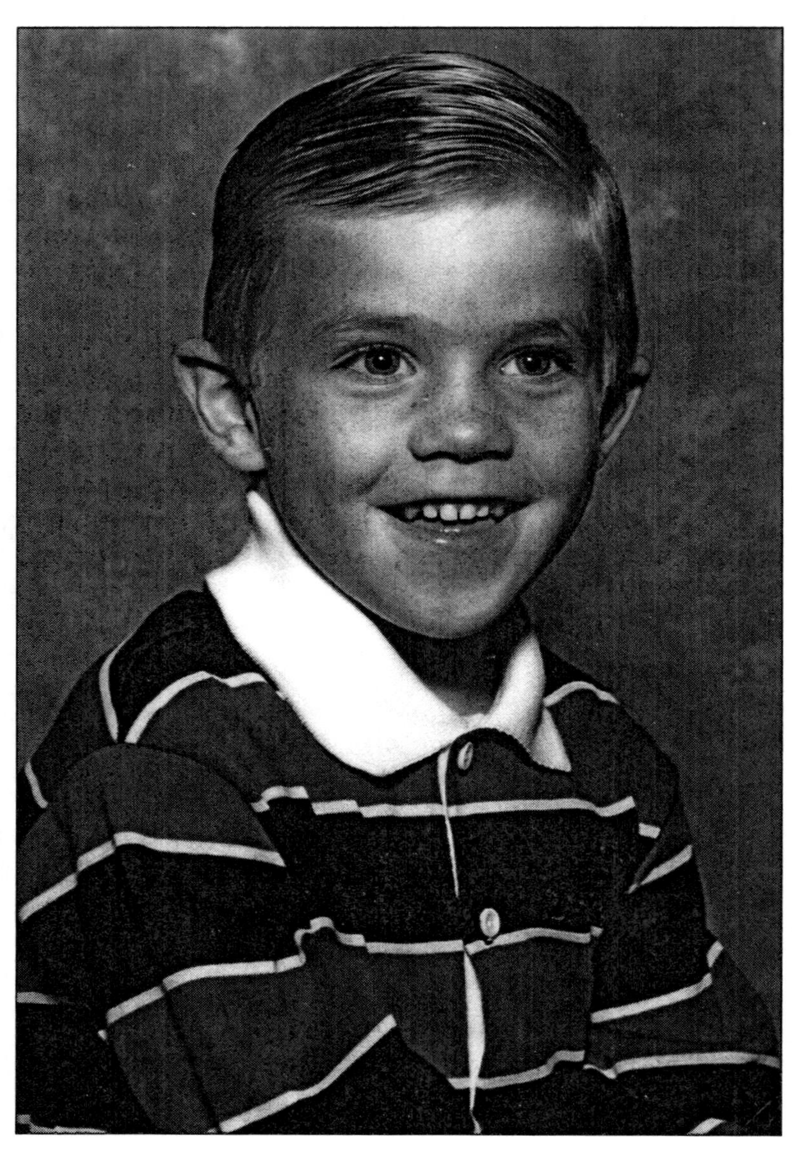

John

Preface

From Eden to Paradise

I was born in a hospital called Eden and will spend the rest of my days in a town called Paradise. The road in between is filled with bruises and hard lessons. On the road to the town of Paradise there are empty fields covered in rocks and thorny grass. On the side there are treacherous cliffs that dive down straight from the roadside. Those cliffs form the nearside of a canyon with a stream running down its center. You can see for miles up the canyon into the mountains beyond.

Most of the year the grass is a dull yellow and the beauty of the landscape is hard to appreciate. But for a season the rain turns the whole landscape into a multi-colored portrait. Wildflowers bloom and even the sky takes on a deeper shade of blue that makes you want to soar like the hawks that float on the currents of air formed by the cliffs. But the season changes and the grasses wither once again.

My life is much the same. There are rocky fields and dangerous cliffs. For a short season things are brighter but it quickly ends. But one thing is certain. The road called Skyway always leads home.

~ John Gilbert

"I'm Writing These Words While I Still Can"

For you created my inmost being;
    you knit me together in my mother's womb.
I praise you because I am fearfully and wonderfully made;
    your works are wonderful,
    I know that full well.
My frame was not hidden from you
    when I was made in the secret place.
When I was woven together in the depths of the earth,
    your eyes saw my unformed body.
All the days ordained for me
    were written in your book
    before one of them came to be.
How precious to me are your thoughts, God!
    How vast is the sum of them!
Were I to count them,
    they would outnumber the grains of sand —
    when I awake, I am still with you.

~ David
Psalm 139:13-18

CHAPTER ONE

As a child I was a great fan of C.S. Lewis. I often dreamed of having been born into a world full of magic and mystery. I imagined that, just maybe there was another universe out there where a child's fantasy was the only true reality. Maybe if I was just lucky enough to find the right portal through time and space I could find that world and meet God in the shape of a lion. However, our world is the only reality I have ever known, except for those precious moments in the pages of thrilling novels and science fiction shows.

This reality has not been especially kind to me. I was born with a destructive genetic disease. The world has given this condition a name that doesn't seem to capture its essence to me. It is simply named Duchenne muscular dystrophy after a French doctor who identified it as something different than other diseases. I have read that in his studies he was shocked at the amount of damage done to muscle tissue by what we now know to be the absence of one critical protein. But the longer I live the more I find out that physical destruction is only half the battle. There is no wardrobe or starship to take me away from here. There is no way out; is there? If this is not the ultimate fantastic voyage, and if there were no passage to another world, I would not have lived my life as I did.

Through my whole life, and even before it began, there has been a kind of gravity pulling me in one direction. This story has been told over and over again in every generation. Long ago it was recorded in the lives of several generations of God's people in the text we know as the Bible. You need only look at Hebrews 11 for a brief outline. It is a story of a world that is out of control. In such a world it seems that circumstances conspire to do evil in the life of a human whose ancestors were cast out and made the lowest and saddest form of life in the universe. There is nothing sadder than a creature that has forgotten its great potential. But God, in his unfathomable love, reached down and pulled some of those individuals out of their misery.

Kinship With Joseph

One of my favorite stories is the story of Joseph. I remind myself often of his life because I feel a certain sense of kinship there. Certainly not every circumstance in his life relates to mine, but I feel that the themes are similar. When Joseph was young he was badly bruised by how cruel the world can be. His own brothers hated him and sent him into slavery. I'm thrilled to say that isn't true in my case because my brother has often helped me out of sticky situations, not put me into them. However, the world can hate everyone in different ways, both intentionally and unintentionally.

It seemed nothing could go right for Joseph for a long time. Many people count God out when things turn ugly in their lives. Others realize they can't help but count Him in. The latter was Joseph's choice and was mine as well. God honored his choice by lifting him up, dusting him off, and using him and his unique gifts. Joseph became the envy of the same brothers, and the same world, that cast him down.

God lifts up the people the world thinks it can't use. As Joseph said to his brothers, "You intended to harm me, but God intended it for good." (Genesis 50:20).

> *This is how the world has left me. Broken and emotionally charred with only my mind to hold on to. I am thankful at least that is left unscathed.*

Present Realities

But what does that same world think of me? Those who know the uplifting God see me the same way He sees me. I am always grateful for their support and love through all the seasons of life. Many others have also been friends and done great things to show their care. When I speak, admittedly harshly, of a hating world, I speak of a land of sin and unfairness that, because of a random accident, left me afflicted for no apparent good reason. I don't think ill of the people who dwell in that land with me. An error occurred in the creation of my body. Only a few molecules didn't come out quite right, but it is amazing what a few misplaced atoms can do to a person.

I am writing these very words while I still can. After nearly twenty-five years of slow degeneration, there is just enough strength left in my right hand and arm to use a computer mouse. Everything else, even the basic life giving function of breathing has to be assisted by machines and other people. This typing that I'm doing, with a special laptop computer and onscreen mouse-driven keyboard, is one of the very last things I can do without help. I don't think most writers would tell you that much of the end of a story at the very beginning, but I thought you should know where things stand. Besides, at the end you will find that this information isn't really going to be the end after all.

This is how the world has left me. Broken and emotionally charred with only my mind to hold on to. I am thankful at least that is left unscathed. Some others have not been so blessed. With me the world was told it could only go so far and no farther, although physically I see no hope and no way out. I am like a prisoner of my own flesh. I place little hope in what this world has to offer. In my case the doctors, as much as I know they care, are like lawyers who have argued as best they could but received no leniency from the local officials. My only hope is a reprieve from some distant ruler. This world is like a country with unjust laws and filled with corrupt officials who seem to be easily bribed.

End Of The Story?

If that were the end of my story I would not have written it. There would be no purpose in it. There are enough books in the world about all the suffering in it without me adding to them. You see, I believe that distant ruler does exist and He has already signed an official pardon with my name on it. The postal service has just been a little slow in delivering the message to the warden.

So what choices are left to me? I could look at the world around me, the people and things I see every day, and choose to be resentful because I don't see why I should be so much worse off than anyone else. But that would only hurt me more. Or I can choose something better, something that has worked over and over again for others.

I find myself in a typical quandary. As invariably happens, I can't improve on Scripture, so I will simply adopt the wisdom of Hebrews' author. At the beginning of Chapter 11 he writes this:

> Now faith is being sure of what we hope for and certain of what we do not see. This is what the ancients were commended for.
>
> Hebrews 11:1-2

He continues by listing the great faith of so many great heroes of the Bible. He lifts up men and women from Abel to Moses as examples for the point he is about to make. Towards the end of the list I can picture him getting out of breath because there are so many! But then he says this:

> All these people were still living by faith when they died. They did not receive the things promised; they only saw them and welcomed them from a distance, admitting that they were foreigners and strangers on earth. People who say such things show that they are looking for a country of their own.
>
> Instead, they were longing for a better country – a heavenly one. Therefore God is not ashamed to be called their God, for he has prepared a city for them.
>
> Hebrews 11:13, 14, 16

There is a better world out there and it is easy to find, you only have to ask for it. All of the faithful people the author listed had their own stories of rocky desert roads that they followed.

§

You are about to read one such story through the eyes of someone who lived it, and perhaps in doing so you will find the way towards living it yourself. We will now start at the beginning of my humble trek down the same old dusty road. I will show you the landmarks and obstacles along the way. Having gone through most of it already I admit that from the outset the road ahead is intimidating. But at the end we can look up and see the fading red light of the autumn sunset beckoning us on to a bright future. I have seen that sight before, and as the thin clouds encircled the horizon I could almost make out brilliant angels dancing on their edges. They know far better than I do what waits past that point where the sun casts its radiance over the high mountains on the other side of the valley. It is too dazzling to look at and even harder to understand. But the thought of it fills me with warm joy beyond the comprehension of my limited senses.

In The Beginning

The cords of death entangled me;
    the torrents of destruction overwhelmed me.
The cords of the grave coiled around me;
    the snares of death confronted me.

In my distress I called to the LORD,
    I cried to my God for help.
From his temple he heard my voice;
    my cry came before him, into his ears.

~ David
Psalm 18:4-6

CHAPTER TWO

The beginning of our own lives is always a mystery to us. All we can remember is what other people tell us. We are told of events from how our parents met to the day we were born but it seems like ancient history. We don't see the events that led to our existence any more clearly than the events beyond. But sometimes those things, once they are told to you, just seem to fit. You often discover that the greatest things in your life began in little and unexpected ways.

Look at the life of John the Baptist, the crazy guy in the desert who ate bugs - yes, the one I was named after. There is no way that Zacharias and Elizabeth could have known that they would, for one, even have a son. They could not have fathomed that his birth would be announced by the angel Gabriel, "who stands in the presence of God" (Luke 1:19). They could certainly not imagine that he would grow up to be the foretold prophet who would prepare the way for the coming of the long awaited Messiah. But God set everything in place long before John was born so that the right person would be in the right place at the right time.

My parents tell me that even before I was born they had definite dreams and plans for both their lives and those of their children. They would try to be even better parents than their own; a familiar story many seem to have in common. There is a story Dad tells when asked why he got started in the business he is in. People ask him that for many reasons. The answer he gives means a lot to me because of how those events shaped the kind of life I would have.

I was on the way and my dad was realizing that the field he was studying was not as interesting to him as he thought it would be. A friend got him an interview with a San Diego based corporation (Jack in the Box Restaurants) where he was hired and rose up the ladder until we were living in San Diego ourselves.

Eventually there was a great opportunity to start a new concept of Mexican food restaurants. This would have all led to a perfectly normal middle class American life. My parents would have provided all that life would require. The concept, however, was not very successful. It was then that life took a turn that no parents could anticipate or handle by themselves. It was a God sized problem that required God sized solutions.

FROM EDEN . . .

I was born on August 24, 1976 in Eden Hospital, Castro Valley, California. That hospital still stands tall in the middle of that valley. Just over the hills on the west you can see San Francisco Bay. Castro Valley is where all my grandparents lived and where my parents grew up. It used to be "in the country" I'm told, but is now as if part one massive East Bay city. We never really lived there ourselves, but it will always feel like a second home to me.

My first five years involved moving to San Diego and seeing my little brother Alan born there when I was three years old. Beyond that I can't share much more. I have vague images in my mind of birthday parties with fancy cakes Mom made in the shapes of "Big Bird" and other kiddie characters. The rest is jumbled.

In many ways my life as I've always known it really began when I was five years old. For as long as I had been walking my parents thought I just had a cute way of getting around. Physically I was slower than other kids, but it wasn't anything alarming. For whatever reason my parents decided one day to take me to a doctor to check me out. I guess as part of a thorough check-up the doctor decided to take a blood test too.

But It's Even More Than That

I don't have any memory of this day, but on my fifth birthday, August 24, 1981, the test results were given to my mom. There was one chemical in my blood that was off the scale and that told them all they needed to know. It was an indicator that something was very wrong with my body. I was diagnosed with Duchenne muscular dystrophy. It is a genetic disease that usually only affects boys. It is a progressive disease of the muscles, meaning it would slowly take away my strength and would destroy every muscle. I was given a life expectancy of sixteen years. My parents were also warned that I might have some mental problems as well.

> *Sure, I've lived; but every single day since then I'm confronted with the cold reality that I'm missing out on some of the best things in life.*

What was the reaction? I don't know how much or how soon I understood. I know my parents didn't hide anything from me because I feel like I've always known. I don't know what my initial reaction was, but I've had a long time to revisit every feeling I could ever have. How does a person handle a life sentence like that? How can I face the fact that my whole life was ripped away without mercy? Sure, I've lived; but every single day I'm confronted with the cold reality that I'm missing out on some of the best things in life.

It takes some thinking at first to realize the consequences of this. The only way to truly understand is for you adults and elderly folks to look back over your life and think of all you would have missed if it had ended when you were sixteen.

But it is even more than that. It isn't like you just suddenly get sick at sixteen. Those years you do live, your body allows you to do less and less. Here is an illustration. One year you can't run anymore so there is no way you can play sports with other kids. Another year you have great difficulty walking straight at all so going out to play involves just watching others. Eventually you are in a wheelchair so you can't go to the high school dances and feel normal. It involves a lot more but that should give you the idea. I've watched the simple things in life just blow away like dust in the wind.

> It doesn't really matter, I think, whether you are given twenty months or twenty years to live. Either way, something has been robbed from you and it is going to stare in your face, mocking you even when you try to close your eyes. These feelings are not easily lived with. It is the only reality I ever remember knowing.

But I was still given a choice about something.

Facing Reality

I have faced the ultimate reality of this world since that awful day. It is like someone with a megaphone in my head has always been declaring the same harsh news that God gave Adam: "For dust you are, and to dust you will return" (Genesis 3:19). You are going to die. Everyone is, I know, I know, just hear me out. It is just that I have never had the luxury of being able to put it out of my mind and live life to the fullest. Who is supposed to go through childhood with that fact constantly in the forefront? Every time my muscles won't do what I want them to I'm reminded.

But I still have at least some life to live. For that I need to be grateful. Some children are not even given that much. And with the life I'm given I still have a choice to make and questions to answer.

I was left with a choice over what perspective to view all this with. At first I didn't understand why this was allowed to happen to me. I still sometimes look down and I'm hit with the realization that this isn't just in my mind. It really happened and it happened *to me*.

My parents started us all on the right path that August day. We could have searched far and wide for the latest guru to sell us the magic cure. We didn't even have to search; some came looking for us. We could have read every self-help book written and tried to cope on our own. But the decision was made that this was all futile. We decided that the best way to live was to trust in God ~ come what may. This was crunch time and this was the choice we made. It wasn't a magic wand that suddenly made me feel better, but it did provide a quality road map that would make a difficult trip tolerable... maybe even better than that.

Childhood

He reached down from on high and took hold of me;
he drew me out of deep waters.
He rescued me from my powerful enemy,
from my foes,
who were too strong for me.
They confronted me in the day of my disaster,
but the LORD was my support.
He brought me out into a spacious place;
he rescued me because he delighted in me.

~ David
Psalm 18:16-19

CHAPTER THREE

---

§

With map in hand, my parents decided that the corporate high life was not the place for us. My dad returned to his old position with Jack in the Box but we moved north to Modesto to be closer to our family in the Bay Area. Modesto . . . that is the first town I remember living in clearly.

MEMORIES

I have a variety of memories living there. It is tough to decide where to begin. When we were there it seemed like an island surrounded by orchards on all sides. Everywhere I went there were endless rows of trees nearby. It was like living in a giant garden. My parents built us a house that was very unique. We had a swimming pool in the back, which was needed on hot summer days. There was a main road that connected a series of maybe four court-style streets. These courts all branched off from one side of the main street. On the other side were nothing but fields and orchards. Today there is nothing but houses.

I had several friends who lived in that neighborhood. In those days I could still walk and would just go out our door and visit them within a few minutes ~ how I'd love to have such freedom now. On occasion the quirky side of kids was a real source of comedy. One time a boy I knew came over to see if I could play. He kept chewing on an apple while he was talking to me. He didn't stop biting it to talk; he did both simultaneously. For some reason I couldn't go and I told him my parents would not let me. At that point the kid finished his apple and gave me the core, informing me I was being given the privilege of throwing it away for him. I walked past my parents, apple core in hand. They asked why I had it and rolled their eyes when I answered. That was just the kind of kid he was and I wasn't the kind to object, I guess. I don't remember his name, but "Old Weird Harold"[1] comes to mind.

There was another kid in our court who wasn't the same age as me. Ours was just a loose friendship that must have developed because we just happened to play in the same neighborhood. I remember his father had a business involving the old arcade video games. As a result there was always a spare one in his garage that didn't require money. My brother and I used to go over to the boy's house with the secret agenda of playing "Donkey Kong" or "Frogger" to our hearts' content. I know it wasn't very nice; I said kids are quirky. The sad thing is I don't ever remember seeing either of his parents around. I think he was alone a lot. I also wonder if the arcade games were there to give him something to do.

Another friend who lived down the street comes to mind. He and his family were Jewish. I only remember that because one day on the bus to school he and I were in the same two-person seat having a deep and interesting conversation. You know those plastic green seats that are supposed to look like leather? In the beginning of summer they got so hot, I would not have been surprised if I came home with a thick green coating on my back. Anyway, he and I were having a deep theological discussion on whether or not Jesus was the Messiah. We were going through the prophecies line by line. . . Okay, now I'm lying. The truth is we were yelling at each other in the midst of the school bus mayhem, "Yes he is!" "No he isn't!" "Yes he is!" "No he isn't!" I don't even know how the subject came up, but I hope my faith sharing abilities have improved since then.

It wasn't always a friendly neighborhood. My brother would probably rather I would not add this, but there were these two girls who bullied us once. They forced us into a portable toilet at a construction site and locked us in. When we finally got out we ran home as fast as we could. Actually, one of us did. Alan dusted me! My parents found the parents of the offending children and told them what happened. I vaguely remember the girls acting sweet and innocent in front of their parents, and blaming the whole thing on us.

My brother would probably rather I would not add this, but there were these two girls who bullied us once. They forced us into a portable toilet at a construction site and locked us in.

Another friendship I developed was with a boy who lived not too far away on his own family's farm. Visiting him was an adventure. To tell you the truth, he was kind of a know-it-all and I was so impressed that I believed almost everything he said! I remember going to his house and playing with all their animals in the orchard. There were all sorts of creatures to learn about. One time we got into the turkey pen. We just chased them all around and laughed at them. Those birds are so stupid. They didn't realize that two scrawny kids (one of which would not have even been able to run away) were no matches for creatures that had sharp beaks and claws within eye level. On second thought, maybe they were not the ones being stupid.

Brian

Now I come to my first "best" friend. I first met Brian on one of the first days of kindergarten. We were in the same class with a sweet elderly teacher named Mrs. Bjornson. Of course, I was only six or seven so she might have just seemed older to me. He and his family also went to the same church we did.

That day was going along as usual until something very frightening happened. The whole class found out that Brian had a severe case of diabetes when he suddenly had an attack in the middle of the day. This is engraved in my mind as one of those things I will always remember. It was frightening for everyone since everything just stopped and adults rushed to help him get some sugar in his system. If the adults were scared, imagine how confused a bunch of kindergarteners were.

After that we eventually became friends. Maybe even as young as we were we just knew we had something in common. We were just friends for a short couple of years. His father got a job somewhere else and we moved to Paradise very soon after. I often wish that had not happened so that I could have had a best friend all through school like so many people do. We wrote one or two letters back and forth but didn't keep it up and lost contact. But I'm getting ahead of myself. I'm trying to get *all* my memories down. I didn't realize how much I remember until I got started!

The School In The Orchard

I remember going to Stanislaus Union School for Kindergarten through second grade. It was a small school with probably one or two rooms per grade. It was surrounded on three sides by an orchard. The family of a girl in my classes owned the orchard; I remember it having walnuts. There was not even a fence between the trees and the field in back of the school. Rattlesnake holes were everywhere.

Because of my diagnosis, my mom had a little trouble getting me into a regular school. But she insisted that I was fully capable of going to a regular school as opposed to a special school for handicapped children. That was one of the best things my parents ever did for me. I would have wasted away in those places. I believe my first grade teacher insisted that I would not make it past the second grade. I can hear those of you who know me laughing, and I'm laughing too. Wouldn't it be sweet justice to send him my transcripts and say, "remember me?" No, that wouldn't be right. I just think it is amazing how people make judgments like that. I even recall being criticized by him along with my fellow students for not coloring inside the lines on a picture. As I remember it, I was trying to blend colors to make the picture look more realistic.

I remember that in the first grade I was often the one to walk with Brian down to the office where he would do his blood test every day. Sometimes we would use this time to contrive evil plots. Before a spelling test once, we schemed to put the correctly spelled words on hidden pieces of paper. Yes, I'm admitting to you that I cheated on a test. I did not do it very well though. I probably thought I was being so stealthy, but my teacher quickly noticed. I was caught but Brian wasn't. I had to sit in the hallway by myself for a time. The real punishment was that I felt so embarrassed and humiliated, even though it was just a ten or twelve word first-grade-level spelling test. I don't remember ever cheating on my schoolwork again.

One day during recess, I was riding a tricycle when I fell backwards onto the concrete pavement hitting my head.

The school nurse checked me out and determined I was fine, sending me home at the end of the day without informing my mom. When I got home I was very tired and my head still ached. My mom called the school, I think, and only then found out what happened. She also called a doctor. Though I did have a mild concussion, the damage wasn't permanent. Needless to say, my mom was pretty upset with the school for the way they handled the incident. She was always my strong advocate.

Another embarrassing time had to do with being manipulated by older kids. At the end of the school day, I went to the usual place to get on the bus that took me home. But before I got to my bus some older kids got into a conversation with me, and convinced me that the schedule had changed and that I was supposed to get on another bus. Well, gullible as I was, I did as I was told. Eventually I was the last child on the wrong bus, confused and very upset. The bus driver saw me and eventually coaxed my name out of me. He called in to his office and found out where I lived. I got home safe and sound, but as a little kid I got one more lesson on how mean the world can be.

Please don't get the impression that school was nothing but an education in hard knocks for me. Despite my first grade teacher's low expectations I quickly began to demonstrate that I really was capable. More than once I received a "Student of the Month" award from that school. The warning of possible mental difficulties was put to rest very soon. I remember the principal of the school would take a group of winners out to an ice cream parlor in town. I would have a special bubble gum ice cream that this place served. This may seem immodest, but I did enjoy being recognized for my achievements, partly because I intuitively knew I was never going to get trophies for things like sports victories. Is it wrong to want to be appreciated?

I don't really take the credit though. I really think this was all an answer to a prayer, the significance of which was not yet fully realized. There would be some tougher times ahead in different areas of my life. But as I look back, I'm thankful I had a time of childhood that was normal. I'm glad I had it all, good times and bad alike.

Family

Blessed are those who find wisdom,
    those who gain understanding,
For she is more profitable than silver
    and yields better returns than gold.
She is more precious than rubies;
    nothing you desire can compare with her.
Long life is in her right hand;
    In her left hand are riches and honor.
Her ways are pleasant ways,
    And all her paths are peace.
She is a tree of life to those who take hold of her;
    those who hold her fast will be blessed.

~ Solomon
Proverbs 3:13-18

CHAPTER FOUR

---

§

Some of the best times in my early childhood were spent with my grandparents. They all lived in Castro Valley where I was born. It was always an exciting trip when we were on our way to that town. We always had fun and I also learned a lot being with them.

GRAMMY & GRANDPA

Of course, we would divide the trip between my maternal and paternal grandparents' homes. That just meant twice the fun. Grammy and Grandpa, my dad's parents, lived in a little white house hidden on the side of busy Somerset Ave. It was on a hill, which caused the driveway and front yard to be very steep. When the road was widened the yard just got steeper and smaller. Add to that a hedge that my grandfather had personally trained for decades and you can picture a little old house that appeared to have sunk below the road.

It was a very small house but it didn't look that way when I was little. Every part of it seemed special to me. The front porch would creak when we walked up to the front door and that rough old metal screen door would swing open to hugs and kisses on the other side. We used to play in the backyard and on the side patio. There was a large vine that grew over a wooden support to give shade to part of the patio. My grandparents had hummingbird feeders, and if we waited long enough one would often come buzzing in. I also remember an outdoor thermometer that had a picture of a roadrunner on it.

My brother and I would always sleep in Dad's old bedroom. Every morning when I woke up I could hear Grandpa out in the dining room rustling his newspaper and whistling. He was always whistling. He was also always awake earlier than everybody else. I remember walking out to the dining room to see him in the same place. He would take us into the kitchen and give us toasted Thomas English Muffins for breakfast.

Grandpa also taught us fun songs and sayings. He would say, "Don't take any. . ." and we would finish it with ". . .wooden nickels." He also taught us what we called the "*Coney Island Song*." Alan and Grandpa and I made a great trio:

Good-bye my Coney Island baa-bee,
Farewell my own true love (two-three)
I'm gonna . . .
Sail away on a ferryboat,
Never to see you any (more) . . .
You can have the hat rack Annie.

Grammy was also fun to spend time with. I remember these toy blocks she made that had ribbons attached which chained the blocks together. The ribbons made the blocks flip around in a way that seemed to defy the laws of physics, as I knew them. Things like that kept me occupied for a long time.

One of the things I loved most about my grandparents was that they were not the kind of elderly folks who just sat around and complained all the time. More often, they complained about the complainers they found themselves sitting with in doctors' lobbies. They would often go on simple trips to just enjoy themselves. They knew how to enjoy the life they were given. It wasn't a glamorous one but it sure must have been better than what they had in their youth. Compared to what they grew up in, we lived in the lap of luxury. I was not ready to express this to them when they were still here, and I think they would rather I just lived this lesson rather than make a speech about it. They had a little sign with an Amish grandfather telling his grandson, "*Ve get too soon olt, und too late schmart!*"

> I want to say ~ Grammy and Grandpa taught me how to enjoy simpler things in life, from Red Skelton's humor to watching hummingbirds enjoy a little drink. I'm out of date it seems, but pop in a tape of Benny Goodman for my taste. I think it's just the greatest music America ever came up with! But more than that, despite how I may have acted as a kid, I learned from them that having the latest, greatest gadget and all the wealth in the world doesn't make you happy. If you have family, a home, and food, you're set with all you need. It's the people around you and the good clean fun you have with them that really put the luxury in your life.

GRANDMA & POP-POP

I also got to spend time with my mother's parents. Grandma and Pop-Pop lived in another neighborhood in the same town. They had another small but nice house in a pleasant cul-de-sac. We could walk from there to the Lutheran church my mom and her family went to. I have just as many loving memories with them as I do with Grammy and Grandpa.

Grandma has always been, in my mind, a quiet, servant-oriented person who was more comfortable in the background of life. When she would serve us breakfast she would often take the extra time to make cinnamon and sugar covered toast into a little house on our plates. She would not sit down until everyone was satisfied with a meal. At their house we often had something Italian to eat. Grandma was a Swede from Minnesota and Pop-Pop was Italian, which is quite a combination at mealtime. I don't ever remember being hungry there.

But I can only wish that I had been given a lot more time to get to know Pop-Pop. You see, I'm not the first in my family to be touched by a life-stealing disease. Pop-Pop had Parkinson's disease even before I was born. It just isn't fair that by the time I was old enough to know him well, the progression of his disease made that difficult. I do know the love he had for me and for all of his grandchildren. That is the most important thing.

Even though he was ill, there was never any question that Pop-Pop was in charge. When he was still living at home there was a day when my three cousins, Alan and I were all visiting at once . . . five grandsons! Well, in front of their house was a very high porch. I don't remember my involvement, but the group all decided it would be fun to jump off the porch over and over again. I think I knew I would break my nose if I participated, but I didn't mind watching. Inside, Pop-Pop found out about what we were up to, and let's just say it quickly came to a stop. He could barely talk and could not come out to stop what was going on, but it was very clear that he did not want this to continue!

When I was in the fifth grade, I believe, we had an assignment to do a biographical report on someone who had an impact on our life. With Grandma's help, I did my report on Pop-Pop. That way, I was able to get to know him better. He was the first of twelve children, six boys and six girls, of an immigrant Italian couple. They were fishermen by trade and settled in Santa Cruz. Many years later when I was little we could go to Fisherman's Wharf there, and upon making it known that we were a member of the Canepa clan we would be warmly welcomed and treated as special. It often meant generous portions at Malio's on the Wharf where Mom's uncle Aldo was a chef and uncle Danny was a bartender!

Later Pop-Pop had to be moved into a convalescent home for veterans. From my limited knowledge I would say it was very nice and modern compared to other places I've seen. We used to have big family outings there with our family and my uncle and his family. This place was out in the hills outside Livermore. The grounds were full of giant wide-open lawns and huge Eucalyptus trees. It had very nice picnic areas where families could visit their loved ones.

Maybe I'm a little sentimental about this stuff, but it was all a sobering experience in my childhood, considering what my own future would hold.

> Even though I only knew Pop-Pop for a short time, and in limited ways, I felt close to him in experience and in the simple love a grandson has for his grandfather. That tie is real no matter what the circumstances were, and no matter the quantity of memories.

Past The Time of Innocence

As he went along, he saw a man blind from birth. His disciples asked him, "Rabbi, who sinned, this man or his parents, that he was born blind?"

"Neither this man nor his parents sinned," said Jesus, "but this happened so that the works of God might be displayed in his life. As long as it is day, we must do the works of him who sent me. Night is coming, when no one can work. While I am in the world, I am the light of the world."

~ The Incarnate Jesus
John 9:1-5

CHAPTER FIVE

This story in John, chapter 9 is one of my favorites in the whole Bible. It shows how much Jesus loved everybody, including those whom the world had gotten used to "crushing at the gate," as Proverbs 22:23 puts it. Very quickly, there came to be a time when I was feeling pretty well crushed myself.

When we were living in Modesto our family went to a church that was a little more formal in nature than what we are used to today. It was called Trinity Presbyterian Church. Pastor Steve Hannah would dress in special robes on Sunday. They had more rituals too. My favorite one was on Palm Sunday when everyone would go outside and carry great big palm branches while singing celebrations of the holiday. They also had a traditional all church dinner where chicken noodle soup was always served. I always looked forward to that.

But don't assume that because it was formal, that the peoples' hearts were not in the right place. The pastor winced as if he were in pain every time someone told him he gave a good sermon. He told my dad once that he would prefer people left his service uncomfortable. That way he knew he was getting to people, and pushing them on to greater growth in their lives.

I remember that they had an excellent children's ministry that really got kids involved and learning. That is the first church that I remember going to Sunday school as well as Vacation Bible School. One time I played a part in a little skit for the service with a cast of other kids. We did the story from Daniel in which Nebuchadnezzar throws Shadrach, Meshach, and Abed-Nego into the furnace. I played Nebuchadnezzar, and I enjoyed learning those names. There was nothing to say, I just had to look perplexed as I counted on my fingers one, two, three ~wait~ *four* people down in the fire!

THINGS ARE STARTING TO CHANGE

But despite the fun times there I was starting to struggle. As I got a little older I began to understand what was happening to me more clearly. Already my body was getting weaker and I was getting angry about it. I could not keep up with other kids and I was frustrated at how hard it was getting just to walk and do whatever I wanted to do.

> *But now I had passed the time of innocence and although I was still very young, it was time to make a decision of my own.*

The barriers were popping up and beginning to make themselves felt more profoundly. But even worse than that, my attitude towards the way my life was going was hurting my family and myself. Just a few short years before, I had been a little kid who didn't fully understand what was going on. I was going through life moment by moment as all kids do. But I had gotten to the point where life was more than fog of experience. I began to take more time to think seriously about my life and how it was unfolding.

I'm sure I had a lot of help working through this process. Knowing myself as I do it probably involved just enough scolding to get my attention. It was time to understand that being angry was going to make life even more difficult for everyone, and at the end of the day I was the only one who could decide how I wanted to live. In former days in the midst of sudden tragedy, my parents had decided that as a family we would turn towards a greater reliance on God. But now I had passed the time of innocence, and although I was still very young, it was time to make a decision of my own.

Heavy Load

My reality was a very heavy load for someone so young to bear. You would think that it would be too deep for a child to wrap his brain around. But the Bible makes it clear that God calls out to us first. I believe He knew what I needed to understand about His desire for my path in life, and gave me the ability to make a decision. Besides, is God's grace really so hard for children to understand, or do they understand it better than adults do? Didn't Jesus say, "Unless you change and become like little children, you will never enter the kingdom of heaven" (Matthew 18:3)?

I can remember a Sunday when I was just sitting in a pew, staring into space, consumed with debate over what my desperate mind thought were its options.

"Can't this pain just go away? Can't I just will myself into health, and not be forced to fear what is coming? No, I can't do that myself. God, can't you just wipe it all away and make it disappear?"

Silence. Nothing changes.

Then comes the cruise missile that hits me right in the bull's eye; fantasies of what might have been. "If I could just go to the beginning and change what happened. Then I could be just the same as everyone else. And then. . . and then. . ." But I just crash back to where I am.

Sometimes I finally wear myself out and stop wandering aimlessly in a search for answers that don't come. But when I'm silent I realize there isn't really silence on the other end. I just wasn't listening.

We have to work with reality, not try to force God to provide solutions for things that are not the real problem; certainly they are not the most important problem. No starship is going to go into a time warp to go back and set things right. God isn't very happy about what has become of His world; clearly He could wipe every slate clean but has chosen not to; not yet. It seems for now He's more interested in teaching us perspective than solving our problems. Think of how He chastised Job[1]:

> Where were you when I laid the earth's foundation?
> Tell me, if you understand.
> Who marked off its dimension? Surely you know!
> Who stretched a measuring line across it?
> On what were its footings set,
> or who laid its cornerstone—
> while the morning stars sang together
> and all the angels shouted for joy?
>
> ~ God
> Job 38:4-7

Before God sets about "making all things new" (Revelation 21:5), He wants to wipe the spiritual slate clean. My disease is going to be here for a long time. I had to accept that. Even if by some miracle God chose to let me be well, there is a more important problem to be solved. This is a broken world that is cut off from God. I too was part of that world.

I was not just its victim. But He wanted me to be reunited with Him no matter what my physical circumstances were. He had provided a way to rectify this spiritual gulf that separated us. And in accepting that gift He gave me a renewed life with a renewed perspective on my pain. I asked Him for help, not for my body, but for my soul.

> Since then God's gifts have overwhelmed me.
> In my relationship with Him I've had a place
> to refresh my mind and feel free. Because of
> that freedom my attitude began to change.

The church we went to had an anointing ritual that my parents let me go through. I don't know if you believe in that or not. I'm not sure how to define it myself. I think of it as a symbol of a point where my life changed rather than anything more. It was simple and nicely done I think. A great deal of the meaning in it for me was that people who loved God would not leave me to wrestle with my disease alone. My pastor(s) and everyone else in God's family would support me when I needed it most. They have been among God's great gifts to me along with a life of significance and purpose that otherwise could not have been.

Hurtful Ignorance

One of the first things the blind man cured by Jesus (John 9) saw was his accusers. They tried to use him to attack Jesus.

In my own way I've faced accusers as well. The moment I tell this story, rather than praising God for the great miracle He *did* perform in my life, they accuse me of not having enough faith because I wasn't healed.

So, was the entire purpose of Jesus coming to Earth to heal people like me? If so, the cross was superfluous! He should have just stayed alive and continued healing sick people for 2,000 years. We would have a world of healthy people. We would all still be going to an eternity separated from God but at least we'd be healthy along the way.

Forgive my sarcasm, but I seriously believe that Jesus came into the world to conquer eternal death for all time. *That* is more important than healing my body presently. And maybe the purpose of my life is to show God's power in healing the *soul* despite any adversity.

> I consider that our present sufferings are not worth comparing with the glory that will be revealed in us.
>
> ~ Paul
> Romans 8:18

> Who shall separate us from the love of Christ? Shall trouble or hardship or persecution or famine or nakedness or danger or sword? As it is written:
>
> "For your sake we face death all day long;
> we are considered as sheep to be slaughtered."
>
> No, in all these things we are more than conquerors through him who loved us. For I am convinced that neither death nor life, neither angels nor demons, neither the present nor the future, nor any powers, neither height nor depth, nor anything else in all creation, will be able to separate us from the love of God that is in Christ Jesus our Lord.
>
> ~ Paul
> Romans 8:35-39

The physical healing that Jesus and His apostles provided was a testament to who Jesus is and His compassion towards those who are most profoundly affected by the world of sin. I do not deny that God can choose to let a person's life go in a direction in which he or she is healed. I simply deny the need for me to feel inadequate because I am not healed. I cannot believe that God meant for us to be slaves to a feeling that we don't have enough faith because we don't have this blessing or that miracle. Through faith I have already been given the *greatest* miracle, which was bought when Jesus died and rose from the grave. If anyone doesn't believe *me* that this was Jesus' priority, just ask Him by looking over John, chapter 6.

> Jesus answered, "Very truly I tell you, you are looking for me, not because you saw the signs I performed but because you ate the loaves and had your fill. Do not work for food that spoils, but for food that endures to eternal life, which the Son of Man will give you. On him God the Father has placed his seal of approval."
>
> ~ Jesus
> John 6:26-27

> Very truly I tell you, whoever believes has eternal life. I am the bread of life. Your ancestors ate the manna in the wilderness, yet they died. But here is the bread that comes down from heaven, which people may eat and not die. I am the living bread that came down from heaven. Whoever eats of this bread will live forever. This bread is my flesh, which I will give for the life of the world.
>
> ~ Jesus
> John 6:47-51

Even so His blessings did not stop there. He has given me everything I really needed, in His timing. Read on and see what God has done!

"People Say I'm Brave, But I Don't See It That Way"

Therefore if anyone is in Christ, he is a new creature; the old things passed away; behold, new things have come. Now all these things are from God, who reconciled us to Himself through Christ . . . .

~ Paul
2 Corinthians 5:17-18 NASB

CHAPTER SIX

§

The year 1985 was busy and adventure-filled for us all. Towards the end of my second grade year my dad was offered another line of work in the same company that would move us out of Modesto. He felt that his current work was keeping him away from his family too much. It was one of those jobs that caused him to say good-bye to us in the morning while we were still asleep, and to come home late when we were back in bed. My parents didn't want this to continue.

Yet another exciting opportunity arose at just the right time. We would move north to a pair of small towns in which a Jack in the Box franchise was available. Now, I know my parents could not have afforded to start such an enterprise on their own. I don't know the details of how the arrangement was made, but a group of folks who had earlier been involved in Dad's career were instrumental in making this change possible. Although I don't know the details of how this began, I do know the result and I continue to be thankful for it.

. . . To Paradise

I believe that this place is where God meant me to be. Looking back, everything I have ever needed has been provided here. I will have to complete this story for you to fully appreciate what I mean by that. I think if my family were to look at their own lives they might find the same is true for them. This isn't a trendy, glamorous, or prestigious place to live, but all our most important needs have been provided. I'm convinced God, through the help of other people, directed our family to the place that was best for us.

Admittedly, my first impression of Paradise was not a good one. My dad had to move to Paradise before Mom, Alan, and I did. We drove up here once to help him move into a cramped little trailer park. I remember the folks were skeptical about renting space to a young whippersnapper like my dad. They didn't want loud parties going on until an ungodly hour, say, 8:00 p.m. That may be a slight exaggeration, but on first glance that is how Paradise presented itself to new up-start immigrants.

Soon we all joined Dad in Paradise for good. I remember that moving day was a very long day for us all. We moved into a house deep in a little ravine with a very steep driveway. It is actually just down the hill from where we live right now. Mom and Dad had an adventure getting our belongings from the narrow gravel road, up the steep driveway, into the house. I don't think they finished before bedtime, so Alan and I camped out in the family room, in our sleeping bags as our parents worked through the night.

It was not the nicest house we ever lived in. It looked like the owners built it themselves, and not very well. It was situated on a hill and was divided into three floors. It seemed worse to me since weak legs and lots of stairs are not compatible. I remember having to pull myself up the stairs to my bedroom, which was on the top floor. The top floor covered only half the house, with the hallway looking out over the family room below. I was beginning to learn the hard lesson that patience was going to be a necessity in my life. I had to take one step at a time, half pulling myself up with my arms clutching the railing. Often on the way down I would trip on the bottom steps and have to wait for someone to help me stand up again.

JERRY'S KID[1]

Even as that year began to reveal the bigger frustrations that I would face in life, I had the opportunity to have a lot of fun too. Since my diagnosis, Mom had been involved in the charity organization that helped people with my kind of disease. The Muscular Dystrophy Association[2] (MDA) would become a significant part of our lives. I know I said earlier that my parents chose not to lead our family on an endless search for a cure to my disease. But in those early days this organization provided for an even greater need as described below. This was before a cure seemed even remotely possible. When scientists identified the gene that caused my disease in the late 80's, the purpose and efforts of the organization began to shift towards the "holy grail" that would make the existence of the organization unnecessary. I do applaud that effort and hope for that day to come to pass for others' sake. But I cannot say it is the same as it was.

When I think of my early involvement in the MDA, I think of the countless professionals and volunteers alike who gave so much of their lives just to help me. Yes, it was meant to help many people. But I always felt that these people were watching out for me in a special way. They didn't seek the glory of the lights and cameras that brought their cause to the attention of the masses. They didn't seek to raise the financial power of the organization they worked for, just to thicken their own wallets in return. They poured out their time, energy, and every inch of their stamina just to give something to someone else without very much recognition for it.

This was a community that greatly supported not only me, but our family as well. There were those in front of the cameras who told a distracted world of the ghastly seriousness of what people like me face. Patient Service Coordinator Nita McCarron never ran out of hugs during Telethons and doctor visits. Volunteer Extraordinaire Mike Crandall, despite his overwhelming responsibilities, always made sure Alan and I were taken care of. Year after year there were dozens of wonderfully caring and talented people on both sides of the camera whose job it was to present the evils of dystrophy, often in great detail, to a culture that finds it abhorrent, and in the presence of those who know its devastation all too well. But these totally un-selfish volunteers never hesitated to drop their heavy workload just to stand by those of us who so desperately needed their help.

I will also never forget my friend Debbie Wacker who was like a second mom when I went to MDA camps long ago. She made sure I had some fun without having to think of anything else. Debbie has become a lifelong friend for me and my family. There are many others deserving mention.

I would give it up in a second just to be another face in the crowd.

In 1985 I was selected to be the representative of everyone in my condition for the whole state of California. Didn't know I was famous once? Yes, I had my fifteen minutes anyway. People who give to an organization like MDA want to understand where their money is going; who benefits, and what is it all for. We took trips all across the state so that fundraisers could be encouraged to keep it up. Sometimes I just had to be present. Other times I was in front of crowds, but always I became the center of attention.

I admit that it was tempting to enjoy the recognition as if it was something I earned . . . because of some great thing I did. But I know that the attention I've received is not warranted, but is rather the result of my disease. So please don't think that the attentiveness has gone to my head. For one thing I feel more than my fair share of pain in return for the attention. I would give it up in a second just to be another face in the crowd. And, if there is anything attractive about me *beyond* my disease, I'd like to think people see in my spirit something God has done, not me. Certainly there is no reason for me to brag about my attitude. Living with this disease has taught me many things, but *self*-confidence is not one of them.

Hope Matters

People say I'm brave, but I don't really see it that way. If I'm confident in anything it is just that I have hope for something better ahead. Not just a future with a better body, but one where all the problems caused by sin have disappeared. I'm thinking of a future where no one is separated from God anymore by anything. This hope gives a lot more strength than our experience on earth tells us it should. Disappointment is part of life. But I believe that the One who defeated even death is a safe support to hold onto through anything. The end of the Bible makes it very clear that the future in which hope is fulfilled belongs to those who *overcome*, not to those who were never scared, never sad, and never disappointed.

This hope is what is really working and "doing its stuff" inside me; I believe it is apparent to others. It is like homemade bread rising under a kitchen towel. Mom used to make bread like that a lot. During the preparation the towel slowly bulges in the middle. You can't really see it growing, but if you go away and then come back after a while you can see a difference. Later it all goes in the oven and the process is out of sight for a time. Then the warm, delicious bread comes out of the oven and you can taste the results.

The biggest of all the adventures was a trip to Sacramento. We were taken to the state capitol for a photo-op meeting with Governor Deukmejian. Down in the lower floor of the capitol we were led through one office full of secretaries into a long conference room where all the big decisions must get made. We waited with some representatives of MDA and a large group of reporters with cameras in hand. As we waited, Alan and I admired the Governor's bronze statuette of John Wayne. Soon the Governor came in and met us. With cameras clicking he sat with Alan and me on either side as he autographed his photo for both of us and probably (who can remember?) said a few words.

After that he invited my family and me into his private office behind the conference room. It was a beautiful room with wood paneling and a big, official desk. The Governor took a big glass jar filled with See's candy and told Alan and me to dig in. We both obediently looked to Mom for approval. She said it was okay to take one, but the Governor said *he* was the *Governor* and we should do what *he* said and take as much as we wanted! Not wanting to disappoint the leader of our state we proceeded to diligently stuff our pockets!

After that we were taken to the Legislature rooms where we were introduced to several legislators and senators we didn't know. They were very friendly and wanted their pictures taken with us too . . . of course.

That was just the beginning of the day. Dad took us to a small airport where we met the man who flew the helicopter for the Channel 3 news station. He took Mom, Alan and me on a helicopter ride over Sacramento. We flew by the capitol building where I noticed the top of the dome was dirty. I had some fun by writing Governor Deukmejian a letter suggesting he have someone take care of the dirty dome. He demonstrated his good nature and humor by writing back, assuring me that he was on top of it! The finale of our ride was a landing at the golf course where MDA was having its prestigious golf tournament and fundraising dinner. It was meant to be a grand entrance to impress everyone.

A Great Gift Indeed

Have you ever been given a gift you could never have gotten for yourself?
Has anyone ever sacrificed a huge amount for you without getting anything in return except to make you happy?

That night we had dinner with some very wealthy, important, and famous people. The NFL was a sponsor and many of their alumni participated. My dad enjoyed introducing his sons to a few famous football players. Some of them showed us their huge Super Bowl rings. The friendliest guys even let us hold one. I could practically imagine putting them on my wrists instead of my fingers. They were also covered in diamonds, which made Mom drool!

We also watched people give away a great deal of money that night. I inadvertently started an incident that has always stuck in my mind. There was an auction for various donated items. Most of them were sports oriented collectors' items, including a basketball signed by the players for the Sacramento Kings. I don't know if you have ever been to such an event, but it does get exciting. I guess I got a little carried away with the fun day and the excitement in the room, because when the basketball was being bid upon I raised my hand, trying to be cute. As soon as it was up it was down due to my mother's quick grasp. Astronauts never felt as many "G's" as my wrist did that night.

Mom wasn't the only one who noticed. I simply watched as the bidding continued, and the price for this basketball went higher and higher. In a short amount of time it got to be an unbelievable figure for an item that was probably not the most valuable thing available. But for one man it became very valuable. Eventually he offered an amount of money no one could match. I don't remember exactly what the amount was, but it was so high that everyone was amazed. The winner stood up on the other side of the room from us. He walked quickly up to the front of the room to claim his prize. But when he turned around he started going in a different direction. Before I knew it he came right up to me and handed me the ball.

It was in my lap and I was stunned. I think it took me a moment to realize what he had done. I remember hearing gasps all over the room and then thunderous applause and seeing weepy eyes. To this day I'm amazed and I don't really know what else to say. Have you ever been given a gift you could never have gotten for yourself? Has anyone ever sacrificed a huge amount for you without getting anything in return except to make you happy and to experience the joy of giving?

I can honestly tell you . . . Someone has.

Later someone told us who the man was. Apparently he was one of the most well-known lobbyists in Sacramento. The tone in the informant's voice suggested he had a reputation for, shall we say, success over his adversaries. Deserved or not, the supposition was that such generosity was unexpected from this particular man. I say you should never be surprised what a person is capable of. I don't like it when people assume the worst about others because of a reputation. True, we all have a hand in building our own reputation, but I've seen low expectations shattered by a deeply moved heart several times.

NEVER ALONE

That Labor Day as the state "poster child" (they later called it "ambassador"), I went to our state capital to appear at the local Sacramento Telethon. Telethons, while still important, seemed like a much bigger deal in those days. The event in Sacramento was the biggest I ever saw. I always used to feel a sense of excitement at both the Sacramento and Chico Telethons. I was never extremely vocal. I just sat there and answered a few questions when I was interviewed. In my room I still have a plaque and pictures of myself with different hosts, from Stan Atkinson and Margaret Pelley to Dino Corbin and Royal Courtain. Each of them was an important person to me, and they always made me feel at home every Labor Day weekend. As I implied earlier, Telethons were not always easy; they invariably reminded me of the realities of dystrophy. Nevertheless, no one ever made me feel like just an impersonal figure on the television screen to help get the job over with. They were always very genuine people and treated me with respect and dignity. I appreciate that very much.

Every year after two long days of fundraising, I found a spot near a television monitor, often with the noise of tired people starting to clean up in the background. All around me people with loving, sacrificial hearts were within view. And then Jerry Lewis would come onto a stage miles away and perpetuate tradition by concluding the Telethon by singing the encouraging words I came to trust . . .

"You'll never walk alone."

You know, in more ways than one, I've never felt like I do.

“Reality Is . . . I’m Always Losing The Ability To Do Something”

Therefore, since we have been justified through faith, we have peace with God through our Lord Jesus Christ, through whom we have gained access by faith into this grace in which we now stand. And we boast in the hope of the glory of God. Not only so, but we also glory in our sufferings, because we know that suffering produces perseverance, perseverance, character; and character, hope. And hope does not put us to shame, because God’s love has been poured out into our hearts through the Holy Spirit, who has been given to us.

You see, at just the right time, when we were still powerless, Christ died for the ungodly. Very rarely will anyone die for a righteous person, though for a good person someone might possible dare to die. But God demonstrates his own love for us in this: While we were still sinners, Christ died for us.

~ Paul
Romans 5:1-8

CHAPTER SEVEN

§

In the fall of 1985 I started the third grade at my new school in Paradise. Once again my mom met a little resistance in getting me enrolled in the normal school system. I don't think it was malicious, it was just assumed that handicapped children went to a "special" school in Chico. I saw the school they were talking about every time I went for physical therapy across from Pleasant Valley High School.

No way.

No offense to those who really need it, but it looked more like a day care center for toddlers than a school. That just would not fit my needs or abilities. My continuing advice is that you don't send your kids where the system automatically says they should go. Send them where *their* needs are met.

Of course, the Third Grade was not academically memorable. I remember a spelling contest to see who could get the most points out of 1,000 on 10 tests worth 100 points each. I was one of a few to get all 1,000 points and the kids who sat next to me were amazed. Other than that I only remember long, tedious hours of learning to write in cursive until my hands hurt.

There were other things that happened that year which were more important. For one thing, we began going to the Evangelical Free Church in Paradise. It was still meeting in rented space from the Adventist Church. It was very small, and very friendly. It was there we first met some folks who have been our friends ever since. My dad started teaching a Sunday school class for myself and the few other children that attended. This church has always had a slightly older congregation and these folks grew to care about us so much—it was often like having lots of grandparents! I learned much from many of them and I appreciate their faith, which inspired me to hang on in some tough times. I knew I had friends there when it felt like people my own age were far away. But we'll get to that later.

Cruelly Observant

Actually, I can remember first having trouble with other kids in the Third Grade. My back was beginning to curve and walking was becoming very difficult. Recess had become a time of day I really did not look forward to. To this day I freeze up when I see balls of any kind flying through the air near me. I should have never tried to play dodge ball! That game is not easy when you can't actually dodge the ball. You think football is rough? Every time a ball of some kind flies in my direction, I just know I can't do anything about it if it were going to hit me.

> Children are cruelly observant sometimes. I feel like saying to some kids that just because you notice something different doesn't mean you have to declare it to the whole world and mock it.

I know I'm not the only one who has felt that way. I also know it is just the way some children are. I have worked hard learning to control my thoughts when I know that most kids are just curious and are clearly not being unkind, despite the temptation to think otherwise. Some have no interest at all that I'm different and are very good at just wanting to be friends. But it is very hard when curiosity degenerates into laughter and cruelty.

Too often kids decided to make life more difficult than it already was. The details of what they'd say and do are unimportant and forgiven. But it happened so often, and it was always the same old thing. Why is it so easy for us to treat each other like that?

My Little Red Quickie

Towards the last part of that year it became clear to my parents, doctors, and physical therapist that walking was not realistic for me anymore. I got my first wheelchair—a "Quickie"—at first for just occasional use, but I soon used it all the time. It was a lightweight black and red manual chair that fit me just right. The swinging arms made me feel like I was in the captain's chair of the Enterprise in the early Star Trek movies. The wheel grips would burn my hands after a while so I wore fingerless gloves when I was out and about. I don't clearly remember feeling sad that I had to give up walking, pretty much forever. I think I just got to the point where I was grateful to not have to work so hard to go somewhere. And, I was young enough that the novelty of having a chair overshadowed regrets that would come later. There are always tradeoffs, but sometimes the few benefits seem to temporarily outweigh losing one's ability . . . like being taken to the front of long lines at Disneyland!

> The simple reality is that I am always losing the ability to do something. As my body got weaker there was less and less freedom to function in basic ways. Sometimes things would get lost in quick succession. Often I would reach a plateau where I grew weaker more slowly.

For a short time I was "on the go" with my chair. There was a large asphalt playing area at Ponderosa Elementary School. At one corner was a steep incline that led to the classrooms. A few times, with friends watching, I purposely wheeled over to the top of the hill and took off full speed. I went speeding downhill for a few seconds and then coasted diagonally across the pavement. It was reckless but fun. Not too smart though. Those wheels shook and rattled till I grabbed the handles with both gloved hands and slowed down by friction.

I had a little bit of fun, but very soon even rolling those wheels got too hard. I was in a manual chair at the end of the Third Grade and in my first electric chair before the Fourth Grade began. But even as it got harder to get around, I began to enjoy non-physical things more and more.

For Learning's Sake

I think it was in the fourth grade that I really began to enjoy school just for the sake of learning new things. It was an earthly blessing that any desire I had to be outdoors doing things other kids did was easily replaced by the fun of learning. I've had adventures inside my mind from reading good books and feeding my God-given gift of imagination. I have always enjoyed good grades in school, but I don't think of them in the way other people seem to. I have always enjoyed the process more than the result. Some of us work hard to achieve excellence in athletics and they enjoy the process as much as the prize. Others are musically gifted and practicing their gift is a joy. I think everyone has something like this in their lives if they really search for it. Reading and learning is just what I enjoy working for. It is also a gift that God could give me that didn't rely on my physical abilities. A side effect is that the more I learn about the world, the more I realize that plenty of people have a much worse lot in life than I do.

Dependence

Nevertheless, losing independence is frustrating. Having to be dependent on people around me for accomplishing simple tasks I should be able to do myself is hard to accept. I am twenty-five years old and have not enjoyed the private use of a bathroom I was eleven. I think however, that such vulnerabilities have provided yet another lesson that leaves me prone towards understanding the need I have for God's help in other areas of life. At first, deep in our souls none of us wants to admit that we need help. But spiritually we are all just as helpless as I am physically. We want to assume control because we don't like to trust that God is capable of taking care of our most important needs.

When someone helps me with something, I don't get everything I want.

Usually I get what I need, but I understand that people are human and can't always perfectly appreciate my needs. Actually, my fears about my needs not being met often turn out to be unfounded. It is just a feeling of insecurity left over from the few times I was disappointed. Despite even those few frustrations, I'm alive and cared for. How much better can God provide for my true needs since He knows the deepest parts of me? He knows my needs before I do. He knew all my needs long before I existed and provided for them. He has even appointed a time for me to stand (and I mean *literally* stand for the first time in at least fifteen years) in front of Him free of every shackle of life and death. That day is coming!

Red-Tailed Hawks, Deer Creek . . . And Friedman!

You say, "I am rich; I have acquired wealth and do not need a thing." But you do not realize that you are wretched, pitiful, poor, blind and naked. I counsel you to buy from me gold refined in the fire, so you can become rich; and white clothes to wear, so you can cover your shameful nakedness; and salve to put on your eyes, so you can see.

Those whom I love I rebuke and discipline. So be earnest, and repent. Her I am! I stand at the door and knock. If anyone hears my voice and opens the door, I will come in and eat with them, and they with me.

To those who are victorious, I will give the right to sit with me on my throne, just as I was victorious and sat down with my Father on his throne.

~ The Risen Jesus
Revelation 3:17-21

CHAPTER EIGHT

When the fifth grade rolled around I was accepted into an advanced class that was a combined group of fifth and sixth grade students. I was not skipping a grade; I was just offered a more advanced curriculum for the next two years. Sometimes the students from both grades worked on the same projects, and other times we worked separately.

This program was about challenging us to be better than we already were. That is a great idea for a school, right? It also took us beyond basic skills. Miss Williams, our teacher, was an art and nature lover, and she wanted to teach us to appreciate those things as well. We all spent a great deal of time on special projects involving art and creative writing. For a long time we knew I was pretty good at drawing based on little doodles that I would make. In these two years I was taught a lot more about painting and drawing.

We studied nature and read books that taught us about the world. One year we took a trip to Woodleaf. Despite being sick in my stomach most of the time, I really enjoyed what I learned there. We met a Red-tailed Hawk who was injured in the wild. We got to get up close to him and draw our own pictures of him. One night at sunset we went with a guide out to the large pond just to watch nature at work at a time that usually gets ignored in our busy lives. We watched, without any artificial light, as it grew darker. I really enjoyed the unspoiled beauty of day turning to night. We saw several bats come out of nowhere and skip across the water. I was surprised how much you could see when you just let your eyes adjust naturally to the dimming light. There were colors and shades all around; we took many trips like that. I wish so badly that I could still go out and enjoy all that God made.

We also read about things that made me appreciate life. The one story we shared that has remained with me ever since was the autobiography of Barry Spanjaard called "*Don't Fence Me In*." It is still on my shelf. We read about the night in his childhood when parachuting Nazi soldiers suddenly invaded his home in Holland. His father picked up his rifle and ran out into the battle and was never heard from again. He and his family were Jewish and they were taken away to those horrible places known as concentration camps. We learned how he survived and ended up in America at the end of the war. It is a good book and I highly recommend it. After we read it, Mr. Spanjaard paid our class a personal visit. It was great to meet him in person. The experience once again taught me that lots of people have had it worse off than me. I'm very blessed and should not feel sorry for myself.

We also had some fun, and Miss Williams was not going to let me be left out despite this being my first year in a wheelchair. Every day when the weather permitted, the class had some outdoor time for exercise. Instead of just letting me sit around and watch she made sure I participated in any possible way. In time I even learned to get involved on my own initiative. As a class we participated in several races held in Bidwell Park. We were not in it to win, of course. Well, at least I wasn't. It was fun to be out there. That park is so wonderful to have around.

We also had an adventure that Dad will never forget. We all went on a trip up to Deer Creek to go hiking through the hills. A few parents went with us, including Dad to help me navigate the trails in my chair.

Now Miss Williams was a very bold, outgoing woman who assured us that I could make it through this adventure like so many other things we had done. I laugh about it now, but . . . . We arrived at Deer Creek and began our trek. Some ways down the trail the path got slowly narrower and the hills got steeper and steeper. My chair was not made for such terrain; Dad carried me much of the way. Others helped him when it got to be too much and soon I was going along like a king in one of those thrones that have servants carrying it on two poles. Only I didn't have those buff movie servants to carry me. I had a group of middle-aged fathers who took a day off work just to take their kids on a field trip. It was a long, grueling day with little to appreciate once we got wherever we were going.

This year was full of challenges for me to overcome. It began with my attitude about my schoolwork. I was becoming an obstinate perfectionist in everything I worked on. I felt that everything I did had to be perfect or else it was worthless. The problem, of course, is that you just can't always be flawless. As a result I was feeling pretty worthless in almost everything. It took some time to learn that seeking to do a good job does not mean I need to accomplish some static version of perfection every time I try something. Right now on my wall hangs my first attempt at poetry written over my first water color painting. I've never been impressed with either, but I did it when I was nine years old. The point is that I tried something new. The more I worked on these abilities, the better I got at it. I wish my hands allowed me to keep practicing. Even if I could, I still would not be perfect at it. But perfection in these things is impossible to define, much less to achieve, anyway.

CCI . . . Boot Camp

That was just the beginning though. For some time we had discussed the idea of getting a service dog so that I could be a little more independent at school. I constantly needed help with things I dropped and items that were out of reach. Quite frankly, it was clear that kids were annoyed at having to help me all the time. I didn't really blame them because I wished I didn't need help myself.

My parents got me onto a very long waiting list with an organization called Canine Companions for Independence (CCI)[1]. We all expected that it would be a while before I was actually put into the training program in Santa Rosa. In very short time, however, we were surprised with a phone call that said there would be an unexpected opening that spring. They asked if we wanted to go through with the process now or wait until my name came up again. They did warn us that they had never worked with someone as young as I was before. The program was designed for teenagers and adults; I was only eleven. We had watched a video they sent us on the details of the program and decided that it was something I could handle and it would be best to go ahead.

The video lied.

We knew it would be a challenge, but I was caught off guard within ten minutes of the first day. I quickly found out what they meant when they greeted us with the words, "Welcome to Boot Camp!"

The program was to last two weeks. My parents decided that Mom would stay with me the first week and Dad would come down for the second week. We had to stay in a hotel and go to their small training center all day, every day. When Mom and I first arrived at the little building we were ushered upstairs to a small square room with other trainees.

We found out that the video they gave us was the candy-coated version, probably on purpose. We were not just there to learn a few commands and learn to function with the help of a dog. Their goal was to break a part of me that seems to come naturally to most disabled people. They wanted to tear down that instinct that tells us to give up and run from the world.

In a way that is a good thing, but it didn't feel good at all at the time. Looking back I better understand some of the points they were trying to make. They went quickly through the rules and expectations for the course. Every morning we would start with a test that required us to memorize commands on our own time. You either passed or were expelled, no exceptions. We would be under the trainer's command from early in the morning until well after the sun went down. As soon as the testing was complete they put us in a circle and brought in a group of dogs that had been intensively trained for the first two years of their lives.

Let me make it clear that the dogs
were not there to be trained; we were.

On the first day, a dog was temporarily assigned to me. In my usual timid way, I asked the dog to do what I needed him to do. He was unresponsive. As other students also failed and were "assaulted" by yelling trainers insisting that they take control of their dogs without really knowing how, I got terribly nervous that I would be next. I did what any novice dog-handler would do . . . I started getting angry at my dog. The room went into chaos while more and more students, including myself, frantically tried to avoid what appeared to be cruel and unusual punishment at the hands of our trainers!

The dog that was with me didn't respond any better to frantic anger than to timid cajoling. He crawled under my wheelchair where he thought the crazy person could not get to him. A trainer noticed this and was right in my ear. My mind was a blur as I tried to figure out a way out of this situation. I also grew stubbornly angry with these people for making me go through Yoda-like mental gymnastics without an apparent solution. I became like Luke Skywalker in his Jedi training telling Yoda that he was asking the impossible. I bolted for the corner of the room and tried to turn my back on the whole thing. Behind me the instructor demanded that I return. Whatever happened next is lost in the category of "unpleasant memories."

Welcome to Boot Camp. That first day was obviously the *Kobiyashi Maru Test*. For those who are not fellow Star Trek fans, that is a test to which there is no solution. Of course they didn't expect me to succeed on my first try. They wanted to see how I would handle myself in the situation and where I needed to improve. I obviously did not do very well. At the time I didn't understand this. I lacked wisdom to be able to see that this might be good for me.

This was a lot to handle in one day. That night, and many nights after, I got little sleep. For the next few days there was a battle inside me. On one side was an urgent desire to go home. On the other side was some undefined sense that if I stayed I might come away with something more than a dog. For the first week the former seemed to win more often. But before I'm too hard on myself I have to remember that on the second day there were a lot fewer students in the room than there were on the first day; several adults had followed *their* urge to go home. I stayed very reluctantly.

On the weekend when Dad came it felt like months had passed. I sat in the hotel lobby and tried to convince my parents that I should go home. Yes, I wanted to give up. I'm not very proud of myself for wanting to quit, but it's the truth. This need to make bad things go away was a part of me that was not going to be overcome in a week. I have an incredible urge inside to run from difficult things. At that time I could hardly think of anything else. Eventually my parents won me over and I agreed to stay. It was the first time I had to make a tough decision to stick with something that was very hard. This was the first time I had to make what felt like an overwhelming decision; the kind that once you've committed to it, it doesn't go away. Looking back I am sure that making that choice—to finish what I had started—helped give me the courage to make similar decisions in the future.

FRIEDMAN

At the start of the second week we were given the dogs that were chosen to be our permanent companion should we pass the course. Here I met Friedman for the first time. He was a spry and handsome two-year-old Golden Retriever then. I know that the trainers sat down and specifically paired Friedman and me together. He wasn't so outgoing himself. I think they chose well. For the rest of the course we were made to be physically inseparable. His leash was not to come off my wrist at any time for any reason.

As the second week progressed things got a little easier but not by much. It always took me several tries to get Friedman to follow my instructions. The television show *20/20* was doing a story on CCI during the time I was there. We still have a video of that segment because for some strange reason they chose me with two others for a close up personal evaluation.

One day Dr. Bonnie Bergin, the woman who founded CCI, was helping with the training. Though I was completely unaware of it at the time, a cameraman filmed her offering me personal instruction as I continued my timid approach with Friedman—rather harshly I might add. On camera it looks like the sun was in my eyes but that isn't really why I was squinting. I was fighting off tears as what I perceived as intimidation was poured out; it had not yet clicked in my mind how to have success with Friedman and I didn't know what to do. I'd like to say that I had a sudden burst of enlightenment and I rose to the occasion and succeeded beyond my wildest expectations.

But this time I was not the star pupil.

An older lady who had been having a similar lack of success with her dog came in one morning bursting with pride! She said she spent the night in a parking lot with her dog "going behind the woodshed" as she put it. She worked and worked until he was regularly obedient to her commands.

But no matter what, Friedman and I were best friends and I could not have gone without him. His companionship made all the difficulties worthwhile.

I passed, but only on probation. They would keep tabs on me for a few months to make sure I could handle myself. This was one of the hardest experiences of my life and honestly I did not fully appreciate it until much later. The truth is, as much as I loved Friedman, I never fully took control, never fully gave him the commanding presence he required to serve me consistent with his training. As a result we both came up short of our fullest potential. As you will see, junior high school, which I entered over a year after getting Friedman, only made things harder. I am willing to take my own part of the blame for this. I should have stopped trying just to get by every day with Friedman and raised the bar for us. I should have been willing to put other things aside and gone behind the woodshed myself. But no matter what, Friedman and I were best friends and I could not have gone without him. His companionship made all the difficulties worthwhile.

Now that I've made it clear that I know I wasn't perfect in this, I'd like to offer a little constructive criticism. Now that I'm older, a little wiser, and able to understand some of the good lessons I learned, I feel I can safely say I don't deserve all the blame for not having more success. For one thing my family and I have always agreed that the training time was too short. Two weeks is not enough time to try to change a person's life so drastically. Later I heard they lengthened it to three weeks but that still seems short. They needed to not try to compress so much information and practice into so little time. I would have appreciated more time for debriefing so that I could reflect in a supportive atmosphere on the progress I was making.

Another thing is that I was only eleven! How many eleven year olds are mature enough to get a hold of these concepts? I would think it would have been okay to drop the military masquerade for a few minutes. It might have been a little easier for someone so young if in a secluded spot they could have shown me they were not evil monsters just making life miserable for me. I know now they were trying to help me, but at that age it was a little hard to understand. This wasn't really boot camp, and nobody was going to die in combat because of a mistake I might make. The very fact that they were adults and I was a child gave them the image of authority. For a few minutes they could have gone without creating that image with the power of fear alone, as might be necessary with fellow adults. I think this is reasonable to ask.

Overall I think these experiences were helpful. I reached a little farther beyond myself and came out a little stronger. There would be far more difficult challenges just over the horizon. I'm positive that God brought even the demanding days of CCI into my life to help prepare me for what was coming. But in the midst of all these earthly and painful encounters He also gave me all of Himself. Not once in the midst of this pain did I turn to God and find no help. I didn't grow stronger through my will but through His. When I asked, a strength I could not have created flowed up from some unseen well. When I was willing, some hard walls I had built up against the world softened and began to crumble. Those walls would have only kept me from pursuing life beyond their seeming safety. They would never have kept anything from coming in and hurting me. God is the only one who knocks at the gate and asks politely to come in.

Fun Is Good

You're off to Great Places!
Today is your day!
Your mountain is waiting,
So... get on your way!

~ Dr. Seuss

CHAPTER NINE

Just a couple of weeks after I graduated with Friedman my hard work was rewarded with some fun. As a family we took a trip to the east coast for some basic American sightseeing from Boston to Washington D.C. It was not just meant for me since the trip was planned before we knew I would be going to CCI so soon. It was actually looked at more as a problem. My family and I had not yet gotten used to having Friedman in our lives when we were off traveling the country.

Things actually went pretty well. I had less of a problem than east coast people who were completely unfamiliar with helping dogs for someone who wasn't blind. The whole idea was new to them, and this was before the Americans with Disabilities Act was in effect as well. We boarded the plane first so that they could get me seated more easily. Friedman laid silently under my feet the entire flight. He was always extremely mild mannered, but able to flip light switches in a single bound. At the end of the flight as people got out ahead of us they were amazed that there had been a dog on board. As we would find out, his good behavior and good looks would always bring a lot of admiring compliments.

American Roots

We arrived in Boston in the middle of the night and saw only a maze of highway on the way to a hotel. For the few days we were there we saw lots of fun things I had only read about. We went on the "Freedom Trail" which took us to Paul Revere's house and grave, as well as old meeting houses where the American Revolution was planned. We got to walk the decks of the USS Constitution and a man dressed in colonial clothes taught Alan and me how to throw tea into the harbor.

From there we drove out to Plymouth Rock. That is a waste of time. There was just an ugly concrete bunker over a garbage-cluttered rock with a date carved in it with modern tools. It was a waste of the space I just used to mention it. We then drove to Philadelphia where we saw the Liberty Bell and Independence Hall. After Philadelphia we drove to New York and saw all we could see in a single day. We went on a ferry to see the Statue of Liberty. It is hard to imagine how tall it is until you are standing next to it. We also saw Wall Street from the car. We stopped nearby to see the Brooklyn Bridge from the riverside. We had real street vendor hot dogs and pretzels for lunch in the shadows of the World Trade Center buildings. At some point things get so tall it doesn't seem to matter anymore how they compare to other things.

(What a shame; how tragic! I wrote these words two months before that horrible day in September. I wish they had not been so tall after all.)

One of the most interesting things we did was to tour the United Nations complex. It turned out that since I was in a wheelchair, my family and I got our own private tour guide. She took us through all the areas that you see on television. Some of it was practically a museum of the world since so many countries had donated artifacts for display.

I remember seeing an amazing sculpture made of a huge amount of ivory under a glass case. I think it was an intricate panorama of an oriental city. We even got to peer into the giant General Assembly room since it was empty. There was a sense of power that I felt as we looked. At one point we had to take an elevator. We all tried to squeeze in but the tour guide got stuck outside. The worried look on her face as the doors closed told us that was a mistake. The four of us just sat patiently as the elevator went higher and higher into the inner workings of the U.N. All sorts of people from all over the world got on and off. We just stayed put and eventually the elevator returned us to a relieved guide.

WASHINGTON

This ended the first week of our trip and we spent the entire second week in Washington DC. That was really the highlight. We stayed in a nice hotel with a room that had a great view of the Mall. Everything there was so educational. We went to the headquarters of all three branches of government.

At that time the White House was not entirely accessible. Mom and Alan went with the tour while Dad, Friedman and I were escorted to a back door area that would accommodate my wheelchair. We passed the president's garbage (amazingly enough, it had TV dinners in it!) and were taken into the kitchen. On a table there was a large pan of fudge cooling. It is good to be the president! We were taken to an elevator that took us upstairs. Who knows, maybe it was the same one President Roosevelt used to get a midnight snack!

During the tour we were taken into a room with a giant Persian rug that must have been a couple of inches thick. It was rolled back behind a cord so that tourists could not step on it. Friedman had his own ideas. He just wanted to lie down for a second and he didn't see it as an extremely expensive rug that belonged to the most powerful man on earth. All he saw was a perfectly comfortable pillow. Mom and I got him off before anyone saw . . . I think.

We also went to the capitol building, which is one of the most interesting and beautiful buildings I have ever seen. It put Sacramento's capitol to shame. In the area we found our local Congressman Herger's office and met some of the people that work there. They were extremely friendly and seemed happy to have people from back home visiting our own little piece of the nation's capital. There was a sense of ownership there. It was an interesting contrast to the feeling I got at the U.N. I felt like if we had gotten off that elevator to try to visit people who are supposed to represent us to the world we would have been seen as causing a problem. At the very least it gave me the impression of being far removed. In Washington, on the other hand, the office that represented us to the rest of the nation cordially welcomed us. Maybe this is unfair to the people at the U.N. but it is the impression I got. At least the government that appoints our ambassador does represent us. So many member nations of the U.N. do not share that freedom. How can the world be justly represented by such an organization?

There are many other things we did in Washington. The Sunday in the middle of our trip was Easter Sunday. We drove to Annapolis to go to church in the giant cathedral at the Naval Academy. They had separate services for Catholics and Protestants and served communion at both. The Protestant service was still very formal and people had to go up to the front to receive communion. When my parents got up there they asked one of the ministers to come down to serve me, which as I knew from going to Grandma's Lutheran church is very common for those who can't go up the stairs to the platform. The process was expected but something else was not. The minister dressed in formal robes came with a decorative cup and thin, round wafer in hand. When it came time to drink from the cup I took a quick and healthy sized sip and swallowed right away, as I was accustomed to.

I am also accustomed to drinking grape juice during communion.

My mouth and throat were burning as I realized that they were using real wine! I said thank you to the minister and looked over to my parents with watering eyes. They could have warned me, you know!

We also saw President Kennedy's grave and the Tomb of the Unknown Soldier. Friedman started softly growling at the Marines during their precision "changing of the guard" ceremony and had to be disciplined a little. That was a very solemn and sad part of the visit.

I came away from that trip wishing I could have stayed longer. I especially could have stayed for weeks just for the different museums of the Smithsonian. This trip gave me many fun memories.

§

These past two chapters basically just cover the time in which I was in the fifth grade. Like I said, it was a busy year. The sixth grade was very similar in terms of school activities. We just spent a little more time getting prepared for life in junior high school - or so I thought.

Purgatory

John knew something about the pain of exclusion. He wrote that junior high — not surprisingly — was perhaps the hardest era of his life. Junior high is difficult for almost everyone, I suppose. Tony Campolo once said that the old Roman Catholic theology is right, that there really is such a thing as purgatory. It's junior high, a place between heaven and hell where you are made to go suffer for your sins.

~ John Ortberg

Therefore, since we are surrounded by such a great cloud of witnesses, let us throw off everything that hinders and the sin that so easily entangles. And let us run with perseverance the race marked out for us, fixing our eyes on Jesus, the pioneer and perfecter of faith. For the joy set before him he endured the cross, scorning its shame, and sat down at the right hand of the throne of God.

Consider him who endured such opposition from sinners, so that you will not grow weary and lose heart.

Hebrews 12:1-3

CHAPTER TEN

Oh joy.

This is it, the chapter of my life I have been dreading to write about. Of course it should be easier to write about than it was to live through. This is where the story begins to turn into a darker version of *The Wonder Years*. Actually you could just about perfectly exchange that kid's home life and school life and it would look about the same. At home everything was great for me, aside from the normal teenage stuff; but school was a different story.

JUNIOR HIGH . . . PURGATORY INDEED!

Paradise Intermediate School. What can a person say about it? People I know up here have struggled to find good things to say about it as it existed a decade ago. In the opinion of some, including me, it was just a place where young teenagers were locked up and adults dare not tread. It has been alleged that the policy of the local school system was not to expect anything from kids at that age and to let the worst of "teenagitis" just run its course. I don't know if it has changed in the last ten years. One can only hope. For those two years, some parents intentionally home schooled some of my classmates. Those kids turned out to be some of the most sane and intelligent of my class in high school.

The problems I had there were not mainly academic in nature. Not all teachers there were to be blamed for anything. I can think of at least five in two years of classes who I really connected with. These were the noble few who actually made room for excellence to be sought by anybody who wanted it. I could get more specific but a few generalities will allow me to tell the truth about my experiences without getting personal. Let me just say that some of the teachers who were most popular with the kids were not my favorites. I personally didn't learn much when the teacher tried too hard to be one of the kids and made the classroom a forum for popularity contests. Ugh, that is a very confrontational thing to say and I hate confrontation so let's move on! I could say a lot more but I'm not in the mood right now. Maybe I don't need to.

The problems I had there were mainly social ones. I still have not completely figured out why certain things happened the way they did. I flip from thinking it was my entire fault to it being everyone else's fault. Reality is somewhere in between.

> A better part of me is slowly learning that it doesn't really accomplish anything to blame anyone for anything. In fact, learning to forgive others and myself is actually a process that leads to healing.

Rejection

I don't remember when or how it started, but somehow I became the target of certain fellow students. Somehow those who crafted the culture at Paradise Intermediate determined that life was not difficult enough for me already.

Especially during lunch hour I was exposed to a *Lord of the Flies* environment. Teachers disappeared behind closed doors. A cafeteria and outdoor eating area became the domain of awkward and fearful teenagers. We all started out like cave men that had no exposure to society. This was to be a furnace fueled by hormones where children were not held accountable for any behavior. Cliques were formed out of desperate attempts to feel accepted. Unfortunately the anger in teenagers also made them feel a need to reject those who were not a part of their own groups.

What a silly species we are! We all need to feel accepted ourselves, but we constantly reject others.

This part I have reasoned out pretty well. I got together with a group of friends myself, but I was also an anomaly. I was different from any other person in the school. I was also a little mysterious to most of them. I stood out so much I might as well have had purple skin. That is dangerous in that environment - an accident waiting to happen.

My expectations were higher. I thought it would be fun to have a dog at school. I thought I would be a kind of popular mascot and friends would come knocking down my door. I had a glimpse of that once in another context when I was exposed to students from other schools. That makes me wonder about what was different here. Why did kids from Paradise treat me one way and kids from bigger cities treat me another way? I really can't answer that. I have had suspicions about this community and its attitude towards all disabled people.

Hurtful Kids & Nice Surprises

The eating area of the school was filthy with discarded food and wrappers. It was extremely tempting for Friedman. I had to spend a lot of time watching him and keeping him from eating the junk around him. In retrospect I should have gone home and done some intensive training with him. I should have taken control of the problem until Friedman could have sat up to his nose in hamburger meat and pizza without flinching, and without me having to ask. That may sound like a fantasy, but that is exactly how well these dogs are capable of behaving. I had the tools to do it; I didn't use them.

I became a favorite target of one particular bully and a few of his friends. This fellow student of mine must have seen me refusing to let Friedman eat the garbage on the ground. I had also been taught by CCI not to allow people to pet Friedman so that he would not grow attached to anyone but me. In retrospect again, if I had cemented our relationship with more training, those precautions would have probably become unnecessary. It was like going on a strict starvation diet to get in shape, but refusing to exercise. I know that not being able to pet Friedman was frustrating for a lot of people. Kind people at least understood the reason even if it was hard. The truth is, as much as people didn't like being told not to pet him, I despised going into public places and having to tell every single person I met that they could not pet my dog. Instead of working hard to achieve the solution though, I got a little angry over the problem and chose to see other people's rudeness as the source of the problem.

That still doesn't excuse the behavior of some people. In their teenage rebelliousness some students resented me for these things. One bully decided to take action against me. He confronted me about this in the middle of lunch hour and started raking me over the coals for "torturing that dog." I "never" fed him and never let anyone pet him. He was convinced that I must not even feed him at home. His friends encouraged him. I was mocked and humiliated. I don't know if it's my paranoia but it seemed like that idea caught on in the school. As I passed by I heard remarks from people. I think out of their own fear of being bullied no one stood up for me, and I didn't stand up for myself very well. Bullying happened repeatedly and got increasingly intense. I became anxious about going to school and started withdrawing from people out of fear.

One bright spot came from an unexpected place at an unexpected time. I was alone in a hallway somewhere and there was hardly anyone around. One of the bully's own friends came towards me. I cringed and prepared for another onslaught. I was surprised. He actually apologized for his friend very sincerely. He told me that he thought the way his friend was treating me was not fair. With my words I accepted his apology simply but graciously. In my mind, while I did truly appreciate that at least one of the bully's friends didn't share that hurtful sentiment, I wondered what power kept him from telling this to his friend. I do know the answer to that; I just don't understand it.

I think that incident is the first piece of evidence that shows that all through junior high and high school I always had more allies than I knew about. I think at some point I might have closed my eyes to that possibility. I closed my eyes to a lot of things because of my very low self-esteem. Certain folks in the school's faculty didn't help the situation. This school did a lot of talking about self-esteem. From almost every teacher we heard speeches about having self-esteem so that we could get along in life as if it was the capstone of the curriculum. They didn't seem to think about building it up in those that didn't already have it.

Here is where their method broke down. That which was meant to help us in fact put fuel to the fire of the problems in this school's atmosphere. Students, and a lot of teachers, confused being "out-going" with "coolness," which seemed to include a need to feel superior to others. Those students who acted cool and superior felt accepted. Those who were "not cool" were rejected and a healthy self-esteem seemed impossible to achieve. I've since learned that a proper and healthy identity can be achieved, even for those of us who are shy. I don't believe coolness can be achieved unless you sell out and change who you are. That is just how it looks to me. In effect the faculty at my school created a hierarchical ladder of acceptance that could only be climbed by denying your own personality.

My parents went to the principal to try to get something done. He said that my bully was a young man who had a broken home that was a hurtful place to live in. He was hurting me because he was having a hard time himself at home. I took no joy in hearing of this boy's very real struggles. The principal, however, thought it would be best if I just hid out and ate somewhere more private. In essence, he was assigning responsibility for the problem to me. The resolution then was for me to disappear rather than to address the bully's behavior. Anyone notice a trend?

HURTFUL ADULTS

Another unrelated problem arose that made me feel equally rejected by the faculty. For some reason I decided to run for Class Treasurer earlier in the year. I think that surprised the teachers in charge of student government. I just wanted to be Treasurer because I thought it would be fun to participate. All the candidates met with the principal to discuss how the election would proceed. I could tell I didn't fit in with the clique that was expected to run for the four offices. I ran against a girl who was thought to be very popular and did fit in.

To everyone's surprise, including mine, I swept the election. The conclusion of my unmemorable speech ended to the sound of thunderous applause . . . yet another clue that I had more friends than I was aware of. I never had proof, but I think the PE coach who ran student government as well as the other elected students resented that I beat a member of their group. My reason for thinking that is just an attitude I always felt from them. In every meeting and everything we had to do together I always seemed to be intruding on their conversations.

They always just knew when the next meeting would be because they kept in constant contact with each other. Everyone except me was personally told there would be another meeting today. I think the PE coach told the president and she made sure her friends would be there. I always had to rely on sketchy and unreliable daily announcements given in our homerooms. Sometimes it didn't even say when or where the meeting would be. Even if it did, I had to race to get prepared to fulfill my responsibilities. I got fed up with this particular problem and finally stood up for myself. I didn't react angrily, but rationally and firmly. At the end of one meeting I stopped the other three and told them I was a duly elected officer of the student council. I asked to be told personally when the meetings would be held, just like everyone else. They said they agreed and from that day on I didn't struggle to check the announcements.

A very long time afterwards I finally got some personal contact, but not the kind I wanted. During lunch hour I was out on the large grass field with a few friends trying to escape bullying for a few minutes.

From behind me I heard "Hey, Gilbert!" from the PE coach. As I turned around he proceeded to lecture me about my responsibilities. I had missed several meetings and he chewed me out for it. In a very immature way he threatened to remove me from office. I really didn't care anymore what he said because I had done all I could. It was clear to me that he and the others didn't really want me there and I didn't think this job was important enough to fight for. It wasn't, trust me. All I really did was to get a piece of paper on the budget for student government from the office and read it at the meeting. I also refused to respond to a teacher who used threats of removing me from office before even hearing my side of the story. I didn't go to another meeting and he never came back after me.

Elusive Friendships

> *I grew tired of fighting to be included in things. For a while I tried asking people why everyone kept disappearing. I got no answers . . . just fewer people to be friends with.*
>
> *There is hope though.*

For all these reasons, and more, junior high school was a very unpleasant experience for me. At times I would find myself choosing a certain path to my next class just to avoid larger crowds. I went to a dance once, but that was a disaster. Things got a little better in high school, but from the seventh and eighth grade on I was a little bit of a loner.

In school I always felt like friendship was hard to hold on to. I got along with plenty of other kids in class, or at least I thought so. But in between classes and during lunch hour it seemed like I would have a small group of friends for a while, but they would soon drift away. It became a pattern.

For several days now I have worried over how much detail to continue with in this section. I confess to you that I am concerned that some people who knew me then might end up reading this and be surprised at how I feel. Please don't take this the wrong way, but these days it seems like every parent of my former classmates I meet thinks I was their child's close friend. My family even gives me reports of meeting kids I went to school with and their glowing remarks of how much they admired me. My first human reaction inside is, "Where were they when I needed them?" It is an ugly thought, but it is there.

In truth, I did feel resentment for a long time against certain people who I thought were my closest friends, and these feelings still resurface often. I felt like they got tired of me. I grew tired of fighting to be included in things. For a while I tried asking people why everyone kept disappearing. I got no answers, just fewer people to be friends with. I withdrew from what I had wanted to be my group of best friends. Right now, I just want to know why. Actually, I'd like to just put it all in the past and not feel the loneliness.

For years I have gone back through everything over and over again. The reality is that not all of it is everyone else's fault. A lot of it is no one's fault at all.

There were several opportunities I had which I backed away from. I met a few people who chose to be obstacles and I made wrong assumptions that that many others would be obstacles, too. Those choices were my own and I live with the consequences. When you keep saying no to people they eventually stop asking.

There are also very real physical barriers that have gotten in the way of friendship. I simply cannot do all the things others can do, especially when everyone else is at an active young age. In retrospect I think I could have done a little more than I chose to do. Compared to my condition now, I had a lot more freedom then. Still, people enjoy the company of others who can join in on their activities.

Young people don't like to slow down so that someone like me can be a part of things, even in a limited way.

Come to think of it, that is probably the single most important reason for this loneliness I feel. I've worried too much about the effect my attitude has had on relationships, probably because it is one of the few things I have control over. Could it be that I have driven people away? I think the Accuser wants me to concentrate on selfish feelings in order for me to tear down both myself and others. It isn't true though; my wrong assumptions about others have often been inaccurate. Look at the evidence. Only a tiny handful of bullies ever had something against me, and that was only because of their own problems. I had little to do with it; I was just in the wrong place at the wrong time. Most of the people who I was worried about reading this never truly gave me any reason to think there was something wrong with me.

These feelings of resentment, however, do come back from time to time. Even in a large crowd there is a part of me that feels alone. But in the end, after I've laid awake in bed worrying over it, I really don't want revenge or justice. I don't hate the bullies and I'm even able to just let go of my own regrets. All I want is not to feel so alone.

I Walked Among Giants

There is hope though.

There is a "latter end" that I have to look forward to. There is a time ahead when no obstacles will exist between anyone and me. No one will be intimidated by something that is different about me. I expect I will one day be reunited with many friends I thought I had lost.

And what, you may ask, has given me this anchor; this very real optimism, even in the midst of turmoil and challenge? What have I had to hold onto? Why not just give up and turn to something that would seem to put all the trouble behind me?

While all these things were going on I had examples to follow. I was acquainted with people who showed me, just by the way they lived, that I didn't have to have what everyone else had in order to be happy. Away from school I walked among giants.

I had read about people ~ pillars of faith ~ in the Bible for years. As valuable as that is for any child, we learn even more by seeing faith lived out in the lives of people around us. In those difficult days I sometimes felt like I didn't have a friend in the world. Just when I needed it most, the Lord provided time for me to spend with people in whose footsteps He wanted me to follow.

We were still going to the Evangelical Free Church in Paradise at this time. It was still a mostly elderly church. These folks were far out of my age group, but that didn't matter to me. When many people my own age seemed out of touch I was given spiritual eyes that allowed me to see and admire in some of them a mature faith that has nothing to do with age.

Most especially the testimony of Irene High was and still is close to my heart. Her husband taught a class where I was taught for the first time the principles of our faith in a systematic way. I was later baptized in their pool behind their beautiful home overlooking the Butte Creek Canyon.

Mrs. High was a faithful servant, always behind the scenes and never saying much. But then she never had to; her sweet spirit and refreshing smile said it all. Here was a woman who, in the cruel tragedy of a driving accident caused by a drunk driver, lost not only so much of her own health, but most importantly she lost her daughter. She has endured so much pain and such difficulty every day of her life since then. But through it all comes a genuinely victorious strength that you almost have to see to believe. That doesn't mean life don't get hard and feel overwhelming at times. She doesn't ignore the many challenges or pretend they don't exist; she just sees *through* them to the goal ahead.

I knew I would do well to try to be like Mrs. High. Let the whole world be far away and let it inflict any pain; just let me be found to have that faith and peace. For obvious reasons her testimony was the one that stood out most to me, but there were others.

My friend—yes my true *friend*—Janiece Wiley, who gave me such respect and treated me as an important person when we co-taught a Vacation Bible School class. Janiece also remains a good friend, now many years later. For a long time now she has been faithfully reading books with me every week. We started when I had to stay home one semester to recover from my last surgery. Now years have passed and we still enjoy each other's company. I can't really think of any other friend who has been around so long and so consistently.

I also think of people who I admired, people who only grew closer to the Lord with age. Some are no longer with us . . . for now, anyway.

I remember Russ Peterson. Our family and his had some fun visits. We even inherited his old Irish Setter named Yeller. But for some reason the biggest memory I have of him was one of the last. The morning that Grandpa was dying and my parents went to the hospital for the last time, he came over and just sat with Alan and me. He and I didn't say much, so there isn't much to tell. I just appreciated having someone I knew cared for us around at that time so that I didn't feel alone.

We also met Pat (*aka* Fence) and John Law there for the first time. They became like substitute parents when Mom and Dad went off on vacation. We had lots of fun together. The nickname "Fence" comes from an infamous Pictionary game. The word was "five" and someone drew the conventional four lines and a crossing slash. She yelled out "fence!" and Alan and I never let her live it down. They are great people who are always there in some of our hardest times.

There are many others who were a part of our lives but last of all for now I want to mention Russ Davis. He was a man who had done such great things with his life for the Lord. He seemed to have such wisdom to me. I waited anxiously for the classes he taught at our church from time to time.

I loved them all. It was through so many of these role models, these giants, that I learned that there were more fulfilling things in life than what I perceived my own world was denying me. However, every church has its problems and for reasons I didn't completely understand we had to leave that church. I was frustrated with that. I had grown comfortable and didn't like going back and forth between strange churches. But I think the Lord knew we needed to be in another place for the near future where I could be better prepared for the challenges I would inevitably face; another church where I could grow even further. I had learned all I could in that place. It was time to take the next step.

§

Ironically it is a line from a science fiction show called *Babylon 5* that comes to mind here. A character said his mother once told him that God, "knows the color of every flower, and the number of leaves on every tree, and He knows just how big your shoulders are so He'll never give you more than you can handle."

His companion responds, "Maybe that's the trick in a place like this . . . grow bigger shoulders."

Death Is Real ~ Death Is Near

How firm a foundation, ye saints of the Lord,
Is laid for your faith in His excellent Word!
What more can He say than to you He hath said-
To you, who for refuge to Jesus have fled?

"Fear not, I am with thee- O be not dismayed,
For I am thy God, I will still give thee aid;
I'll strengthen thee, help thee, and cause thee to stand,
Upheld by My gracious, omnipotent hand.

When thru the deep waters I call thee to go,
The Rivers of woe shall not thee overflow;
For I will be with thee thy troubles to bless,
And sanctify to thee thy deepest distress.

When thru fiery trials thy pathway shall lie,
My grace, all sufficient, shall be thy supply;
The flame shall not hurt thee - I only design
Thy dross to consume and thy gold to refine.

The soul that on Jesus hath leaned for repose,
I will not, I will not desert to his foes;
That soul, tho' all hell should endeavor to shake,
I'll never- no, never- no, never forsake!"

How Firm A Foundation

CHAPTER ELEVEN

§

That is one of my favorite hymns.

When I began attending Paradise High School in the fall of 1991 things began looking up in some ways. A lot of the same problems remained but I could at least eat my lunch in peace with some friends. The high school actually had this brilliant idea of sweeping the floors in the cafeteria. Kids also finally realized that food belongs in your mouth, not on the floor where service dogs can be tempted.

Seniors were a pain to be avoided though. Some of them thought the rule of not petting Friedman should not apply to them. I made the mistake of signing up for a basic first year freshman science class. It was actually mostly used as a remedial class for seniors who were not going to graduate unless they passed a science class. They didn't care about that though. They thought they had the system figured out. The school would not dare refuse to graduate them because of this one requirement and the poor teacher and I heard that from them every day. They were more interested in what happened on *Beverly Hills, 90210* that week. During half the class or more they sat on the tables with their backs to the teacher.

Except for that one class the quality of school went up considerably. I had many more quality teachers. Some of them became my all-time favorite teachers. I was even able to learn from teachers who were popular with students. Something was different in high school and it allowed me to excel. I rose to the higher challenges and began making up for lost time in junior high.

Here is the best example of what I mean. In junior high I had trouble getting ahead in math, but in high school I excelled at it. I had the same math teacher for algebra and geometry in my freshman and sophomore years. He was kind of a sports/jock type of guy. He liked to tease and roughly cajole his students like we were on the basketball team. When he called, "All right Gilbert, what's the answer?" I had better hope I have the right answer or be ready to feel the heat. That isn't the most compatible personality with mine, but I learned because that's why we were there.

He had a picture on his wall of a seaside mansion with a huge garage filled with expensive cars. I sat near the back so when we got our tests or homework back some other kids would see my grade as they passed my papers back to me. Some of the guys near me would have fun with me because they were convinced that someday I would be the millionaire owner of that mansion and they would be my personal mechanics taking care of my cars. An amazing thing began. It was possible to be appreciated, even by other kids, just for being a good student.

I also got to go farther with my artwork than I had before. I took Mr. Wroble's class for all four years. He was a great guy who made art fun for his students. His class was always a nice break in the day where I could do something relaxing that I enjoyed. The square picture of a woman's face in our living room is the first picture I drew my freshman year. He also put together a yearly art calendar to raise money for the art department. All students could vote for which pictures were put in the calendar. My picture got put in that year.

Personal Responsibility

I am digressing from what I had intended this chapter to be about. I wrote everything above yesterday. After thinking about it and sleeping on it I have decided to move on. My life is about more things than school. It is enough to say that I started enjoying school again for the most part. I say "for the most part" because I still had trouble with friendships, but I have covered that subject already. I don't want to go on and on about that because I feel that it isn't important to blame anyone for anything.

On the way home from church just now (August 5, 2001), I realized something that is extremely important for me to include here. I have to confess . . . I feel convicted because *I have blamed people* for the way they've treated me. In the past I have had the exact same conversation with Jesus that a sick man had with Him about 2,000 years ago. This conversation is recorded at the beginning of John Chapter 5.

> Now there is in Jerusalem near the Sheep Gate a pool, which in Aramaic is called Bethesda and which is surrounded by five covered colonnades. Here a great number of disabled people used to lie—the blind, the lame, the paralyzed. One who was there had been an invalid for thirty-eight years. When Jesus saw him lying there and learned that he had been in this condition for a long time, he asked him, "Do you want to get well?"
>
> "Sir," the invalid replied, "I have no one to help me into the pool when the water is stirred. While I am trying to get in, someone else goes down ahead of me."
>
> Then Jesus said to him, "Get up! Pick up your mat and walk." At once the man was cured; he picked up his mat and walked.
>
> ~ John
> John 5:2-9

I hear in that man's response to Jesus the same things I often think. I know full well what that man's situation was. Some things don't change in thirty-eight years, or in two thousand years. Often when I was younger, and sometimes even today, just when I'm about to go and do something someone stronger and faster gets there first. All of what I complained about in the last chapter and the beginning of this one is just another version of the same thing.

I hear this man and myself saying, "It just isn't fair, Jesus. Look at all these people who won't bend down for two seconds to help me. For so long I've had to grovel and beg for help, for friendship. I only get dirty looks, rolling eyes, or worse yet, ignored. They make it so much harder than it already is, and I'm angry about it."

All He asks is, "Do *you* want to get well?"

It would be so easy to choose to get even angrier and direct some of it at Him too. It would be convenient to insist that He just fix everyone else first. I could justify my anger by saying that I would not be so angry if they would all just shape up.

> *But I still see Jesus' penetrating, pleading eyes staring straight into mine.*
>
> *He is searching out this lost sheep!*

I could do all that, but I still see Jesus' penetrating, pleading eyes staring straight into mine. Right here, right now he is searching out *this* lost sheep! He and he alone will worry about the others in their time. Suddenly I am made aware of an intrusive log in my own eye. I have sinned against them as much if not more than they have against me. The issue now is whether I want to give it all up to Him and be well.

Deep inside, though I fail at times, I decide to agree with Jesus that I too am a sinner who needs His healing forgiveness . . . and a part of me is getting well.

DOCTORS

In the summer between my freshman and sophomore years my doctors in Sacramento began talking to us about something very serious. I have not spoken about that part of my life yet but it seems appropriate now.

My experience with doctors did not end with my diagnosis; not by any means. I sympathize with that woman in the Bible in Jesus' time that "had suffered a great deal under the care of many doctors" (Mark 5:26).

I've never been angry with the vast majority of the doctors who have helped me, especially not those who have followed my case for a very long time. I am sometimes shocked, when I go to a clinic where other kids who have my same disease are around, by the variety of attitudes I see. On the other side of thin walls I heard such anger expressed towards anyone in range. I was dismayed, and then determined to try as best I could not to be like that.

Some of my earliest memories are of events that took place at the UC Davis Medical Center in Sacramento. I have sat and waited for hours and hours of my life in that hospital's waiting rooms.

When I first went there, we would go through two waiting room experiences to get to the tiny Physical Medicine and Rehabilitation clinic (PM&R) in the basement. Then we would wait in a very tiny windowless room for the doctors (and there were many of them) to study my files and give a briefing on what was to be accomplished that day for the sake of three, four, or five student doctors.

Visiting a teaching hospital when you have a condition like mine is an interesting experience. I have been a living, breathing model for countless young doctors. I was always asked if I would mind if they participated. I never objected because, despite the frustration of having to repeat everything, I knew deep inside that if I helped them to learn they would in turn help others who were in the same condition. I take some comfort in that. A lot of the time there has not been much doctors could do for me except attempt to delay the deterioration that is inevitable. Maybe someday the base of knowledge that my own case has contributed to will help others more.

Over the years I saw several of the physician professors themselves come and go. One of the benefits of living when and where I do is that I have had the personal attention of some of the best, most brilliant doctors in their fields. In the beginning we used to see Dr. Fowler. He was an older man who always smelled of his pipe, which he carried around with him. On his nametag he had a little pin of Kermit the Frog. He would stretch my joints as far as they could go to monitor the progress of my disease. He used to admonish my parents and me to keep up my physical therapy so that I could remain as limber as possible.

That is another thing that I had to endure. I used to go to weekly sessions of stretching and pulling. It was very uncomfortable but necessary for my own good, the more the better. I should have done it more like my doctors said.

Eventually Dr. Fowler retired and the next generation took over. Dr. McDonald became the leader of the team of doctors who worked on me.

Over the years my files have grown into mountainous piles of folders. It has become a running gag to see so many doctors drag in those thick overflowing volumes. A lot of my life is written in those pages. These volumes of doctors' notes and test results are like scrapbooks of all the physical pain I've ever felt. They are a detailed account of my history with this disease. They contain the records of every blood test that I tried to avoid. There are results of many exhausting breathing tests that began after Dr. Bonecat started working on my case. He has turned out to be the doctor I see at UCD the most now. He is an intelligent, caring man, not just for me but also for our whole family.

In my life, these were the days where the rubber began to meet the road in every exhausting moment, not just when doctors were testing me. It is one thing to say all these wonderful things about what I believe. But it was at these times that my faith was fired and refined. Whenever my body was tired and had nothing left to give I could only sift through my emotions and appraise where my spirit was concerning these things.

> But just when I thought I had gone through so much, I learned that there was much more to endure. When I came to the end of myself I found that no matter how far things went there was something firm on which to stand. I was firmly in the grip of Someone who had endured far more to reach a far greater goal. Now, in the beginning of high school, that belief was going to be tested in the extreme.

Scoliosis

One of the symptoms of my disease is a very crooked back. Even when I'm sitting I do not sit at my full height. I really have no idea how tall I am. Like most kids, I used to get measured at a doorjamb by my parents or grandparents when I was younger. I stopped walking before the normal growth spurts of adolescence and since then we lost track. Maybe it is just vanity to even care.

It is also a matter of comfort as well. At this point in my life I was beginning to get uncomfortable just sitting. My doctors knew it would only get worse with time as my body, lacking any of the larger muscle groups, began to collapse in on itself. They wanted to intervene in what sounded like a radical way to me. They proposed a major surgery in which two metal rods would be fixed to my spine to slightly correct the curvature and prevent it from getting any worse. I have to tell you the very idea of having that kind of hardware in me was not appealing at all. The doctors urged me to do it by explaining in detail how much harder things would be without this procedure. I never did like the idea but eventually I agreed at least to talk to the doctors who would actually do the surgery.

We went to see the orthopedic doctors across the street from the Med Center. Here was a whole new team to work with. The head of them all was Dr. Benson who looked just like you would expect a brilliant surgeon would. He had the confident demeanor of one too. He and his assistant explained in more detail the procedure they would perform. They discussed the risks and benefits with us. They explained that I was a little older and farther along than most boys that were recipients of this surgery. They were more comfortable doing this with someone a little younger and stronger. I personally don't know why it was not done earlier. I don't remember the subject ever being brought up.

After laying me on a table and stretching my back out as far as it would go they explained that they could only correct my spine so far because my spine was already starting to get rigid in a deformed state. Still, even with just a slight correction, we could be sure the situation would not get any worse.

Through it all they never expressed doubt in their ability to pull off this task with success. They were clear that this would be difficult for me. Even with complete success there would be a long and difficult recovery. But these men were experienced and convinced that they were capable despite the few difficulties in my case.

In the end the final decision was mine. I was convinced that it was the right thing to do. In the same way that I knew my case might help others through those student doctors, I believed that they knew this would be the best thing for me because of their experience with others. I decided to go ahead with it.

The hospital did a great job of trying to help me prepare in advance as best they could. A woman who worked for the hospital came to several of my doctor visits with us, and from time to time explained things I might not understand.

She brought samples of some equipment that would be used at different stages of my recovery so that I would not be too surprised. It was a service meant for kids a little younger than me (I was sixteen), but truthfully I think it would benefit people at any age. Most of all she was a friend in a strange place. Doctors can be authoritative, and technicians aloof. She became a familiar face among strangers and made an intimidating environment feel a little more "down to earth."

I took a little too much comfort in the confidence of my doctors for a while. This was their job, which they were certainly experts at, and I assign no fault to them. I was just overwhelmed and absorbed in the technical issues of the whole thing. At first I wasn't letting myself think too hard about the seriousness of the choice I had made. Putting walls up defensively was easier than dealing with it at first.

We were now regularly attending this new church in Chico called Grace Community Church. Having visited several different churches, Grace began to feel like home after our first few visits. The most convincing reason to settle there, at least for me, was the obvious love of the people. When I entered that church for the first time I felt embraced by people who greeted everyone at the door. I am sad to say that seemed to be a unique feature of this church.

When I went to the then very small high school aged Sunday school class, I was immediately welcomed by the Roberts who taught the class. I hope they know how much I appreciated that. Nobody here ever hesitated to make us feel like we mattered to him or her. Allow me to make a note here. Because of this, I believe that our church has the ability to grow into the evangelical church that the Lord wants us to be. We have the foundation laid, not because of a new building, but because of the genuine love in this church. None of us is inadequate to the task if we commit to it. We just have to extend the love outside the church doors a little farther than we have in the past. God's love doesn't stop at the doors; ours shouldn't either.

Anyway, even though we were newcomers, my parents arranged for Pastor Dave Workman to talk with me about my upcoming surgery. My dad also talked to me alone about this, but I don't remember the order. I met Pastor Dave for some time alone at the Leatherby's ice cream shop that used to be in the shopping center across from the old mall. He asked me what I thought about the whole thing. I proceeded to tell him the facts of the matter, how I believed the benefits outweighed the risks and so forth. He asked me, "But, John, how do you feel?"

I don't remember the details of the conversation after that. I do believe that is when the walls started cracking though.

Have you ever been so afraid
that you didn't want to think about the fear?

Another time, Dad and I sat on the back deck having a similar conversation. He pointed out frankly the dire truth that this was something I could actually die from. He wasn't trying to scare me, just to focus my attention in the right place. It had never really hit me that hard before. The doctors' confidence in *themselves* was no longer a confidence I could share. I still thought it was important to continue, but I realized that if I was going to get through this, not just physically, I wasn't going to be able to rely on any doctor's talent no matter how great it was. They could not take care of the other things that mattered.

The question was, "Am I ready, if necessary,
to end my life at sixteen?"

Where was my trust, no matter what happened? When faced with that reality, it became a whole different game. I could not just gamble with this and let the chips fall where they might. I had to put my immediate and long-term hope in the only One worthy of that hope - regardless of the outcome.

FAILURE . . . HUMANLY SPEAKING

Eventually the sands of time poured down and I could not slow them down or wish them away. October rolled around and on the final Sunday before my surgery, although I was very nervous and not sure of many things, I was confident that I was not alone in this. I remember the whole church praying for me and that I tried to hold on to every song we sang. This was one of those times when you feel that every experience you have is something that might slip away if you don't appreciate all of it adequately. There is really nothing you can do though, and part of that is distressing.

The morning of the day before the surgery we all went to a local photographer to have a nice family portrait taken. Mom and I left directly from there to Sacramento. Dad and Alan would catch up and meet us in the hospital parking lot with the Petersons' RV, in which Mom and Dad planned to stay. Mom and I spent the early afternoon at the Sacramento Zoo just for something interesting to do.

In the evening we found Dad and Alan waiting for us in a parking lot, which today is filled with new buildings. Friends had lent us their RV so that Mom, Dad, and Alan would have a place to sleep during my time of recovery. My family busied themselves for a few minutes getting the temporary home away from home settled. I just sat and watched the orange autumn sunset. For some reason an image that has always stuck with me is a large flock of crows, dark black against the brilliant sky, flying to their nests for the night.

We then went inside to check in. It had been previously decided that I should stay in the hospital the night before so that they could do some final work and be sure I was ready first thing in the morning. They did the few things to me that they could still do while I was awake and then tried to let me fall asleep, which in my anxiety took longer than expected.

> *In seconds an effort designed to improve my life became a battle to save it.*

Even when we were just doing the paperwork my emotions began to get bigger than what I could control. When I was finally lying down and surrounded by no one but family and nurses I broke down. I was more afraid than I ever have been. There was no one to put on a brave face for anymore and I didn't care to try.

Eventually I fell into a light and exhausted sleep, probably with the help of some medicine. I wasn't going to try to be brave the way some people mistakenly define bravery. I think if you need help you should just take it and not try to keep things under your own control. That was basically the last coherent memory I have. When someone retrieved me in the very early morning I was only half awake. I vaguely remember a voice telling me not to try too hard to wake up because I was just going to be asleep again in a few minutes. I have an even more vague and brief memory that in no time at all I was in a cold room filled with echoes of voices and nothing but bright electric light all around.

Without any reference of time, it is strange to write this story now. It seems I just slipped from unconsciousness to a "buzzed" wakefulness and back again. When I was awake, if you can call it that, I could not move or talk and could only see through a fog. I could only feel that very unique feeling of very powerful drugs fighting a lot of pain. The only way I can try to describe it is that it's like floating in an ocean inside your body without any way to swim away from the water, which seems to soak energy out of you. There were voices around and at some point the voices told me some very bad things.

> I was told that the doctors had been hours into the surgery. My back was wide open and my spine ready to receive the metal rods when something went wrong. Apparently my body could not withstand the stress and my heart stopped for a couple of minutes. In seconds an effort designed to improve my life became a battle to save it. The surgery completely failed and the doctors decided not to try to complete it. The worst very nearly did happen, but I was revived.

The fight did not end in the operating room. I've been told that the nurses and doctors at one time were measuring the rate of my blood loss by marking the size of the spreading stain on the sheet underneath me. I was given a lot of blood.

During the whole first week of my recovery I was in an ICU ward. The fog slowly lifted, though I soon learned to wish it hadn't. During those first few days I have memories of individuals visiting me but I can't clearly identify most of them. I do, however, remember my grandmother standing next to me for a few moments. The room was kept dark and the shades were closed allowing just a faint amount of sunlight in from my left side. She was standing between the window and me so I could not make out her face. My grandmother had a lot of health problems through her adult life. It was not that long afterwards that I was visiting her in the hospital all too often. She was a very special person to me so it doesn't surprise me that I recognized her more than anyone else besides my parents.

The recovery was a long process, but I was slowly getting better. When I was more aware I was able to make requests by scribbling short words on the pad of paper resting on my chest. It was a frustrating way of communicating for all of us. Mostly I would just ask for more pain medicine; it came out as ***PAIN ME!*** Mom and Dad would encourage me by telling me about all the people who were outside but were not allowed to come in, especially our friend Kathy Machuga who was there for a very long time.

Unfortunately the more awake I was as the days went on, the more I was aware of how much pain I was in. I didn't even care who the new president was in early November. I saw that news on the television for a few seconds and went back to sleep. My days consisted of counting the minutes until I was allowed another dose of morphine. It was a welcome relief every time a nurse put it in my IV.

It felt like a cool and refreshing liquid going up my arm and into my body.

I was also aware of how futile it all seemed to be. I was going through all this pain without the satisfaction of having a beneficial result. I was very sad when my doctors came in and discussed the situation with us. They did not think it was worth the risk to make a second attempt. I understood and knew it was the right decision. It was still probably the biggest disappointment of my life and the lowest I've ever felt.

I was upset about this unexpected turn in events but for the time being I was anxious to get better. There was so much finality to it that I just wanted to get on with my life. I was also still on heavy medication and had a hard time concentrating even on regrets. You might think I would have felt more distressed at such a horrible thing in my life. All I can say is that no matter how upset I've ever felt about this event, there has always been a sense of peace about it. I've felt like I nearly died but I survived and at least am still alive today. I've come to have a healthier attitude about it over time. For a while I just had the general feeling that because something was so terribly wrong in my life that there might be something wrong with me. I toyed with that idea far too long actually. I have decided that this is a lie in my head meant to separate me from the truth that I was refined and made into a person of stronger faith because of this. When I identified that lie and gave it over to God I was set free from it. In its place grew convictions that were stronger than ever.

> I did wonder for a long while what the point of all this was. On the surface it seemed so useless. What was the meaning of going through all this pain with no result? If I had gotten those metal rods in there, I can tell you for sure I would be a lot more comfortable now. Remember how the doctors told me how much more difficult things would be as they convinced me to go through with the surgery? Everything they said was true.

When I finally got home, I had a lot of time on my hands with which to think about these things. For several months I was practically home schooled. A teacher, who became a good friend, would bring my assignments to me. I would work every day but I spent many hours spaced out on the couch with codeine coursing through my veins. At some point the drowsiness would wear off, but I would still need time to rest. In those times my thinking shifted to these questions about the lack of meaning in the pain I had gone through, not just in those past few months, but also in my entire life. In reality, I did not come to firm conclusions right away. Some of it took a few years.

I felt that there just might be some meaning to this if I tried to look for it. There was some choice in the matter. I could have decided to get bitter about it. Instead it seemed better to turn this back over to God and see if there was anything He could do with it. Some might say God abandoned me, but after this event I am more convinced than ever that I was in the right place spiritually and I only want to know more about Him. Maybe that sounds strange to you but it feels perfectly right to me. And if my faith could hold through this, don't you think maybe there just might be something to it? What greater test can you devise? I believe in something bigger than all the trials I face, and it held firm through the worst thing anybody could ever go through. I'm not deluding myself by trying to set right in my mind something that was wrong. I know of the power of which I speak, and it didn't come from within me. My beliefs were tested and came through with flying colors.

> *What in the world could possibly make all this pain worthwhile?*

If I've done one thing well, it is that I've learned to be a trustworthy person. People can tell me things in confidence and I don't repeat them to anybody. Partly that grew out of necessity because sometimes people confide in each other as if I'm not there. I've played the part of the fly on the wall and there is no sense repeating confidences that were not meant for my ears. When given permission to share I do so without exaggeration. And when I share that which is important and appropriate from my own beliefs and experiences, I can do it faithfully and without exaggeration as well. So when speak of a growing faith in the wake of serious challenge you can believe me when I tell you these things are true.

Is There A Bigger Picture Here?

What in the world could possibly make all this pain worthwhile? I have certainly not benefited from it physically. Someday it will work its final handiwork on me and accomplish what this surgery didn't. I am confident that there is value even in this apparent failure. As useless as it all seems, God can use this experience for a greater good. And the only good reason for it that I can think of . . . is you. He can prove to you that the hope He provides and the faith He perfects can overcome every obstacle life can throw at us. Now, I'm sure there are people in the world who suffer more than I ever have. But God has led me to write this and live as an example for you who I'm in contact with. If you have suffered less than me or about the same amount then this whole story is here for you. There is nothing arrogant about that because the same things can be true about anyone's life. I'm not unique. If you know me or read this, then my pain and how I've overcome it is meant to tell you that there is hope available for you too.

Perhaps you don't know God like I do. If so, then maybe something is tugging on your heart right now as you read these words. It is telling you I am right and that no matter how similar or different your pain and mine is, there is something here that will help you overcome too. Please don't ignore it. I felt the same a long time ago, and when I got to know the source of that strong pull it never let me down.

Maybe you do know God, but doubt whether He can really be relied upon with your troubles. If you are afraid for your life, I can tell you I have been where you are - and He is reliable. If you are somewhere short of that, then I hope you will see that if He helped me, He can and will help you. I know it is hard to keep your focus. When I have met new struggles I have sometimes gone back and doubted, yes, even though I went through all this myself. However, with each new trial, when I put my whole trust in Him, even for earthly things, He never gave up on me. But even if He does not rescue me from physical danger, when this disease steals my life once and for all, you need to know that my ultimate hope has already been secured. My story won't end there; I just won't be able to write about that for you.

No matter what happens, this is the only purpose that is worth it all. I can see what the end result will be, and to be sure, I would rather not be going through this. I don't really completely understand it. There are ways for peoples' lives to impact others without this much pain and difficulty and the fear of death. All I can do is trust and believe that what I experience now can't even begin to compare with what I'm going to experience later in a very real heaven. I did recover, despite the discomfort of a huge and sensitive scar down the center of my back from the base of my neck to my tailbone. I got cards from some of my classmates wishing me well and I worked hard on my schoolwork, unwilling to fall behind. Sometimes I would push a little too hard and Mom would have to tell me it was okay to stop for the day. I was able to complete that school year and moved on with my class until I graduated on time in the spring of 1995.

“Would You Mind If I Ramble Awhile?”

Now listen, you who say, “Today or tomorrow we will go to this or that city, spend a year there, carry on business and make money.” Why, you do not even know what will happen tomorrow. What is your life? You are a mist that appears for a little while and then vanishes. Instead, you ought to say, “If it is the Lord’s will, we will live and do this or that.”

~ James, Brother of Jesus
James 4:13-15

CHAPTER TWELVE

§

Since those days, I have been blessed with things I might not have experienced at all. There have also been very hard things to go through. The back surgery took place at the end of only two thirds of my life until now. Looking back it is hard to believe how much of life has happened since then. For years I felt like I was just coming out of that experience, but I've had to realize that that was just the beginning of what has been a long road of maturing faith. I've gone through many ups and downs since then. There are long plateaus in between sudden events that test my resolve and then lead me farther along than I thought possible. Through it all it's like I'm on a train ride that has a certain number of connections ahead. I am much more aware than a lot of people my age that I don't know how many of those places I'll make it to. I've seen more of them than I expected and still don't know how many more I'll get to see. Of course, there are some I wish I had never seen.

Unfortunately, being so unsure of my future, and living with a degenerative disease, I spend far too much time convinced that this is as bad as things will get and as far as I'm going to go; there can't be much more over the horizon. Only God knows the whole story from beginning to end.

Actually, I do know all I really need to know. I know how He has helped me in the past and I have the best view of the future any human can have. The things in between, the things I can't see at all, is the only stuff that bothers me the most these days.

After the infamous back surgery I continued to deal with the difficulties of this disease. I lost a lot of weight because of that experience and had to deal with new ways of trying to stay comfortable. Throughout my junior and senior years we went through a number of seating systems to try to find a way for me to stay comfortable through the day. Just like the doctors said, I would continue to deal with that for the rest of my life. It really wasn't until we went to the Wheelchair Center in Sacramento years later that we finally found people who gave me a system that has worked reliably.

It also was not long before breathing began to be more difficult. The disease started to take effect on muscles that can't be seen, like my diaphragm. Though my exterior muscles would continue to decline in strength, the vast majority of that damage had already been done and the rest of the decline would be very gradual. The process would continue inside, and still does. Dr. Bonecat became the primary doctor that I would see in Sacramento. In the latter part of my high school years, or soon after, I began to need help with my breathing. For a brief period after school and through the night I would have to put on a mask attached to a ventilator and oxygen generator to help me breath better. It was just one more thing to think about. I did appreciate Bob King, whose company provided the equipment for a few years. He recognized my ability to think and always helped me to understand what was being done for me.

§

In the last two years of high school I began to focus on classes that challenged me even more. I always enjoyed my honors English classes with Mrs. Jones and Mr. Ellison. I hope my writing skills in this endeavor would meet with their approval. My favorite project in Mrs. Jones' class was an anthology of science fiction work I put together. I found examples of science fiction writing in everything from short stories to poetry, if you can believe it! I worked very hard on that and enjoyed it too. I also enjoyed our class trip to Ashland, Oregon that year to see a few plays including a great one called *You Can't Take It With You*. Unfortunately we also saw the worst play I ever saw in my life. I won't even dignify it by complaining about it further. Poor Mrs. Jones was sorry she took her class to that one.

In Mr. Ellison's AP English class during my senior year I learned to strengthen my essay writing skills. I found out for the first time that if a class really pushes me I learn the most from it. We went to Ashland again that year. This time our whole family went along. I think Alan was in Mr. Ellison's freshman English class that year. We went to see Shakespeare's *Twelfth Night* and *Hamlet*. Dad and Alan dosed off during the first one. Personally I'm not a big fan of Shakespeare's comedies because I have little frame of reference with which to understand the humor. I'm not sure I would want to understand most of it anyway.

The last few weeks of high school were the best time I ever had during my education. I felt the satisfaction of having accomplished something important. My friends (I never meant to say I had none) tried to convince me to let them pet Friedman before we graduated. Since it was the last time they would probably see him I finally gave in. We'd been together so long by then, Friedman and me; there was really no harm done. Our teachers let up on us when they could and let us enjoy the time. When we graduated, our class was the most accomplished class Paradise High School had ever seen.

On graduation night . . . all of my classmates . . . and all of their families stood on their feet . . . applauded me and cheered me on.

On graduation night, Friedman and I went through the whole graduation ceremony just like everyone else. It was held outdoors in the school's football stadium. We had worked with the school to figure out how I could participate fully. They used the ramps my grandfather had bought so that I could get into his house in Magalia. I was the first to receive my diploma. Some folks helped me up the ramps and onto the stage. Friedman and I went right up to Mr. Stout, our principal, and received my diploma. As he congratulated me and I began to turn to go back down I saw something that shocked me. All of my classmates, even the ones I didn't know, and all of their families stood on their feet applauding me and cheering me on. I was terribly flattered and realized I had more friends than I have let on. Was I so blind in these school days that I didn't let myself realize this? Oh well, what's past is past. In the end I knew that I was proud of getting through it all and lots of other people apparently are proud of me too. I hope some will come to understand that my joy is grounded in what God did *for* me.

After we were officially graduated, we all celebrated and my few closest friends and I congratulated each other. It was late for me, and I went home and crashed on the couch in the middle of the party we had. Lots of people came, including a few of my favorite teachers such as Mrs. Kelsey. She was my health teacher for half of my freshman year. She was a wonderful lady who helped me out a lot. My whole family, my grandmother, and even my mother's cousin Bernie Carpenter and her husband Bob were there as well as at the ceremony. They surprised me by coming all the way from Texas just to see me graduate. I was very honored by that; they are very generous people.

§

After this it was time for college at Chico State. It started on a bad note. Friedman was getting a little older and grayer by now. He had been with me for seven years through some of the toughest times in my life. Suddenly, during one of the first few weeks of school his health took a quick turn for the worse. There was little question about it, he was very sick. My parents took him to the veterinarian and I spent a very miserable hour or so waiting at home on the couch. When they came home, without him, they told me the doctor said there was nothing to be done. They quickly took me to see Friedman at the vet's because I wanted the final decision to be mine. As the very solemn staff led me into the back room nobody needed to say anything to me. Through my tears I saw him lying there in terrible pain.

I looked into his eyes,
but they were glossed over and he just wasn't there
anymore.

I told them to do what needed to be done to end his clear agony. I wasn't that eloquent, I just nodded when they asked quietly. It wasn't a terribly hard decision to make since he appeared to be in so much pain that extending it would require a cruelty I never had. But losing him left a hole like I lost my best friend, and that he really was.

§

If you think about it, most towns don't have a university nearby. If my dad's business had taken us to some town that was farther away from the nearest college, I would have been pretty much stuck at this point. I would have had to settle for never going to school again after High School. At most I would have been able to only continue my education through correspondence courses or my own reading. What happened instead nearly gives me goose bumps.

I have a real college right where I need it to be!

If circumstances were different, my abilities in academics might have allowed me to go to many far-off universities. But since my abilities are what they are, I believe that we were led years in advance to a place that suited my yet unknown needs. Call it coincidence if you want but personally, I don't believe in coincidences like that.

§

I've discovered that thinking and worrying over all the "what ifs" is a useless exercise. I still do it too much. Sometimes I imagine having gone to some far off university and being a stellar student, then moving on to an accomplished career. But for me, it is sometimes simply a dream of being able to sit at a desk comfortably, taking my own notes, and being able to devote my full attention to my instructors without being distracted by a pain in my side or in my hip or any other physical need.

It has been so long since I was able to relax so much that I could just enjoy the moment! Always there is something screaming for attention so that I have to devote a large portion of my mind to it. Even choosing to ignore the distractions takes so much energy. It truly drains me until I finally fall asleep at night. I used to love to lie in bed early on a spring morning and listen to the world waking up. I drank in the cool, refreshing breeze through the open window like it was candy. I think I remember sensations like that because now my senses are so dulled by the distractions I feel. When it is a chore just to breathe it is hard to enjoy things like that.

I think about all that—about my limitations, my painful distractions—and then I think about when I'm told that God sustains every moment of our lives. I think about Jesus saying to me, "So do not worry about tomorrow; for tomorrow will care for itself. Each day has enough trouble of its own" (Matthew 6:34, NASB).

I prayed sincerely for help when life started to get like this. A disease of inconvenience became a disease of constant daily trouble, and finally a disease of pain. I asked only that the distractions would not get in the way when it really mattered. So far that has been given to me. The problem hasn't magically disappeared, but somehow I can work past it enough to absorb the important information. When I'm sitting in school or in church or any other event, I come away having grasped all I really needed. There is the answer to all you who wonder how in the world I retain so much knowledge despite how much else I have to deal with. The question answers itself I think. There *is* no way in the world it could be done. I appreciate the compliments people give me about how smart they think I must be, but though I may have been originally made with some intelligence, I could not have done this well on my own.

The most important result is not how well I do in school. I think the real reason God blessed me with this gift is so that no matter how much brain power I have to set apart for the distractions of my life, they could never distract me too much from Him. You may see me having to leave for a few minutes during church. As much as I hate going, I am confident that God has let me hear what I needed to hear most the same as everybody else. The same holds true every single day. In fact, sometimes the kinds of distractions I've dealt with have actually only worked in His favor.

§

Let me tell you of a great example. I'm a little sensitive about this, so I didn't mention it before. A lot of people can be unintentionally insensitive about it, so I never talk about it.

Notice anything missing in the last few chapters about junior high and high school? No "romantic" type of relationships, right? That is because there really never was one. It's not that I never thought along those lines, or even because I was too shy. More important things distracted me and the hassle and time consumed by a first attempt early in junior high led me to believe it wasn't worth the energy. (That's all the detail you're getting, sorry! This is as vulnerable as I want to be in this format!) While I've at times regretted that decision and though it probably cost me some healthy, wholesome "growing up" experiences like a couple of high school proms, I've realized there could have been some benefit from that. The way things are these days, the good might outweigh the bad. I'm trying to say that all the time I might have spent in the dating scene was used up by more long-lasting and valuable pursuits. I basically sacrificed short-term and shallow relationships for a stronger relationship with God, and I think that is a fair trade.

I'm not against others going through the normal teenage stuff, as long as it is within the bounds of integrity and obedience to God's perfect design for human relationships. For me the circumstances are just different, and I deal with much bigger problems on a daily basis. Most kids will grow up into much more mature and important relationships with

God and people over time. The crises of my life just put me on the fast track towards the former and the silliness of junior high "relationships" were meaningless compared to my devotion to Him.

§

When it was time to start thinking about my future in college, I formally enrolled in the Computer Science major because I enjoyed working with computers in high school. I thought about what I wanted to do with the rest of my time in life. To be honest, I made some bad assumptions and based my decisions on them. Looking back this part of my life is irritatingly similar to those stories of Jesus' disciples when they just were not getting it. You know the parts, when you imagine yourself chastising them for being so dense. After all, Jesus had just given them a glimpse of the reality of how trustworthy He was! Couldn't they remember anything?

If we are honest with ourselves we have to admit there are times in all our lives when we act exactly the same way. We also have to realize that no matter how many mistakes we make, the Lord doesn't give up on us either. He even used their mistakes to instruct us. If they got everything right what would there have been to write about? Could we really have related to the lives of twelve perfect men? The gospel is about one perfect man and a bunch of other bozos in the same shape as you and me. So in return I offer you the truth about my slightly wrong attitude and how it changed, not because the circumstances changed but because my attitude is altered.

I decided I was a little worn out from working so hard to keep up with where I should be at my age. I know, earlier I credited God with my accomplishments, not *my* "working hard." Like I've said, we all take our turn being the dense disciple. Maybe I could enjoy just a *little* credit?? In any case, the fact is I was getting to the point where I could not have kept up completely. I don't believe that even with the right attitude I would have graduated in four years. College classes do demand more work than high school does, and I just could not physically handle taking a full load and stay up till all hours of the night doing homework. That decision to not try to take a full load wasn't the real problem.

I was also despairing with a conviction that
even if I tried, I didn't even have four years left.
It is a morbid idea, but that is how I felt.

So what is the point of working hard for a career that will never get off the drawing board? I didn't give up; I just decided to only choose to take classes I would enjoy with the few semesters I had coming. For two plus years I did just that. Unfortunately, as much as I did enjoy those classes I was in despair about my life most of the time. I didn't see the real point of going on with it all.

That feeling is just a part of living with this disease. I still don't know how long I have and whether I'll even make it to another graduation. I would like that for myself. People talk like it is going to happen just because they don't really know what else to say about it. I don't blame them even though it tends to make me a little sad. It is not as if I always want people to qualify talk of my college graduation with, "if you don't die first." This is a basic morbidity in the back of my head whenever I think about any future plans I try to make. It is one of the hardest things I have to overcome in this season of my life.

§

I've learned to be patient with myself over the feelings I had during the first two years of college. The reason for that is that I was going through some pretty heavy physical difficulties during that time that probably had some effect. My breathing problem only got worse and worse. Ever since my back surgery I've not been able to eat enough to keep up my weight; I began dwindling away. The problem with my breathing was that I could not inhale very well and could not exhale enough used air, so CO_2 just built up all day long. That is a terrible feeling, and it does cruel things to the body and mind. It is hard to keep the right perspective on life when you experience sleepless nights and a constant nagging ache in your head all day, every day. For a while I would actually wake up screaming in the middle of the night. In the morning I never remembered anything. It became clear that the breathing machinery and treatment I was using at the time were losing the battle.

There is one thing that came along that changed my perspective and physical deterioration. My doctors told me about another surgery they wanted me to consider. The very word . . . *surgery* . . . sent rivers of fear flowing through my mind. I didn't exactly have a great track record. They were extremely patient with me about this. I would not be surprised if they toned down their personal advocacy because of my last experience. Still, they assured me that there were nowhere near the same risks as there were before. They told me there are always risks, but those associated with this surgery were relatively minor.

They wanted to take a more direct route towards helping me breathe by performing a tracheotomy[1]. At the same time they wanted to put a tube into my stomach so that I could get the nutrition I was lacking. Just because it was a relatively minor surgery didn't mean it was easy to make a choice about whether to do it or not. The thing that made it most difficult was that my doctors could not tell me exactly what all the benefits and drawbacks would be. Different people have different results from this surgery. I might or might not be able to speak afterwards. Losing the normal breathing through my nose and mouth, with all of their natural defenses, might make me more vulnerable to illness. On the other, hand it would be easier to recover from an illness with the trache rather than without it. People's bodies also react differently to having plastic where it doesn't belong. Some people need to have the resulting fluid in the lungs removed often; others hardly need suctioning treatments at all. On top of it all there was the possibility that if I didn't choose to do it, someday I might get so sick that they would have to do it in an emergency situation. All of these possibilities made it hard to come to a decision.

It all came down to a choice between extending my life at the risk of it being filled with monotonous and unpleasant tasks versus letting nature take its course. It felt like a really bleak future either way. I was never convinced that the best-case scenario would happen. I didn't have that much optimism. I didn't really expect the worst either. I believed the result would be somewhere in between. In the end, after agonizing for a long time, I chose to try to get the help I needed. It was pretty much a decision of practicality. It seemed like I didn't have much to lose, but I could gain a lot even if there were some tedious things that might slow me down.

> *If He can be trusted with the good, why not the bad?*

This surgery was scheduled for July of 1997. The time passed too quickly, just as before. I entered this surgery with a little more calmness than the first one. I was nervous about what would happen though. I wondered if maybe I just was not meant to succeed with surgery. Maybe my body just doesn't react well to the things the doctors have to do in these situations. No matter what my fears were though, I had the same sense of peace that always seemed to come at the most unexpected times. It was like I was the victim of a shipwreck. The life raft that kept me afloat was that part of me deep inside that knew the whole world could fall apart but I would still be safe. I didn't even see death anymore as the point where the life raft was finally overcome by waves and sank with me in it. Rather, it will be when the rescue ship finally arrives and ropes are thrown down to lift me up completely out of danger.

There was another factor in my life that fed this almost tangible conviction. In earlier times people who believed these things pointed me in the right direction. I followed because they seemed trustworthy. But at Grace Community Church I have gone beyond just following out of a kind of obedience, as good as that was for me before. After years of Pastor Dave's teaching I grew to a newer level of faith that had given me a firmer personal grasp on what all this means. I gained from this church and its total reliance on the Word of God for direction a new set of glasses that allowed me to see more clearly. This gave me the tools I needed to be transformed from just a "follower" to a "do-er." For example, for a while I was very afraid of death because I didn't really understand what was beyond. That fear reappears from time to time. People had always talked of heaven in nebulous terms. I was afraid because I didn't really understand. I thought it was not understandable.

> But by simply going to what God said, instead of what people have said about it, I learned that while it's true we can't understand everything, God has given us a glimpse of what is to come. It was enough of a glimpse to blast my biggest fears out of the water!

I've learned that when God promises something good, He doesn't mess around. If He can be trusted with the good, why not the bad? I've also learned the Bible isn't just something for religious "goody-two-shoes" to carry around and make them good people by osmosis. It is a real tool for real life. The more I use it the stronger the foundations get. Actually the rock was always strong enough; I just needed a light so I could see it under my feet.

For this surgery we spent the previous night in a hotel in Sacramento. I slept acceptably well that night and woke up early to go to the hospital. I was very nervous, but still pretty calm. This time I was awake until I got into the operating room and the doctor put me to sleep. Getting an IV in was an adventure. I had become skin and bones since the last surgery; finding my veins required the skill of the most experienced nurse. When they finally got it in, they gave me something that calmed me down and relaxed me. That is pretty much everything to tell until I woke up in the ICU.

I was in some pain and drugged up but I was aware of my surroundings. I think my mom and nurse were there when I came to. The first thing Mom said was not to worry, everything went as expected. I was surprised by the sense of relief that gave me. I didn't mind the pain as much because at least it was worth something! I also met Nurse Love for the first time. No kidding, that was her name. She was one of the best nurses I ever had. I didn't really understand all of what I was feeling. It was disconcerting at first not to be breathing through my nose or mouth. Right away she just made me feel like she knew what she was doing and I was in good hands. After a few days the equipment was adjusted and I was able to talk, in a strange new way.

Most of the recovery time for this surgery was not about healing from the wounds. My body had to play catch up because of the years I had spent not breathing well. There was a lot of fluid deep inside that finally had the opportunity to escape. In fact, after the first few days it wasn't the pain from the wounds that bothered me the most. It was the feeling of being sick both because of the buildup in my lungs that was finally coming out and because it took a while before my stomach would accept the food I was now eating. Most importantly though, the hospital was not going to let me go home until my parents could take care of my new needs. They had to be taught how to do a lot of what the nurses were doing. I had to get used to living with it all too.

Since I was more aware of the goings on around me I heard some interesting things outside my ICU room door. A couple of times I was startled by loud alarms and people rushing by with big machines. Often I saw police officers through the glass wall. There was a convict in the room next door getting medical treatment. I judged from nurses' expressions as they came in my room from time to time that he was an extremely difficult patient. One night I woke up to people in another room talking very loudly, almost screaming. Since I could hear the conversation so clearly I figured out that a man had been in an accident. He must have been encased in some medical device and the doctor was yelling so that the man could hear him through it. The doctor was asking him if he wanted extreme measures taken to save his life or if he just wanted them to let him go. I didn't get back to sleep very easily after hearing that.

After a couple of weeks it was time to go home again. I experienced a strange sensation. For many long, boring days I had anxiously waited for the doctor to say I could go home and for the pharmacy to get its act together and give us enough supplies to last until we set things up with a supplier at home. When the day finally came and we were waiting for an ambulance from Chico to drive me two hours to our home, a part of me became very nervous about leaving. I had gotten used to the security of having all of my new medical needs met in the hospital. I was anxious about us being on our own, but as soon as I actually got home I felt better. Being lifted out of the ambulance, it was nice to look up from the gurney at my own blue sky and majestic trees. There were also people here waiting to take care of things. There was a new bed for me to use and a nurse to help make the transition. For a few days nurses came for a couple of shifts and stayed through the night.

Even though I was home it took a while to get my strength back up. As the summer came to a close I decided I wasn't quite ready to go back to school, so I skipped one semester. We went back to the ear, nose, and throat (ENT) doctor's office every other week to see how I was progressing. Unfortunately the tracheotomy was not healing very well. The first time they tried to take the equipment out to check the site was yet another time when a doctor's overconfidence was put to the test. It had not healed like it should have so with the plastic came blood, and lots of it. Dad says the poor guy's eyes bulged out, as a simple procedure became a mini crisis. Somehow, with me choking, he and his helper got things back together and immediately suctioned the blood out of my lungs.

It was a process that was repeated with more caution, but still with little success, several times. It became obvious that things were not going as they should. The doctors finally decided that they had to fix the problem with another surgery. This one would be even more minor because the site already existed. I quickly agreed to this with some disappointment. I wasn't happy with the idea of having to keep going through painful trache exchanges.

There is very little to tell about this surgery. It was scheduled and came very quickly. We went down to UC Davis the same way as before. They didn't put me to sleep as deeply because I was awake in the operating room before the surgery and woke up again a few minutes later in the post-op room. I think a couple of nurses wished I was asleep sooner because I kept peppering them with questions.

I finally felt drowsy and suddenly found myself in another room with a new pain in my neck. Everything went as expected—again. I even did so well that I spent just one night in ICU and went home the next day. I was pleasantly shocked when the nurse told me that I could go home.

Unfortunately, this time I lost the ability to speak out loud.

The ability to speak still exists; I just would not be able to breathe at the same time. We never have found a way for me to overcome this obstacle. I'd like to be able to talk like you see Christopher Reeves doing, but every system was tried without any success. We continued to return to the ENT doc every few weeks; my stoma eventually healed nicely. . .just no voice.

From then on this breathing assistance has been a part of my life. It has usually helped me breathe much better than I could before. I could sleep easier and for the first time in five years I actually began gaining weight. In all I gained about half of what my weight was before the stomach tube was put in, which made me feel a little healthier even though I'm still skin and bones.

Even accepting those blessings, living this way can be frustrating at times. I don't think I fully appreciated the ability to communicate freely with people until I lost it. Suctioning mucus from my lungs many times every day gets monotonous and inconvenient when I'm trying to go out and enjoy an event of any kind. Every time I try to do something special like going to church or seeing a movie the concern of missing something occupies my mind. Of course, that has always been a part of my life to some degree.

When Peace Like A River . . .

I can do all this through him who gives me strength.

~ Paul
Philippians 4:13

Nothing less than life in the steps of Christ
is adequate to the human soul or the needs of our world.

~ Dallas Willard

CHAPTER THIRTEEN

Life the last few years has had its high points and low points. Sometimes the two awkwardly overlap and uncomfortably coexist. I have seen things I didn't expect to see. While I've enjoyed school and the interesting things I've learned there, those lessons are not the ones that stick out in my mind most now that I look back. I saw people rise to levels that they didn't expect of themselves, including me.

I don't get around much anymore so every trip I do take is a big deal to me. The last big trip I took was to San Diego to see Alan graduate from Marine boot camp. It was obviously the real thing, not some "wanna be" imitation for overzealous dog trainers. Did I say that? I'd be silly to say, "I can relate to it" just because of CCI. On a side note, as Janiece would say, I think it is often a symptom of the desire for victim-hood when every tragedy draws a mob of people who want to say they relate to it just because they want to have

> *But most importantly I was deeply proud of my brother.*

something significant to say. Sympathy is a good thing, but it should be expressed for the benefit of others, not oneself. I especially believe this when I hear car dealerships telling us in commercials how significantly the events of September 11th, 2001 affected their desire to sell us a car. Really!

Let's get back to the important stuff. I was honestly excited to be going. I gained so much respect for my brother and what he had done. Some of the ideals of the Marine Corps, which were introduced to family in the two or three days prior to the graduation, were very noble. I also admit that the military pomp and circumstance, which is not without meaning, was thrilling to me. But most importantly I was deeply proud of my brother.

HARRY

Another person I feel a mixture of pride and love over has been on my mind since I wrote the very first sentence in this story. I've been debating how to present this since then because wounds over these events still run very deep for people I care a lot about. I'll just present it with the integrity it deserves; besides, many people close to the subject have probably already guessed who I intend to talk about.

Just a couple of short years ago some people we knew got the most disturbing news anyone could ever get. Seeing that from the outside was a new and sobering experience for me. Harry and Kim Hernandez had become good friends since they moved to Chico and became involved in Grace Community Church. For anyone who doesn't know, Harry was the young new Associate Pastor for our church. I always enjoyed Kim and Harry, and especially how much he enjoyed learning about what I was doing in school and comparing notes with me on everything from Hebrew to History. I always felt we had much in common.

After several years of them being an integral part of life at church something happened that even today has a sting of shock in the memory, at least for me. Harry suddenly had cancer, and to make a long and painful story short, there was never anything that could be done. In a short time I went from thinking we had a few things in common to feeling closer to him than I've ever felt to anyone, even though I hate the reason it happened. And it has nothing to do with facing horrible diseases. All the things I've tried to say in this story were embodied in him until the very end. Never anywhere else have I seen, except on the cross, such a healthy model of what God intends for us to become. And now my only regret is that I didn't express what I felt better when I had the chance.

What I personally carried away from this probably goes deeper than I understand myself, at least for right now. I didn't meet a perfect or euphorically religious man; I met a *faith-full man* who could, at this most important time, *trust* beyond his circumstances in a world made new with love—a love beyond what any of us can understand.

I went to see Harry one last time on a brisk Halloween afternoon, and that is where I saw it: the inexpressibly beautiful sunset I described at the end of the first chapter. I was given a chance to say my last farewells as Harry lay very sick in his bed. As we were leaving Kim and Harry's house, I turned my wheelchair around in their hallway so I could back out over the bump at the front door on the way out. And there was Harry! He followed us out of his room, walking very weakly on someone's arm. As I looked on, smiling, he insisted in a moment of confusion that he should help get me over the threshold. Everyone told him it was okay, that they could take care of it. But I think even in his last days he just wanted to help someone else. That is just the kind of person he was. Maybe this experience was God's way of letting Harry help me over my last and ultimate obstacle.

As I turned around again I saw him in the hallway beyond that open door, and then immediately saw that awesome sunset. It is something that remains with me.

§

Mostly the issue I continue to deal with is that same trust, the kind Harry so clearly enjoyed. It comes up over and over again. I face trial after trial, leading me to trust God more for everything in this world and the world beyond. Last year my parents went away for thirty-six hours, leaving me apart from them for more than a day for the first time in a very long time. It may sound silly to have your sense of security dashed because of such a trivial thing. But for someone like me it is not very trivial at all. I struggled with this, mostly until my friend Linda Beadle wrote me this message:

> John,
>
> I've been thinking (dangerous thing to do!) and praying about you and this coming weekend.
>
> God says, "Trust me, aren't you my child? Didn't I save you and keep you unto me? I have you and your life in my hand - trust me." This is what I keep hearing in my spirit, John. I know it is hard to trust your care to someone besides family and to release your mom and dad for the weekend. . . but you are God's child and He will not be gone and He will continue to care for you.
>
> Linda

As Linda has gotten accustomed to doing, she hit me right between the eyes with this one. Actually, I felt right away that it wasn't necessarily her talking at all. It is a feeling I had that I can't explain. I can't say I enjoyed the weekend, but I did learn something from it.

I have faced similar growth experiences since then. I'm facing one now, having been sick for nearly three months and trying to overcome gnawing doubt. But every single time, I come to a better understanding of the God who loves me, and what He deeply desires for me.

Trust is the theme of the following poem, which in the form of a song has carried many of us through very hard times. For some strange reason I have never heard the last verse of the poem sung as part of the hymn. It seems integral to me, especially after hearing a sermon recently by John Ortberg. He pointed out the story of Joshua leading the Israelites across the Jordan. The Levites who carried the ark were told by God to set foot in the Jordan before He would pull back the waters as He did at the Red Sea. This seems simple enough until you realize that the Jordan was in flood stage that time of year. The banks of the Jordan where they were being asked to walk in was so steep that usually a man's first step in was his last as he fell under and drowned. But we have an unusual God. He invited those men to trust Him—that He was going to provide a firm foundation for their feet. And so He invites each of us.

And so He invites me.

When peace, like a river, attendeth my way,
When sorrows like sea billows roll;
Whatever my lot, Thou has taught me to say,
It is well, it is well, with my soul.

Though Satan should buffet, though trials should come,
Let this blest assurance control,

That Christ has regarded my helpless estate,
And hath shed His own blood for my soul.

My sin, oh, the bliss of this glorious thought!
My sin, not in part but the whole,
Is nailed to the cross, and I bear it no more,
Praise the Lord, praise the Lord, O my soul!

For me, be it Christ, be it Christ hence to live:
If Jordan above me shall roll,
No pang shall be mine, for in death as in life
Thou wilt whisper Thy peace to my soul.

But, Lord, 'tis for Thee, for Thy coming we wait,
The sky, not the grave, is our goal;
Oh trump of the angel! Oh voice of the Lord!
Blessed hope, blessed rest of my soul!

And Lord, haste the day when my faith shall be sight,
The clouds be rolled back as a scroll;
The trump shall resound, and the Lord shall descend,
Even so, it is well with my soul.

It is well, with my soul,
It is well, it is well, with my soul.

It Is Well With My Soul
Horatio G. Spafford, 1873

On an April morning in 2000 Pastor Dave Workman asked John to speak on the topic of "How I Face the Future." John would take center stage in his wheelchair. As his written thoughts were displayed on a large screen above his head, John spoke to the congregation in a computer generated verbal monotone through his laptop.

Dave taught clearly about an eternity available to us through a risen Christ.

"You can face your future with or without God in your life . . . the choice is yours. God says His way is the way in which He masters the circumstances of your life instead of letting your circumstances master you."

And then our pastor tearfully introduced John:

"But this morning," Dave said, "I don't want you to take my word for this. I want you to listen to the testimony of a young man, John Gilbert, and how he faces his future. He has a disease that has destroyed his life . . . one inch at a time. As a matter of fact he has no remedy and no recourse but to face it. He's already out lived his life expectancy; he's here by God's grace. John can't talk anymore, but thanks to modern technology he's going to speak to us through his computer. So I want you to listen real carefully . . . and hear how John faces his future."

How I Face The Future

I have been asked to speak to you about how I face the future.

Because of this disease I have called Duchenne muscular dystrophy I know I am facing a difficult future. For those of you who don't know me, this disease will someday cut short my time on earth. It is a genetic disease that does not allow the muscles to grow at all. I have already been through difficult things I did not expect and I did not want to happen.

Seven years ago I faced one of the hardest things I ever had to go through. I was sixteen then. For most sixteen year olds their biggest concern is passing a driving test. My biggest concern was staying alive. That year I had some major surgery that was meant to straighten out my back. In the middle of the procedure my heart stopped for a while and I had a long and difficult recovery. Many of the people here will remember that time and they helped my family and me through it.

Recently I had surgery again. This time the purpose was to help me breathe by giving me a *trache*.

As a result I lost the ability to speak which is why I am using this computer today.

I cannot tell you exactly what will happen in the future because I don't know myself. Sometimes not knowing feels like the hardest part. It is like watching the last few minutes of a really exciting movie for the first time. You can sense an ending coming but you don't know how it will end. In some of these movies you are not really sure the good guys are going to win. Sometimes I don't feel so sure they are either.

There is no way I could survive these worries and feelings of being overwhelmed by how bad the world is on my own. Fortunately, I don't have to. Have you ever asked yourself if God could do one great thing to help you what would it be?

I have.

Obviously the first thing that comes to mind in my situation is to be cured right this minute. But that is not what the greatest thing would be. Jesus said, "These things I have spoken to you, so that in Me you may have peace. In the world you have tribulation, but take courage; I have overcome the world."

Two thousand years ago before I even existed and was able to know what I needed, Jesus did something that would help me more than I could possibly imagine. He defeated the world and all the horrible things it has to offer . . . the least of which is a disease like mine. Because I believe in who Jesus is and what He did, I can have peace about my future. I am at peace with the future because while the immediate future is full of difficult things, the more distant future is full of wonderful things. My pain is only a temporary situation. In other words, that movie I've been watching is almost over. It has not really been a very good movie, but Jesus has been signed on as the producer for the sequel, and He promises it will be great. I believe Him. In fact, I have staked my life on it.

Knowing these things doesn't take any of the very real suffering away. But the peace Jesus offers is just as real and gives me the ability to face the future with confidence in the final outcome.

Thank you for the opportunity to share these things with you.

§

John left the stage to an honoring applause,
followed by a deafening and sustained silence.

That's how it is when we're privileged to witness a transformed life.

In These Last Few Days . . .

Twenty five years of life . . .

- ~ of being sick . . . increasingly very sick,
- ~ of being different and alone,
- ~ of being trapped in a body that would not respond to the desires of a young boy's heart,
- ~ and of knowing an inexplicable joy.

John originally intended his quoting of Horatio Spafford's *It Is Well With My Soul* to be the final thought in his book. However . . .

It was not all well with John's soul. Uncertain what tomorrow would bring, uncertain what heaven would be like, John wrestled with his imagination as it wrestled with truth. As months passed and death crept closer still, John enjoyed a fresh perspective . . . an insight that comes from *knowing*, from *remaining*, from *abiding* (John 15). And as his life neared its premature end, John penned these final thoughts reflecting a depth of humility and contentment that come from a life fully surrendered to Christ.

Something Stronger Than Time

Humble yourselves, therefore, under God's mighty hand, that he may lift you up in due time. Cast all your anxiety on him because he cares for you.

Be alert and of sober mind. Your enemy the devil prowls around like a roaring lion looking for someone to devour. Resist him, standing firm in the faith, because you know that your fellow believers throughout the world are undergoing the same kind of sufferings.

And the God of all grace, who called you to his eternal glory in Christ, after you have suffered a little while, will himself restore you and make you strong, firm and steadfast. To him be the power for ever and ever. Amen.

~ Peter
1 Peter 5:6-11

CHAPTER FOURTEEN

I have been reminded in the hardest possible way that the choices we make affect our lives in every way. One of the biggest choices of my life is swiftly approaching like a dark storm cloud over the valley.

Twenty years ago my parents made a decision that affects me every day. It was an unusual decision that astonishes people who know what it means, as well as those who think they could never imagine having the devotion it demands. They decided that, come what may, they would take care of their son. Dad is the first to point out, even to me when necessary, that it is my mom who bears the brunt of that burden. And she has carried it so very well.

Not long ago a woman at church asked me to pray for a family at the beginning of their long hard road. The short tale stopped me in my tracks, brought a burden to my heart and made me regret every ounce of self-pity I've ever felt. She told me about a young boy who was diagnosed with a terminal disease. She told me his father had gone into long-term military service just to avoid watching his son die. Right after the woman left me alone, I just sat by the lawn in front of the church doors and said a prayer for their healing as a family, and one of gratitude for my own family.

Nurses often are amazed that my mom does all of the care for someone in my condition. They also say that this is highly unusual. I can say without the slightest reservation that she does a much better job than most professionals do. I owe the quality of life I've experienced for most of my years to her. I'm sorry that in my frustration and humanity I don't express that gratitude more readily. But I choose to display it to the world now.

I also thank God for this blessing: that though I am often lonely, I have never been alone. He has provided love when I needed it most, and although some would observe our family and say my dad is the more "sensitive" parent, God often in times of dire circumstances provided that love through my mother. When the world seems to crash down around me she is often found to be holding on to me and crying through it with me.

Winding Down . . .

For five months now a battle has been raging in my body. I have had a persistent lung infection that has developed into pneumonia twice. I have had a fever every day since Halloween, and now winter has passed into spring, and summer is fast approaching. I have been on some very powerful antibiotics, but at most they only seem to accomplish a stalemate.

In January, after several failed attempts with antibiotics, my doctor suggested it was time to move on to more powerful IV antibiotics. That may sound simple enough, but with me, IV's are no simple matter. There is no place on my arms where an IV appropriate for antibiotics can be used. The best alternative was a central line into my chest. There was risk in this though. While a trained surgeon would do everything he could to prevent this, with the deformity of my upper body there was a chance that the desired vein could be missed and my lung could be punctured and collapse.

Once again, out of the blue it was time to make a big decision. This one was different from all the others though. Beyond the choice over this procedure, I had to begin thinking about how badly I wanted to fight this infection and how much I was willing to go through to try to get well. At this point I had a matter of hours to make a decision. The weekend was approaching and because of doctors' schedules I could not wait for the first of the week to decide. That isn't the best way to make such a decision, but sometimes the world gives us no choice. At this time all I could do was try to rely on the wisdom of others and trust that, even though it seemed the world had given me too much to handle, it wasn't too much for God. So with some prayer and a little courage I decided to have the procedure done. My condition was that if the worst did happen, I did not want extraordinary measures taken to save my life. That was the best compromise I could come up with in the time given.

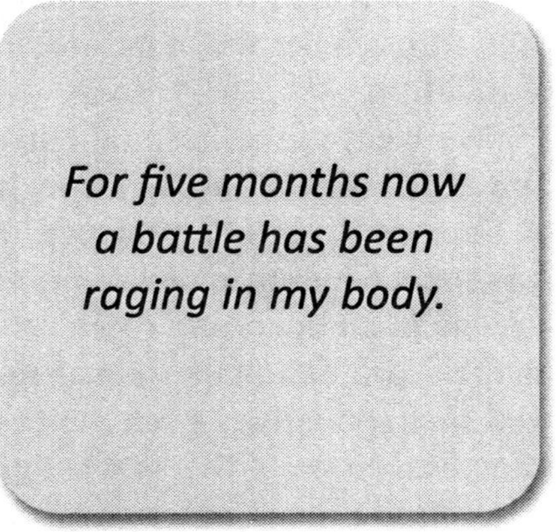

I also had to realize my limits. I could not decide everything concerning life and death in two hours. I could only face what was directly before me and leave the rest to God for now. I don't think I was indecisive. I knew that should I come out of this procedure successfully the big issues would still be there. I believe that we should not expect too much of ourselves. Such a decision had to be made in due time, without unwarranted haste.

I was probably more nervous about this procedure than was necessary. Doctors have to give us the worst-case scenario even when it is an extremely unlikely result. But having been through the worst before, it is hard for me to put it out of mind.

We went to the hospital early in the day. I had all those dire possibilities running through my head. But in the lobby of Feather River Hospital, affiliated with the Seventh Day Adventist Church, is one of my favorite paintings. It depicts a scene in an operating room full of medical equipment and medical professionals trained to save lives. I know all too well that sometimes even the best of both can't avert some tragedies. None of that is what grabbed my attention. In this painting the focus is Jesus, who is standing beside the surgeon with one hand on his shoulder while the other steadies his hand as they both reach for the patient. I said a quick prayer, "See that picture Lord? That's what I'd like, that says it all." Most of all, it said that no matter what happens, He is in control. I was a little more at ease after that.

We spent the vast majority of the day just waiting in a corner of the pre-op room. Friends came to visit and waited with us. My procedure got pushed back a little later in the afternoon. People with different problems came and went. I even watched an old lady have some blood drained after she had taken too much of a sleeping pill. Eventually my brother and his girlfriend came back. He tries to hide it, but I could tell he was even more tense and nervous than I was. It is one thing to be going through all this, and quite another to watch someone you care about going through it and not be able to do anything. Finally, when it seemed the place was shutting down a nurse came to get my dad so he could get cleaned up to go in the operating room to get me comfortable on the table.

Soon he was in surgical clothes and we followed someone back to the operating room. Before I could finish explaining to the anesthesiologist how much trouble it is to get an IV in my hand he had it done already. Dad lifted me onto the table and as soon as I was comfortable other people in blue suits and masks surrounded me. A nurse asked me if I wanted my dad to stay as long as he stayed back. (Paradise is a small town; I went to school with the surgeon's son, and one of my nurses was Wilma Landers, a friend from the Evangelical Free Church days!) After some mental haggling between "Hey, I'm twenty-five years old!" and "Please, yes!" The "Please, yes!" won—I wanted Dad with me. Before I knew it, I was in Dad's arms being swung back into my chair. In a foggy blur I made out the sound of his voice saying, "Everything went great, John, you're fine."

Somehow I got from there to a side room and Mom was holding me up so a man could take an x-ray of my chest. Soon I was back in the pre-op area, finding the gray paint on the wall most interesting. As I came out of the stupor, I found out that the surgeon decided to use an IV catheter that can stay in for possibly two years without infection. Everyone told me the best part is most blood tests can be done through it; there would be fewer needle pokes were in my future. Hallelujah! Praise the Lord!

After this experience I went home and began using more powerful drugs to try to beat this thing. Within a couple of weeks I went in to have yet another x-ray taken. When the results came back the doctor said the word I've dreaded every time I've gotten sick in the last five years: Pneumonia.

. . . And Down

Not long ago I spent a few days in Feather River's ICU so that my doctors could keep a closer eye on me. A local pulmonologist joined the case in an effort to determine what if anything could be done to help my damaged lungs. Truthfully, I know my general doctor, Dr. Thorp, was as frustrated with this as we were; he cares for me very much. On the third day of my hospital stay the pulmonologist, having examined my lungs thoroughly, came in and gave us a stark appraisal of their condition. He said I had a strain of bacteria that is extremely resistant to antibiotics. The one antibiotic that would help me the most was the one I had a bad reaction to the night before and could not take. Furthermore, much of my lower left lung had become useless. It only has about 20% of the breathing capacity of my right lung, and the tissue that had become useless would only serve as a trap and breeding ground for illnesses.

> This was not good news. I did not receive it very well, nor should I have. It was another time in my life when I needed the security of someone nearby, because the storm was raging again. I knew I had to expect this someday. I know enough about my disease to say that long or short; this is the last battle to fight. But no amount of knowledge prepared me for the day it came.

It Was Becoming Clear

That week the question of how to engage this last battle certainly did not go away, it became more pressing. Certainly I did not intend to give up on life in despair because the future seemed suddenly dimmed. It just became clear that I had to begin thinking along those lines. The weight of the whole thing terrified me. I didn't know where to begin. This was not helped by the fact that I had been experiencing fear and doubt over God's promises for the life to come for several months. I am now seriously suspicious of the timing of that, and the verse I chose for this chapter explains my concerns—the devil has indeed been prowling around.

For a long time I had doubts about my existence and what it is meant to become. At times I have found myself inescapably afraid of the very idea of eternity. I even doubted God's love and ability to take care of me through a period that seems so alien to me. When the reality of facing that future came all the nearer, it became overwhelming. I could not get through this alone and knew I needed help. I needed to reach out to a community that could bear me up when I was down. I think God knew that I needed this too. For one thing, my parents seemed to know and they helped me find time to talk to people and ask my questions without shame.

Another way He provided was really unexpected. My mom had sent generic letters to many people informing them of my condition. The response was pretty amazing. I started getting messages from people who were a part of my life long ago, many of whom I have mentioned in previous chapters. Even people who didn't get the letter, but heard through the grapevine, responded. For the first time I had to scroll my e-mail box to read all the messages. People informed me of how my life mattered to them. They told me about the impact my life had made, and sometimes they surprised me.

> In all of it there seemed to be a veiled message from Someone else, "Look at what I've done out of love in this life, and feel how much it matters. If all that can be done through pain, how much more through endless joy?"

Still I had questions, and as I said I talked with people I thought could help. I could not just let nagging questions ferment. In reality I already knew the answers to many of the questions I had. I think I had just lost my focus in the quagmire of the pain I feel. It is very hard to look up when all around there is nothing but the constant pressure of worry and pain.

Sometimes I asked myself, "If I really believe, shouldn't at least a part of me be joyful about heaven and an eternity in a new life?"

And that was just the problem. It felt like joy and peace were hard to come by when I could have really used them most. I knew I'd felt peace before, and I knew it was real then. But at times I got so low that I doubted, as irrational as it sounds, whether I really wanted to get well and feel peace again. Could it be that God was hiding some secret agenda? Could it be that eternity really was something to be afraid of?

In talking to trustworthy people and thinking and reading my Bible, I at least came most of the way towards believing this is a problem with me and not with God. Even so, it was still a frightening place to be in, and I felt trapped between the fear of continuing to fight this illness in pain and fear of the unknown.

What began to heal my thoughts in this area were reminders of how God asks us to train our thoughts in times like this. One day I was sitting in my room when a little bird landed on the tree outside my window. As it hopped around digging under the bark in search for food, I was reminded of Jesus' own words. "Look at the birds of the air; they do not sow or reap or store away in barns, and yet your heavenly Father feeds them. Are you not much more valuable than they?" (Matthew 6:26). I realized that the Creator God provided for every creature within the context of its existence. He didn't forget anything, nor did He leave His creatures discontented. We did that to ourselves when we listened to the original lie, which was that God was hiding something from us. That is the root of this sinful, evil world. It is why the world is the way it is.

God also chose to describe our eternal future by emphasizing what it is not: "He will wipe every tear from their eyes. There will be no more death or mourning or crying or pain, for the old order of things has passed away" (Revelation 21:4). I think that waiting to understand everything else is a useless exercise. I believe God chose these words because He knows the limit of our mortal minds. He knows we can comprehend doing away with our tears and pain. Can any of us really comprehend eternity? Don't you think it is a little dishonest for any of us to try to pretend like we can? Some might feel deep inside that they had better sound like they believe by speaking of something as if they understand it. I think that we should admit that God and His vastness is far beyond our comprehension and show true faith by trusting that His plan is the best. We truly need to humble ourselves under His might and let Him work, not try to reach some superhuman state of enlightenment that will cause us to lift ourselves into a higher existence.

Most of all, it helped simply to know I wasn't alone. Other people were going through the same thing. In fact, most people who don't die in a sudden accident do go through a similar process. The possibility of death is not easy for anyone to face. Whether you have a long-term terminal disease or live to a ripe old age, everyone has to deal with some kind of doubt about whether their life has followed the right path. They also have a choice about how to spend their last days.

Final Choices

Like I've mentioned several times in this chapter, the issue of how hard to fight a losing battle has been inescapable these last few months. Today as I write it is just about the only thing on my mind. After a couple of rounds of IV antibiotics my condition only worsened into more pneumonia and fluid building up on my lungs. Emotionally, I have been a little uncertain about the moral distinction between choosing to deny further treatment and the much talked about "euthanasia." There is a lot of misconception and confusion on the subject. Unfortunately, I think too many Christians have based their thoughts over the subject on the self-motivated sound bites of politicians and ratings motivated television shows. As for me, I was more interested in what God says. I offer you what I've learned.

First of all I needed to be clear about what my choice actually was about. There is a big difference between causing your own death and realizing that even though you have done everything you can, death is on the way. I don't believe you must necessarily try every possible treatment before coming to that realization. What is the distinction?

I am facing the fact that the best medical treatment
is only prolonging my life, not saving it.

The treatment itself can often be worse than the disease. The real choice to be made is how much quality of life makes life worth prolonging. Let me be clear. Evaluating your quality of life does not entail comparing yourself to a perfectly fit Olympic athlete. I think my own life proves you don't have to have it all to have a decent quality of life. However there does come a point when prolonging one's life becomes an exercise in futility. Doctors today are capable of keeping a person alive but very unhappy with excessive pain. I simply can't find any reason that is necessary and I seriously doubt that God has some secret need for people to live in pain for as long as possible just for the sake of being alive.

So the question is, what does God really think? Want to know the truth? I don't know. But I do know that when God has a moral objection to something He makes it clear to us and points out the consequences of disobedience. He simply didn't do that here. I don't believe that means we are left alone to decide a deeply moral question. I'm not saying God has abandoned us in something very important. I'm saying His ways are not our ways. Maybe we should not think of it as such a deeply moral problem and that God might be angry with a wrong decision when the real issue is our own fear of death.

Psalm 116:15 (NASB) says, "Precious in the sight of the LORD is the death of His godly ones." God didn't use some ugly, frightening word to describe death for those who love Him. He called it *precious*. He didn't say it should be avoided at all costs when a person becomes so sick that it is clearly inevitable. And thankfully we are blessed with medicine that makes it less painful when it does come. These medicines don't cause death, they make it painless. Where is the moral issue in that?

But even if you feel you are justified in making that decision, it certainly isn't easy. Death isn't ever going to feel right even if you are in so much discomfort that you feel anything is better than this. I've had to stop looking for that non-existent emotion that makes you feel like it is a wonderful thing to die. At least that has been my experience. I've learned that what I really am looking for is that point when my frustration with the ordeals of this life overcomes my fear of death.

Even though I have that natural fear of death, I believe that as a Christian I can face this with far more courage. The reason is that I have confidence that death can be more than just a tragic ending. I also have a different perspective on what makes life worth living in the meantime.

Would you believe that the apostle Paul went through the same things I'm going through? He talked about this in his letter to the Philippians, although I admit I never fully understood the subject of this passage until I was going through this myself.

> Yes, and I will continue to rejoice, for I know that through your prayers and God's provision of the Spirit of Jesus Christ, what has happened to me will turn out for my deliverance. I eagerly expect and hope that I will in no way be ashamed, but will have sufficient courage so that now as always Christ will be exalted in my body, whether by life or by death. For to me, to live is Christ and to die is gain. If I am to go on living in the body, this will mean fruitful labor for me. Yet what shall I choose? I do not know! I am torn between the two: I desire to depart and be with Christ, which is better by far; but it is more necessary for you that I remain in the body. Convinced of this I know that I will remain, and I will continue with all of you for your progress and joy in the faith, so that through my being with you again your joy in Christ Jesus will overflow on account of me.
>
> ~ Paul
> Philippians 1:18b-26

First of all, for those of us going through these trials, let us stop and take comfort from these words. Notice that even Paul didn't know what the right thing to want was. He knew that to die meant to have something better than what he had here. But, no matter the reason, he also wanted to stay. It is natural to be feeling a

> *It washed over my soul and mind that the resolution of what lies beyond death is simply not my battle to fight.*

dilemma right now, and Paul himself wasn't given a divine revelation as to what the right or wrong decision would be.

Still, let's take a close look at what his motives were. Paul defined the quality of his life, even at the end, as a measure of how he could contribute to other peoples' lives. That was his priority. So it is mine. That is why I am trying to spend this time in my life; no matter how long it might be, sharing with you what I've been going through so that maybe it will help you someday. I'm sure it isn't any easier to read than it is to write, but it is what makes all this worthwhile.

But if life was not to be, Paul's hope in Christ was sufficient to overcome his fears. He believed as I do that death wasn't a loss, but a gain if he believed in Jesus' death and resurrection for his sins. If you believe in that, you must believe His promises for your future with Him because we follow His footsteps. If this story I've written about myself means anything to you, then you can't walk away from it without at least considering whether the things I believe are true. I don't believe I'm going to heaven because I suffered unfairly and that God owes me something better now. I'm going because I believe that Jesus, who is the only one who really did suffer unfairly, took on what I deserve and provided a way to heaven. Amen!

Deep In My Soul There Is Calm

In these last few days I've realized a better peace over my fears. It washed over my soul and mind that the resolution of what lies beyond death is simply not my battle to fight. The battle has already been waged and won! God says to me, and to you, "Cease striving and know that I am God" (Psalm 46:10, NASB). I found out that the Hebrew word 'raphah' translated here into 'cease' literally means 'relax, let go.' That is exactly how I feel spiritually right now. It is like one of those nice warm summer evenings coming home from watching a church softball game in Chico. That feeling of my skin having been warmed by the summer air, and then cooled by the breeze through the car window. What beautiful horizons we saw! And when we rolled into Paradise it felt like the world was truly peaceful as the sun crowned the pine trees with golden light.

Yes, deep in my soul there is calm. I am relinquishing my fears to Him in trust. What am I going to do? Am I to walk into the afterlife and tell God what my needs are during this eternity thing before committing? Foolish nonsense! How could I possibly plan heaven based on my fleeting emotions? He is the God who created me. He knew what my needs for this life were before I was born. Even now, in the midst of the birth pangs of the life to come, He has all my needs planned for and is waiting anxiously in the delivery room (Note: added 4/18/02, 4:15 pm).

§

Reality will be unveiled; as the feeling of losing something transitory will be replaced by the firm embrace of Another.

And what joy will fill my heart!

I don't know what is ahead of me today or tomorrow. If I must go soon, I am confident that my life counted for something despite the discontentment. I am even more confident that where I am going is a place where my life will count for even more, with nothing but contentment and joy. The desire to enter God's rest grows within me as greater pain in this world makes me desire to hold on less. But even as I reach that final peak and I fear the sheer cliff on the other side, which bids me to jump, I hear a voice, which teaches me that you have to jump first in order to fly.

The image of letting go of something solid is just an illusion. As soon as I feel myself letting go of something solid for something ethereal I will realize the exact opposite is the case. Reality will be unveiled; as the feeling of losing something transitory will be replaced by the firm embrace of Another. In *a moment of something stronger than time* I will stand with immeasurable humility and awe in the presence of the King of the universe. As His attention suddenly turns to me, and just before I realize that the burden of that interest is more than I can bear, His Son will stand beside me and claim me as His own.

And what joy will fill my heart . . . as I finally understand that I simply had no idea and could never have found the words to explain how wonderful it would be. All my cares and worries will be wiped away like so many tears on the fingers of the scarred hand of a carpenter. I will stand there before Him in complete comfort like I've never known and He will be the first one I will embrace with new strong arms. Or perhaps better yet, I will kneel at His feet and unload all the troubles I've carried once and for all. Others who got there ahead of me, some who knew me and some who from afar could not wait to meet me will welcome me. We will join the chorus to praise the one who reunited us all with each other and Himself. And I hope, before I even know anything we once called time could have passed on Earth, you will join us there.

All my love in Jesus Christ,

John Gilbert

Part Two

A Father's Reflections

In the Middle of a Thousand Nights

Bruce Stuart Gilbert

These reflections are dedicated to . . .

Cathy, My Bride

Who has shared the burden
and tasted the wine.

Does Jesus Live in Your Home?

May, 2002

A local prayer group, mostly Roman Catholics, asked me to talk to them about eternal security (although they did not know the term). The following day I had several phone calls expressing appreciation. One call in particular was from a lawyer who said, "For the first time in my 77 years I can think about death without being terrified." In God's wonderful timing, the next time we were able to attend the group, I had just received a letter from a young man called John. John is in his middle twenties, and has only a few weeks to live. He was diagnosed with muscular dystrophy at age 5, and the prognosis then said he would not live beyond 16. He is now in his 20's thanks mainly to his mother. It is a wonderfully positive letter, full of triumph and expectancy.

This brings me to the thought that I particularly want to leave with you. When Jesus met Zaccheus He said, "I must stay at your house today" (Luke 19:5). Do people invite themselves to your home? Does Jesus stay there? Does He enrich the relationships? Decide the decor? Preside at meals? I have had the privilege of staying in hundreds of homes. The one where Jesus is most evident is the one where John will soon die. John and his family with him have suffered the indescribable. Their whole lifestyle and financial structure have been drastically changed as he has been progressively disabled and disfigured. They faced this with enormous courage, deep tenderness, and shining faith. Please pray for them at this time, and make sure that Jesus is thoroughly at home where you live.

~ Ken Needham
Trans-Mission

From My Perspective ~

But if I knew everything, there would be no wonder,
because what I believe in is far more than I know

~ Polly O'Keefe
An Acceptable Time

The slow but urgent journey[1] . . . I like that phrase. I've borrowed it to reference the process of being ever so gradually but nonetheless decisively transformed by the life, death, resurrection, and character of Jesus. I hope it reflects something of my life; certainly it reflects much of John's.

The following pages include a number of reflections on John's life and that of our family; my hope is that they will compliment what our son has written in *Eden*. Perhaps they will provide a helpful context for parts of his story; perhaps they will offer some perspective of which even he was unaware. In any case, they are not offered assuming any particular wisdom or corner on truth. They are simply part of the process.

New Information!

I came to faith in Jesus Christ while a senior at Castro Valley High School—go Spartans! At the invitation of friends, I was introduced to the gospel through a local Young Life Club where Don Close spoke to my young heart every Wednesday night. This was new information! Don's house became our hang-out (The Ranch); we played pool and laughed and met early in the morning to learn something of the Bible and its truth. I was included in something very different than I had known—it felt good. To be included; it felt *very* good. Before long I was sitting with George, Bob, and Tom in the pews of the First Baptist Church listening to Paul Ratcliff teach me about God. He was wise; I could trust him. An alter call was tradition each Sunday; I never saw anyone respond. But as I was exposed to the simple truth of the gospel message as expressed by Don and Paul, I knew it was more than a good story; it was Truth—a Truth that required *my* response. And on a Sunday morning in the spring of 1965, I stood up and walked forward in response to Paul's invitation. Nothing else has ever felt so right.

It Was Home

I enjoyed a *wonderful* childhood. I was deeply loved by immediate and extended family. Mom and Dad expressed their love in very different ways, and their devotion and the unconditional nature of their love for me was never in question. It was the 50's and we were a representative post-war American family. I was raised by model citizens of Brokaw's "Greatest Generation" —Al and Elsa Gilbert— with their high school educations, prudence born of the Great Depression, and humility displayed in sacrificial service. They lived lives of simple needs and simple dreams. Character, integrity, hard work, and honesty were values held high in our family.

Plenty of belly laughs and lots of baseball offered balance. Our modest house was clearly home. Life was good! There was no frame of reference to suggest otherwise.

God, however, was not in our home. He was not consciously missed. Christmas was about rich family time and the exchanging of sensible gifts. Easter was about coloring eggs and a nice ham dinner, again with extended family as the highly valued center piece. And in between these two events we lived out a blend of "*Father Knows Best*" and "*Leave It To Beaver,*" albeit in a considerably less affluent neighborhood. God's absence was never a tension. My folks never had anything negative to say about God or church or Billy Graham. Spiritual things simply weren't on the radar. That is, until I returned that Sunday morning from Paul Ratcliffe's church and announced that I had become a Christian. My decision was met with minimal interest or curiosity. Mom seemed happy for me; Dad politely ignored the issue. As the years unfolded, I came to learn that it was Dad who had consciously kept God from our home . . . issues (disappointments, abuses?) from his youth he refused to discuss. Mom, always loving, always supportive, came to my baptism. Dad, however, stayed home; we never discussed it.

It has always interested me that so much of what I learned early on about what it means to live life as a "good Christian" were the very values instilled in me—expected of me—in my youth as I was being shaped and molded in our non-Christian home. That is, the living of a wholesome and moral life where integrity, responsibility, and ethical behavior were considered the norm. These were at the core of my parent's message to their children. But no God.

Spiritual Heritage ~ Maybe?

A parenthetical thought:

I was in my forties when I first learned of my Jewish heritage. My maternal great, great grandfather, Salomon Totzek, was a Russian Orthodox Jew and part of the "Fiddler on the Roof" culture who apparently fled his home in the midst of anti-Semitic turmoil. The story is told that Salomon took his family from Russian danger to the relative safety of Eastern Europe, eventually settling in Germany where his son Siegfried was born. Siegfried later became determined to abandon his father's faith and the persecution it attracted, protecting himself and his family from the predictable trouble that came with being a Jew. Siegfried's son Bruno, my maternal grandfather, arrived at Ellis Island on September 8, 1892 as an eight year old accompanied by his mother Rieka and sisters Else and Irma. In his early adulthood Bruno followed his father's footsteps into Freemasonry. If Bruno believed in God, his faith was kept hidden in the Mason's jar.

Could it be that only a few short generations ago I had family that read the Torah and prayed to Yahweh? Of course, family history—Jewish or otherwise—is unrelated to the opportunity we each have for a personal relationship with Christ. Nevertheless, how I would love to know more about my heritage. To whatever extent faith existed in my family tree, it apparently remained in hibernation until my conversion to Christianity in 1965.

War and Choices

Vietnam was raging and the draft was active. I had two kinds of friends. Several were excellent students with specific goals. They attended Stanford and Cal and educational deferments were easily attainable. Other friends headed for Canada. It was not uncommon. I, on the other hand, came from a heritage of proud military service. School was of little interest, but Canada was for cowards. I enlisted in the Air Force and served four years, primarily in Germany.

I was a new Christian, eighteen years old and away from home for the first time, with all the freedom that provides. My faith was real but not grounded, and the temptations of life were readily available. This was my first defining moment of faith. How would I respond and why?

I learned that the God I had said "yes" to really did live inside me. His Spirit would not let me go. When I was tempted to cross some serious lines, I experienced a very real sense of guilt and shame *before* I acted on the temptation. I began to understand my Christian faith as being a *mutual* relationship—a covenant—with my Creator. It was not only about me being faithful to God. It was also about God being faithful to me. Certainly those years included flawed judgment. But when I consider how my life might have unfolded had I taken advantage of all the opportunities for fleeting pleasures before me, I thank God for protecting me in very real ways.

Dreams

Certainly, God created each of his creatures unique from the next—as many combinations of variables as there are thumb prints. While I've labeled my childhood and youth as "wonderful," its normalcy included pride and fear, self-doubt and hormones. Much of my youth and early adulthood was spent contemplating self-imposed comparisons: he's faster; he's taller; he's better looking and smarter; her family has money for fancy vacations; learning comes easy for her. Oh, no! She's faster, too!

Where would I fit? How would I blend in? Convincing myself that I was average at best and that a life of mediocrity was not only inevitable but acceptable was an underlying obsession for years. The laundry list of "nobody understands me" scenarios is not unique to current youth.

As teenage years unfolded and confusion about life set in, only one dream had clarity: Someday, I wanted to be a father!

I wanted a child. I wanted many children. I wanted to love them and train them and play with them and discipline them and nourish them... and most certainly, I wanted to be loved by them. I wanted intimate, rich community with my kids.

I wanted family.

The requisite wife? Hmmm. . .didn't have that figured out. Girls scared me. And to think one could fall in love with *me* was preposterous.

But kids—WOW! The most beautiful word I could ever imagine was "Daddy"!

§

I met Cathy and fell in love. I had dated other girls. But they were just, well . . . girls. Cathy was different. Neither of us glamorous, neither particularly "cool," but—we *connected.* I knew it and it scared me (she's quick to remind any who will listen that it took me a month to call her for a second date!). We fell in love, married in June of 1974 and began to live the American dream. Our future was uncertain, but life was good.

A career path I could never have imagined was born in need of a paycheck. I left an unfinished Master's program in counseling psychology to wear a paper hat in a hamburger joint represented by a clown. The irony was not lost on my father. However, a career that began with some reluctance grew into an opportunity filled with rewards and accolades.

Then . . . John was born. I knew joy in a fresh way.

Professional opportunity took us to corporate headquarters in San Diego, the "opportunity of a lifetime!" Look out American Dream, here we come!

Then . . . Alan was born. More joy!

Two sons . . . I have two sons! We're just beginning. And now life was really good again, although in a very different way from the "really good" of my youth. Once again I knew the joy of family, this time "my" family. Now however, unlike my mother and father, I had little time for them. This was not the simple life I had known and wanted. This life was growingly complex. This was a life of wanting more, getting more, being more. Just a few more years, and then . . . .

DIAGNOSIS AND DECISION

August 24, 1981

John was diagnosed with Duchenne muscular dystrophy[2] at age five. Within hours of being informed of John's disease Cathy and I found ourselves at our kitchen table. . ."what now?" Our world had been rocked; *everything* was different, every hope shattered.

We talked for hours, and in the process came to understand that, actually, everything had *not* changed. We determined that God had not changed. That we had largely ignored him in the early years of our marriage did not alter who he was. And we determined that our love for each other had not changed. In fact, the time we had spent uncontrollably sobbing in one another's arms in the wake of our new reality began a bond that would prove to be among the unforeseen demonstrations of God's grace in the face of seeming tragedy. Clearly, the God who formed John and Alan in Cathy's womb would be the foundation on which we would move forward. Faith was now no longer a theological concept or philosophical ideal; faith was now the life raft to which we would hold on for dear life. Faith became real. The joyful trust I experienced that day I walked forward to Paul Ratcliffe's embrace was tangible once again. These were benchmark days. Cathy and I had chosen to become followers of Jesus—we had become disciples of Christ.

Spiritually Marked

I asked Jesus to be the forgiver of my sin during my senior year in high school. It wasn't until many years later that I acknowledged him as the leader of my life. Lord and Savior. Theologians argue about the timing of such things—let 'em argue. God's love is unconditional and salvation is without merit. Growth and character, however, learning to live as Jesus modeled life to be lived, that's hard, tearstained work!

The journey of having Christ's character formed within is never predictable or steady, but is marked by "fits and starts," seasons of life that materialize, develop, and pass—always leaving an indelible "*spiritual marking*" that can grow us if understood, or cripple us if not. My spiritual trek since the kitchen table has been rich, filled with memorable people and moments, insights and truths, and notable *spiritual markings*, each shaping me in valuable and significant ways.

A Generous Gift

Ted Faris was a valued and highly respected boss/friend in San Diego where he had invited me to join him in the development of a new restaurant concept seven years earlier. For a number of reasons, the concept failed. In its wake, and coinciding with John's diagnosis, Ted became the company's first franchisee while I returned to Jack In The Box management in Modesto, California where I oversaw the operation of several restaurants in the Sacramento Valley. And while I was genuinely grateful that Ted and others made arrangements to accommodate our family needs in those days, returning to Jack operations was a significant reversal from a career perspective. That leadership was sensitive to our needs was then, and remains now, most appreciated. Their accommodating generosity, however, meant that someone who had earned the right to be promoted into the position I was given had been trumped by an outsider. And, beyond my intrusion were the demanding expectation placed on multi-unit supervisors. Seventy-plus hour weeks invested in the name of "desired results" were commonplace. Those were challenging years.

The phone rang; it was Ted.

"Bruce, how'd you like to get into franchising?"

I'm pretty sure my response was something like, "Don't tease me, Ted!" But he was not teasing. He was inviting me to join a partnership that would purchase two restaurants with the promise of building more, with me as the Operating Partner.

"It would be a dream come true," I said. "But that requires the kind of money we just don't have."

"How much *do* you have?" he said. "I mean, if you sold *everything you have*, how much could you invest?"

The question seemed silly really. I knew the kind of purchase he was talking about would require many hundreds of thousands of dollars—*way* out of our ballpark! I answered his question to be polite; the math was not hard. We could sell our house, keep one used car, and then there was a very modest savings account.

"If we sold *everything*," I told Ted, "we'd have about $30,000." I'll never forget his response:

> "Bruce," Ted said, "that's precisely
> the amount that's required!"

I'll never forget those words. Ted and his partners had plenty of resources. What they didn't have was a trusted partner who would be fully devoted and unquestionably loyal to the team and its project. They didn't need my money. But they did need all I had. That would be *precisely the amount that's required.*

That's the Christian message, isn't it? God invites us into his eternal family, and the only condition is total surrender—all I have. That would be *precisely the amount that's required.* C.S. Lewis says it like this:

> The Christian way is different: harder, and easier. Christ says "Give me All. I don't want so much of your time and so much of your money and so much of your work: I want You. I have not come to torment your natural self, but to kill it. No half-measures are any good. I don't want to cut off a branch here and a branch there, I want to have the whole tree down. I don't want to drill the tooth, or crown it, or stop it, but to have it out. Hand over the whole natural self, all the desires which you think innocent as well as the ones you think wicked – the whole outfit. I will give you a new self instead. In fact, I will give you Myself: my own will shall become yours."[3]

What a gift! John said it well (*Eden* Six) when Denny Valentine placed the prized basketball in his lap: "Have you ever been given a gift you could never have gotten for yourself?" Ted was offering us a life that not only complimented my abilities, but would allow me to be the husband and father that my current seventy-plus hour weeks denied. And at a price that would be significantly less than my fair share.

And yet, while the dollar amount of my investment was relatively paltry, it *was* all I had. This wonderful opportunity, this unprecedented gift, would cost everything I owned.

> The imagery of Ted's offer did not go unnoticed. Christ gave all he had for my benefit, and he requires nothing less of me when I chose to be his follower. *Everything I have* . . . precisely the amount that's required.

Depravity

Dallas Willard was once asked if he believed in total depravity. He responded by saying that he believed in *sufficient* depravity. He explained sufficiency to mean that when we get to heaven we will never be able to claim responsibility for our being there.

I saw the ugliness of our depravity when my dear father suffered from clinical depression late in his life. He was admitted to a psychiatric ward for several days and underwent shock therapy. I was with him there when he behaved in unthinkable ways and said unimaginable things totally alien to his nature. Just a *glimpse* of Dad's depravity had surfaced; it was grotesque and repelling. It caused me to cringe.

Now depravity was not only a theological term; it had become real and observable and repulsive. I came to understand that my own sufficient depravity was no different than my father's. It's just that through a chemical imbalance in his brain brought on by a deep fear, Dad's depravity had surfaced while mine remained visibly and apparently managed. It has been remarkably sobering and spiritually marking to recognize that my depravity is quite real—it is always there and inclined to surface with very little prompting. And yet, I have become profoundly aware that my inherent corruption has been eternally trumped by the *power and blessing of God's grace*—a grace that overwhelms my sin, loves me in spite of it, and offers me triumph over it.

ETERNAL CHOICES

Mom became a Christian in her fifties. She had always been a loving, compassionate person, and now she would celebrate eternity in the presence of God. Dad was a wonderful man who had many traits and characteristics I would do well to emulate. But he chose to reject God.

Mom had suffered two mild heart attacks and multiple stokes in the last third of her life and seemed to grow old rapidly. I visited her at home one night after an abdominal surgery and long convalescence. When it was time to leave, we stood and embraced for the longest time. With tears in her eyes, her face inches from mine, she said slowly, "I don't know if you'll ever know how deeply I love you." But I did know! She had always loved me like that. When I first heard about God's unconditional love, I could begin to grasp the concept because of my mother's love for me. That night she died in her sleep. Of course I wept. Of course I missed her. But *her* faith allowed for *my* joy. I would see her again.

A hundred days later, Dad died. His reason for living had vanished. He went to church with us on Easter Sunday and heard a clear gospel message. The next morning he was in the hospital with labored breathing. The following Friday at midnight, the oncology nurse called to say I should come . . . he likely wouldn't make it through the night. When I got there he was barely able to talk. But he could listen. With his eyes closed I told him again how much God loved him . . . how much I loved him, and that even now in the quietness of his heart he could say "yes" to Jesus. And I told him what a great father he'd been, why I respected him and listed all the good things he'd given me. A long, long silence followed. And then he opened his eyes and I saw in them a sorrow and regret that haunts me still. In a barely audible but clearly understood voice, Dad said, "I gave you everything but the thing you wanted most." With that he fell back under the mercy of morphine and died many hours later.

Within the period of one hundred days, the promise of eternity in the presence of God was ruthlessly countered by the tragic reality of a Christless eternity. It has been a *spiritual marking* to know firsthand that *choices have consequences*—eternal blessing; eternal curse; it's the core theology of Scripture[4] up close and painfully personal. The death of my mother was difficult. The death of my father was devastating. With Mom I knew hope. With Dad, only despair. I had seen those eyes before in the psychiatric ward, and now again on a literal death bed. They screamed *hopelessness*! The heart of an evangelist began to grow within me; I didn't ever want to see those eyes again.

WURZBURG

Another marking ~

Cathy and I accepted an invitation to spend time in the home of dear friends Ken and Eva Needham on the first anniversary of John's death. Their humble Irish abode is nestled among sheep and stone walls in the shadow of the Mountains of Mourne. Overlooking the Irish Sea in the near distance, this home offered an isolated solace; the perfect venue for consolation and reflection with those who may well know us best.

We left Ireland for some Italian sightseeing with our friends Dan and Linda Beadle, and concluded our trip with Cathy and me reminiscing for a few days near Wurzburg, Germany where I was stationed with the Air Force in the late sixties. It's a remarkably beautiful city in northern Bavaria. The Main River runs through its middle and the medieval Marionsburg Castle sits on an overlooking hill. One afternoon Cathy and I hiked to the castle wall where we sat high above the river, looking out at the red tiled city roofs that marked the landscape.

Without warning a tear formed in the corner of my eye; then another. There was an annoying lump in my throat and I began to feel a very heavy, though undefined burden. Cathy noticed and asked what I was feeling. "I don't know. . .really."

"I think *I* know," she said. "The last time you were here you had your whole life in front of you. You expected all your dreams to come true. And now, thirty-five years later, your dreams haven't come true, and it hurts."

Of course, she was exactly right. She's often exactly right.

There is a rudeness to life; a brutalness. Jesus said that in this life we would have trouble. Of course, he too was right. That moment on the castle wall was yet another marking. Life *is* unfair, almost always unfair. The hope of the Christ follower is not to live a happy life because the dreams of our youth are being fulfilled, but *to live a life of hope in Christ* in spite of the fact that they are not.

And Now . . .

Clearly the present and future are influenced and molded by what has been. It would be dishonest to suggest that the wounds of life have been thoroughly healed or that the blessings and markings noted have come easily or without significant cost. Grace is continually sought and gratefully received; it is the fuel required for every next step. How grateful I am that its supply is endless; like ocean waves repeatedly, albeit slowly, rounding off the rough edges of the jagged shoreline rocks. God's grace just keeps coming.

I have, however, been promised not a life of regret, but a life of abundance born out of faith and obedience! Clearly there has been much abundance! And while I seek continued healing from sin's effect in my life, I also seek to appropriate the present and future blessings God has for me, most particularly manifest in the person he dreams of me *becoming*.

Clearly I am in the process of continued transformation—exactly what I seek. Like physical exercise, the benefits are accompanied by the aches and pains inherent in the process. There is great value in having been stretched, to think through the *what* and *why* of my values and beliefs. I have confronted sinful attitudes and behaviors that linger still—that seemingly elusive balance between truth and grace. Pruning is an uncomfortable process, but grace is powerful and prevailing. God is faithful to finish what he's begun. This is very good.

Yes, the abundant life. That is the promise, isn't it. Perhaps for too long I have convinced myself that that is what I *sought* (always future), when in reality it is exactly what I *have* (always current), were I only to recognize it in the moment. Life is best lived not busily pursuing what is *far*, but tightly embracing what is *near*. "Rejoice," Jesus said. "The kingdom of God is *near*."

§

And then there is the future—what we so often think about as what we will one day "do." As the seasons of my life rapidly pass, I find myself increasingly comfortable with the present . . . with *being*.

Of primary importance is faithfulness to my calling as a child of light—Paul's language in Ephesians 4 and 5—pursuing conformity to the character of God's Son. The balance of my life will continue to be marked by the disciplines of prayer and study, silence and solitude, as well as those seasonal disciplines sprinkled throughout my life in response to need of and care for my soul. Like every disciple, I am called to be a lover of God and people—to be a giver as well as a recipient of grace. My prayer is that I would be increasingly marked by God, and that I would represent him well.

For Cathy and me in this next season of life, we desire simply to be faithful to the words of the psalmist . . .

> As for me, I will always have hope;
> I will praise you more and more.
> My mouth will tell of your righteous deeds,
> of your saving acts all day long –
> though I know not how to relate them all.
> I will come and proclaim your mighty acts, Sovereign LORD;
> I will proclaim your righteous deeds, yours alone.
> Since my youth, God, you have taught me,
> and to this day I declare your marvelous deeds.
> Even when I am old and gray,
> do not forsake me, my God,
> till I declare your power to the next generation,
> your mighty acts to all who are to come.
>
> ~ David
> Psalm 71:14-18

§

John wrote much, said much, drew much, gave much. Insights and perspectives offered through water colors and pencil drawings, poems and limericks, essays and short stories—I want to share it all. It strikes me, however, that another John modeled wisdom when faced with a similar urge. That John wanted to tell the world about his friend Jesus—his Lord and redeemer. He wanted to tell every story, quote every word, relay every remembrance Mary shared over the years as John cared for her in the wake of her Son going home. But at the end of his Gospel, the disciple whom Jesus loved writes this:

> Jesus did many other things as well. If every one of them were written down, I suppose that even the whole world would not have room for the books that would be written.
>
> ~ John
> John 21:25

The Apostle John limits his writing to that which serves his purpose:

> Jesus performed many other signs in the presence of his disciples, which are not recorded in this book. But these are written that you may believe that Jesus is the Messiah, the Son of God, and that by believing you may have life in his name.
>
> ~ John
> John 20:30-31

Our John's purpose in writing *Eden* was to tell of the hope he had in Jesus from the perspective of a life seemingly devastated by dystrophy.

Those of us who knew John Stuart Gilbert and love him still are richly blessed. Our hope is that many more will come to know him through this effort. Clearly, however, while we honor John, we *worship* only God—Father, Son, and Holy Spirit—and tell this story for the purpose of reflecting on the life available to each of us, regardless of our dealt hand, because . . .

> The time has come. . . . The kingdom of God has come near.
>
> ~ Jesus
> Mark 1:15

. . . and we can be part of it if we want to.

Reflections . . .

To tell a story like *Eden* is to begin at the beginning,
and to end at the end.

To reflect is to think slowly, and again slower still, in contemplation of what was, in order that its truth might gain clarity and its value might offer perspective.

To reflect is not to tell a story,
but to complement the story told.

Reflections 1...

Early Days

Dreams too often remain dreams . . .

For the first twenty five years of his life, John lived with us. He died June 3, 2002. He now lives in the presence of God awaiting a new and resurrected body. He is greatly missed. We'll join him before long.

John was born on a warm August day; the abundance Jesus promised (John 10:10) seemed clearly evident. Life was rich and full. It was about everything good. It was love come to fruition. Watching my firstborn take his first breath; being invited to sever the lifeline to his mother; a fresh soul, my blood, Cathy's blood, entering eternity future . . . how could a moment in time possibly be more fulfilling?

Four toe-tapping grandparents were paying their dues in the waiting room. Emotionally drained but never more alive, I surfaced from the delivery room to announce that they had a new grandson: John Stuart Gilbert.

Sounded noble. Little did I know.

Exhausted after a twenty-two hour labor (Cathy was tired too!) I raced to tell friends and strangers alike. No one was too distant to be told the good news. I'd never need to sleep again!

THE BAPTIST

Names mean something.

Our first born was to be named after John the Baptist. We prayed that he would grow to be a truth teller like his namesake, a prophet sacrificially committed to the cause of the Christ he had yet to meet. We hoped our son would be submitted as well.

After four hundred years of silence, Israel finally received a messenger. John the Baptist, born to Elizabeth and Zechariah, proved not only to be a miracle for this previously barren couple, but for the Jewish nation as well.

God's hand was on him from before conception. As he grew, John "became strong in spirit" (Luke 1:80). The calling on his life was clear and he remained faithful to it throughout his life. His message? "Repent, for the kingdom of heaven has come near" (Matthew. 3:2). He spoke of God's kingdom being readily accessible in the person of Jesus, and stressed repentance rather than laws. The people had long lived in darkness. But now, finally, John came "as a witness to the light" (John 1:8b). The Baptist knew his place and sought no prominence. Francis of Assisi wisely wrote,

> "Blessed is the servant who esteems himself no better when he is praised and exalted by people than when he is considered worthless, simple, and despicable; for what a man is before God, that he is and nothing more."[1]

The Baptist readily deflected any notion of celebrity, claiming instead, "He must become greater; I must become less" (John 3:30). He did so enthusiastically dedicated and with a sincere joy.

At the heart of Dietrich Bonhoeffer's *The Cost of Discipleship* is this:

> If our Christianity has ceased to be serious about discipleship, if we have watered down the gospel into emotional uplift which makes no costly demands and which fails to distinguish between natural and Christian existence, then we cannot help regarding the cross as [*nothing more than*] an ordinary everyday calamity, as one of the trials and tribulations of life.[2]

The "costly demands" Bonhoeffer speaks of are required by Christ and by the biblical text, but are volitional on the part of the Christ follower. That is, obedience is always a choice. Such was the volitional life of the Baptist who chose to sacrifice his comfort and image for the proclamation of, and in the service to, his coming Messiah. He eventually sacrificed his life.

And while asceticism suggests a voluntary suffering,[3] what of that suffering which is not volitional; that which is thrust upon us in the form of, for example, terminal disease? Is this kind of suffering not also capable of bringing one to a proclamation of and service to, his Messiah? John the Baptist had a strength of spirit allowing him to see himself not through the eyes of his contemporaries and critics, but through the eyes of God; to live well under grace as only the sacrificially and volitionally submitted can.

Both the Baptist and our son lived under the shadow of Genesis 3, as do we. The oppression and consequences of sin—*disobedience*—are very real. And yet both Johns answered the call on their lives by rejecting the concept of self, dying to sin, and pointing simply to Jesus—for the cause of Christ and for his glory.

We named our son after John the Baptist.
Names mean something.

~ FAST FORWARD FIVE YEARS ~

Opportunity

Cathy and I had been Christians when we married. Though my salvation was real, at thirty-four years old I had yet to seriously follow Christ as the leader of my life. Cathy was much the same—we were the "cultural Christians" so many would later describe. The corporate ladder was proving climbable. Hard work, long hours, and favorable results had earned a certain degree of hope for a promising future. Recognition and opportunity were plentiful. It was not easy, but it was fun.

What a whirlwind! Buying and selling houses. Working very hard, but enjoying its fruits in the form of raises, promotions, and lots of "Atta Boys"! Surprise recognition came when my boss' boss was offered an opportunity to develop a new restaurant concept in San Diego. He asked me if I wanted to join him. What a compliment! What a privilege! No promises, but a ground floor opportunity! Of course . . . let's pack!

Life was good in San Diego. Sun, and surf, and salsa that made you salivate. Alan was born there in 1979. Two boys, two cars, home ownership, and a loving wife—the American dream was alive and well in southern California. And while the new concept opportunity eventually fizzled, it remained a unique and priceless career experience.

Spiritual conflict? Not really. A beer or two (sometimes more) after work now and then was just part of corporate scene. Consider it a rung on the ladder. Besides, it was fun and fed a need to belong, of being part of the core . . . very satisfying. It provided an opportunity to meet influential people—today we call it networking—you never know when they might come in handy. Family responsibility? No problem. After all, this was *our* dream, wasn't it? One day I had no idea how I would support my wife and future family. The next day I'm a respected member of a billion dollar company earning reasonable money and being invited to participate in a special opportunity at headquarters. I kissed the boys forehead when I left the house at five in the morning and I kissed them again when I got home in time for the ten o'clock news. They were already asleep, but hey, this was only temporary. Think of where we're going—as a family, of course.

Oh, by the way . . . John had developed these huge calf muscles. "Football legs" some said, and at such a young age. Ahh, an athlete—every father's dream! And he walked with this delightful little gait. Different for sure . . . but curiously cute.

Crisis

Peggy buzzed . . . an incoming call on line one.

"Mr. Gilbert?"

"Yes, this is Bruce Gilbert."

A somber, authoritative voice introduced itself.

"Mr. Gilbert, this is Dr. Schultz at Sharps Memorial Hospital. I'm calling to inform you that your son's lab tests are in. John has Duchenne muscular dystrophy. His life expectance is 16 years. If you have any other children, bring them in for testing immediately. Your sons all have a 50/50 chance of having Duchenne dystrophy and your daughters have a 50/50 chance of being a carrier. We'd also like you to schedule an appointment for genetic counseling that will help you understand your options [read abortion] if your wife should become pregnant. Any questions?" Click.

It was John's fifth birthday.

Staggered . . . I began to feel nauseous and my legs felt like Jell-O before I could return the phone to its cradle. The thirty minute drive home to face the reality of my bride's face would be filled with growing emotion and countless questions. I've listened to others who have received similar news and they tell of immediate and angry outbursts toward a God that was supposed to take care of them: "Why, God?!" "Why me?!" "Why my son, daughter, husband, wife, friend . . . ?!" "So much for a loving God; I hate you God!"

For me it was different.

As I drove home it struck me: this will be the defining moment in our lives that would never be the same. From that moment on, every relationship, every consideration, every decision would be indelibly marked by the reality of John's life and death.

How do I face Cathy?
What will I say to her?
How will this impact Alan's life?
Does dystrophy hurt?
Will John know pain?
Will he grow up angry?
Will he hate God?
Who tells John he's sick?
Who tells John he's going to die?

This is really happening! Cathy and I would face the unknown challenges of being the parents of a terminally ill child. Just a toddler, Alan's life would never be normal. What about family and friends? How would they react; could we count on them; would we scare them? As the father and leader of this young family that had been so ruthlessly derailed, what exactly was my responsibility? What am I supposed to think? How was I to react; what exactly was I supposed to *do*? How do I make this go away; was there a life raft anywhere in sight? Was there some foundation on which to stand? This is Harry Truman's buck[4], buddy. And you, Mr. Gilbert—husband, father, alleged spiritual leader—appear to be in charge!

Oh God! Our son is going to die!

§

So how *would* I react?

More importantly, would Jesus be sufficient to see us through this ordeal? I didn't blame or hate God. I didn't even question his allowing this to happen. But deep in my soul, in those first moments, I found myself wondering if what Cathy and I had professed for so many years would be validated in the midst of this catastrophe. Would Jesus indeed be enough?

And who would we be in private—when no one was looking? Who would we be in the middle of the night when the tears came? What kind of husband would I become for Cathy, father to John, father to Alan? And Cathy . . . mother of a dying boy! How does someone prepare for that? Who would she become; how would she be marked? Would our marriage survive?

§

I don't know if you ever hear God speak to you. I confess to a healthy skepticism when someone begins a conversation with "God told me _____," and even more with, "God told *me* to tell *you* _____." Nevertheless I certainly believe God desires to communicate to/with us through his Word, his creation, and certainly through his Holy Spirit. I can't see or hear him—it's not a "five senses" kind of thing. It's a spirit level kind of thing; his Spirit speaking to mine, the undeniable existence of God's presence.

I don't know how to write this without sounding stereotypically pious, but in the early days of John's diagnosis, when the shock waned and the fear dissipated, I experienced that *presence*, very real, very tangible. I sensed God's Spirit speaking to my own: "Don't be afraid. I will not leave you alone."

§

Pulling into the drive-way, I was overcome with fear. Inside that house was a waiting nightmare: John, my dying five-year-old son; Alan, my yet-to-be diagnosed eighteen-month-old son; Mom and Dad visiting from the Bay Area to celebrate John's birthday; and Cathy, my bride.

> Halfway up the walk, the front door opened slowly. . .and I saw her. Stunned and speechless, her tear stained face, assaulted spirit, and broken heart looked at me through haunted eyes. She was thirty-one years old, exhausted, hopeless, defeated, and desperate for me to share this inconceivable nightmare with her.

No words were spoken. As Alan's afternoon nap continued, my folks stood quietly, anxiously, and grief stricken behind Cathy. They desperately wanted and needed to express themselves; to hold us and protect us, *their* children. But because of who they were—noble representatives of their generation—they disappeared as if never there, somehow understanding that this young father and mother needed time alone to absorb this cruel turn of fate.

Cathy and I embraced as if letting go would cause the universe to unravel. We found our way to the sofa and cried for hours, laying a foundation of oneness that would sustain us through unthinkable challenges for the next twenty years and counting. We wept and gushed uncontrollably. Our reservoir of tears was bottomless. I experienced a vulnerability and transparency I would have never thought possible. No pretense, no answers, no emotional deception; no "manning-up." There we were, spiritually and emotionally naked before each other and our God.

Choices . . . Now What?

Alan's blood test came back positive. With an acceptable CPK[5] range of 200-400, Alan's results were in excess of 12,000, much like John's. We're two for two. Two sons with bright futures one day, two death sentences the next. We later learned that Alan's results were in error; the lab had confused his blood with John's. Alan was fine, but *that* night . . . .

Four days after John's diagnosis and with Alan's lab reports freshly in our hands we sat at our kitchen table discussing a topic of critical importance. We were Christians. But while Jesus was our Forgiver, he was not the Leader of our lives. We were reasonably good people, friendly neighbors and almost never kicked the dog. Saved? Yes. But we couldn't say (not with a straight face) that we were pleasing God or bringing him glory in the way our lives were being lived. We were far from any kind of genuine fellowship with the one who had voluntarily and sacrificially paid the debt we rightfully owed. And while we were beginning to accumulate the trappings of the upwardly mobile, we were far from the kind of abundant life Jesus had promised to those who follow him.

The question before us was the simple but preeminent question before us all.
What are we going to do with this person Jesus?

Forget how we've treated him since our "conversions," what are we going to do with him *now*? If Jesus was who he said he was, wouldn't that have significant implications for our lives? If he was, in fact, God's Son, wasn't he worth being worshipped and followed rather than simply being acknowledged (and thanked, of course) for getting us into heaven? But, if he were to become both Savior *and* Lord, Forgiver *and* Leader, what would that look like; how would we pursue that kind of relationship? And, what would it cost?

Dangerous Prayers

To clasp the hands in prayer
is the beginning of an uprising against
the disorder of the world.[6]

Karl Barth

When do we tend to pray? I wonder if there's much difference between the Christian and the not yet convinced? We pray when we need something, don't we? To pass a test, to get a car, to fix a hurt . . . "Help me God!" Too often it seems we only call on God when we need something. The God of Convenience, the AM/PM of spiritual benefits, open twenty four hours a day.

It had been too long since I'd really prayed. I don't remember being embarrassed. I don't remember feeling hypocritical. I needed God to hear me and I very much needed to hear from him. But it wasn't that I needed him to fix John; I needed him to fix me! To fix us! Now, it seemed, I had finally been broken. Anger, hatred, doubt, even fear were somehow not reasonable responses to John's disease. Fighting it would not solve it, nor would escape. The only reasonable solution, it appeared, was surrender.

At the kitchen table that night we uttered our first ever dangerous prayer, Cathy and I. A dangerous prayer is a prayer that, when answered, will have a radical and conspicuous impact on your life. Dangerous prayers are the catalysts for life change.

Our prayer at the table asked God to penetrate our lives starting at the deepest part of our souls. From there he could work his way into every aspect of our lives, providing a refuge throughout our unpredictable future, and providing a spiritual kick in the fanny so that we might truly be salt and light for him within our sphere of influence.

> Our most hopeful prayer was that our boys would become men of God; followers of Jesus. What else matters beyond the destiny of a soul? Really . . . what else matters?

Surrender to the power and authority of Jesus Christ is the only reasonable response to the human condition. It is the single most important decision a person can make. That my life and the lives of those I love most would be marked by surrender to God was the great hope of my dangerous prayers.

Hands

Sunday, October 17, 1998
Willow Creek Community Church

I confess. I had come to hear Bill Hybels speak. I confess not because I disapprove of Hybels . . . on the contrary. It's just that I hadn't come to *worship*. He came to the platform, but only to notify the gathering that on this morning he would defer to Nancy Beach who would be sharing some thoughts regarding "The Hand of God."

I looked forward to Hybels teaching and the whole "Creeker" experience and was disappointed that having come so far I would be hearing someone else. I was unfamiliar with Nancy Beach; God, of course, was not. Turns out, Willow Creek is no more primarily about Bill Hybels than John's life was primarily about dystrophy. Hybels took a back seat, allowing God, not Nancy Beech, to take center stage . . . and so he did.

Nancy's message was a series of reflections on five pencil sketches, each displayed on a massive overhead screen. The "Hand of God" . . . each sketch depicted a strong, masculine hand providing various kinds of support for, and interaction with, a childish, gender-neutral figure. The youth never changed its appearance from one sketch to the next, yet each picture reflected on a unique season in the child's life.

> Drawing One - The child is standing in the palm of the Hand as the Hand rests gently against the abdomen of God. Certainly there is a sense that there is much more to the picture left unseen, just as there is more to God, as yet unrevealed. The child, arms extended, is stretching out, reaching up, seeking the loving affection of its Father.

> Drawing Two ~ Hand in Hand, walking with God, the child seeking his guidance as he provides his perfect direction, support, and leading. Hand in Hand—each *in* the other, each *on* the other—committed not to let go. When the child's hand resists the firm grip of the Father's Hand, it risks danger. When it holds on tight, there is safety.

Drawing Three ~ The artist shows us a child at play, somersaulting in the Hand. Refreshing ~ I'm reminded that the God to be feared is also the God of joy and humor. He is a God who wants balance in my life. He likes to hear my corny jokes; to hear me laugh 'til I cry; encouraging me to be silly and physical and enjoy the myriad healthy opportunities he provides.

Drawing Four ~ We see the child triumphant, standing boldly on the Hand which is drawn in the "Thumbs Up" position. Achievement, victory, the child has *overcome* because the Hand belongs to the Overcomer. Interesting to note that the child, even with his fist thrust skyward not unlike a victorious athlete, *remains in the Hand*, leaning, in fact, on the protruding thumb of the Hand—for balance, perhaps—even as it proclaims victory. Victory is too often the season of life when we tell the Hand, "Thanks for the lift, but I'll be getting off now." This child knows better.

Drawing Five ~ The final drawing reminds us of our frailty and ultimate dependence on God's unyielding and unquenchable capacity for compassion toward his creation. It shows the child nestled in the gently cupped Hand, head lowered almost in the fetal position. This is the season of pain; the season of suffering.

And the Hand provides refuge . . . always.

There is no attitude here. No "Take it like a man!" No "Get a grip!" This is not a Hand that *requires* anything from the child. Rather, this is a Hand of safety. You can rest here. You need not fear here. This is a place of shelter and comfort . . . nothing threatening or scary gets in here. This is that place of unconditional love where merit has no value . . . a love that spiritually and eternally can only be provided by the Father.

Nancy spoke simply and elegantly of the Hand/child relationship. Yet, I noticed a constant throughout the drawings not mentioned in her reflections. In each scene, in each season of life, the child is naked . . . stark naked. There is no sense of shame or embarrassment. After all, this *being*, with its childlike innocence, is also simple. Its needs are pure and uncluttered. Its nakedness is not provocative. Rather, it speaks to our opportunity for complete vulnerability before the Creator of the universe. The word for that is *freedom*. . .wonderfully complete transparency, just the way he wants our relationships to be!

The gathering at Willow was reminded that while this Hand of refuge for the weary soul is always readily available, we should stay there as long as we need to, not necessarily as long as we want to. Healed, we are to get back into the race.

We can have great confidence that when we are weary and burdened, when we face chaos and tragedy, YAHWEH will not abandon his children. Our flame of hope may flicker, but even in the strongest wind God *will not allow it to be extinguished*.

Pain is inevitable. Misery is a choice.

Reflections 2...

A Dreaded First

But Jesus was quick to comfort them.
"Courage, it's me. Don't be afraid."

~ Jesus
Matthew 14:27,
THE MESSAGE

When I decided to ask Cathy to marry me, I wanted it to be special, and I wanted to offer honor and respect to her parents. I knew I would only do this once in life, and I wanted to do it well.

Cathy's father, Manny, was very sick with Parkinson's disease during the second half of his life. Just before Christmas 1973, I volunteered to drive him across the Bay to his doctor's appointment in San Francisco. While it may have appeared to be a generous gesture from a kind boyfriend, my true motive was to get Manny alone to ask his permission to marry his daughter. I'd not yet popped the question to Cathy—first things first.

We drove an hour to the Med Center, saw the doctor, and drove an hour home. My knees were knocking the entire trip.

I waited and waited, until we were almost back to his house! Pulling into the neighborhood, I swallowed hard and asked the question. He was delighted . . . enthusiastically joyful, and began to welcome me into the family.

That was the good news. The bad news was that Manny's enthusiasm overflowed as we entered his house where Cathy and her mom Doris were waiting for our return. Unable to contain his joy, Manny announced to one and all that Bruce and Cathy were going to be married!

Surprise over; proposal destroyed; dream shattered.

Over the years that story was told many times, always to the delight of the family. Wasn't it cute that, in his advancing years and confusion, Manny had spoiled the surprise? Quaint, huh? But in my heart, I was always saddened. Frustrated and cheated is more honest. I'd never get that moment back.

§

There are a few precious opportunities in life, moments of great value, which are placed before us only once. And when they are gone, they are gone forever. No editing; no mulligans; no second and third takes. Gone forever.

Firsts are usually pleasant lifetime memories. The first kiss. The first base hit. The first fish caught. The first time a young girl is told she's beautiful. The first time it dawns on you that you're really good at something. The first child born; the first step; the first word; the first . . . .

I had a dreaded first . . .

I had to tell my son he was going to die.

The harsh phone call from Dr. Schultz left no uncertainty about John's mortality. Telling John when he was five years old, of course was too soon. When *would* be the right time? When he was seven? Would ten be too late? Perhaps when he got his first wheelchair? Or when his body began to twist? *How* would I tell him? Would I be as blunt as Dr. Schultz had been with me? Would I fumble the words unable to get them out? Would I cry? Would John cry? Or would we be tough? You know . . . real men.

Three things were important to me:

It was my great hope that John would come to know Jesus personally and genuinely before he learned of his shortened life expectancy. He was a child; his faith might well be simple, but my hope was that it would be sincere. I wanted him to trust in his heart that the God of the universe loved him unconditionally before this news would make such a radical thought difficult to believe. Of course such a choice would have to be John's. No one mandates the faith of another—but I could hope.

It was important to me that John hear truth, lovingly offered, couched in spiritual relevance; but truth nevertheless. His life, for however long he would live, would require great courage and character. Now was no time to lob softballs.

And, it was important that John hear this truth from *me* . . . his father. Life's most difficult moments are painful in very real ways, and running away is a great temptation. But telling John he was going to die prematurely was my responsibility; I would not shirk from it. It is when you stay and do the honorable—that which integrity demands—that you know you're most alive.

How Could I Have Waited So Long?

It was the Muscular Dystrophy Labor Day Telethon of 1985. John was nine; Alan almost six. John had been California State Poster Child that year. Earlier TV exposures had made both boys familiar faces with familiar stories to many northern Californians each Labor Day. They were cute, appealing, and very spiffy in the little three piece suits Cathy had made them for this special day. Stan Atkinson was the long established and beloved host of the annual Sacramento event. We'd gotten to know Stan a few years earlier at the first of many Telethons. He and his charming co-host, Margaret Pelly-Larson were kind and loving folks; professional news anchors at KCRA TV and people who dedicated many hours, many years, to MDA for all the right reasons.

Stan's job was to create an environment that would "make those phones ring!" The telethon was about educating the public about dystrophy and defining the needs of its victims. And of course it provided lots of great entertainment with Jerry Lewis and all the celebrities. But in the end there was only one measuring stick for success . . . money! "A dollar more than last year" was the annual war-cry.

At Telethon, more money is raised in the last ninety minutes than the previous twenty-plus hours together. That's when most folks watch; that's when hearts are most touched. Cathy has often said you can watch the last two minutes of any basketball contest and see the whole game. And so it is with Telethon. In those last few moments you bring out your biggest hitters, your ace in the hole.

That was John and Alan. Lights, camera. . .it's heartstring time!

An Early Telethon with Stan Atkinson and Margaret Pelley Larson.

Stan was, and remains still, a genuinely loving and tender man. He's enjoyed a well-deserved reputation of being a "giver" in the Sacramento Valley community for many years. God bless him! But in his zeal to do his job well, he crossed a line.

"Back from Jerry and his friends in Las Vegas!" . . . Betty Vasquez, Stan's co-host that year, introduced the local segment this way:

> "Every time that phone rings, it means one more dollar. And that's going to help not only the adults but the young people who have neuromuscular disease. And one little person, one precious child, is with Stan right now, and you're helping him with every single pledge you make. Stan . . ."

John was sitting on a small chair with Alan standing to his right, both boys looking very poised in their dapper suits. Stan knelt beside them in front of hundreds of thousands of viewers. The camera came in close—the plea had to be personal. Here are his words:

> "We're talking about John Gilbert, our California State Poster Child this year. This is a case in point: John is nine years old. He was five when it was discovered he had Duchenne muscular dystrophy. Duchenne dystrophy *is the one that kills young boys.* It gives them a life of sixteen, eighteen, twenty years. And so far, nobody as yet has found a way to stop it.
>
> Now here is the case in point. Johnny is nine and his little brother Alan standing alongside him is five . . . the same age as John when he was diagnosed. Alan is perfectly OK. The doctors say there's no chance he'll ever have muscular dystrophy.
>
> We need to know so much about this. Because never in the Gilbert family . . . in Bruce's or in Cathy's side of the family (the father and the mother) has muscular dystrophy existed, at least as far as they've been able to trace. And they've gone back four or five generations. Can you imagine being frustrated by the mystery of something like this? To all of the sudden have it come out of left field and indiscriminately choose one child. In this case Johnny. One child lives; *one child dies.*
>
> You do this year after year after year, and you keep thinking that it just shouldn't be. We can make it so that it will not be! We can start right now. You can start right now so that it will "not be" by dialing the number at the bottom of your screen."[1]

Pan to the tote board.

When Stan told John he was going to die on live TV, I was sitting on a staircase immediately behind the cameras, and I witnessed something about my son I would see many times in the years to come. Stan's words *jolted* John, but at first I could only see it in his curious eyes and tilted head. Then his brow furrowed; his lips pursed. His curious eyes, now sullen, sunk deep into his face, and slowly looked to the ground, thinking, contemplating, considering what he'd heard. He knew he had a disease, he knew it was hard to walk . . . but death? His eyes searched for me and he gently bit his lip as he processed Stan's words:

> "It gives them a life of sixteen, eighteen, twenty years. And so far, nobody as yet has found a way to stop it."

John did not panic or overreact; he remained silent and respectful. At nine years old he demonstrated a character and composure that would come to be synonymous with how he lived his life.

Segment over. John struggled to stand. . .pushing on his knees, then his thighs until up-right, fighting for balance before attempting to walk. In that waddling gait that every Duchenne parent knows too well, John made a bee-line for the staircase where his father sat numbed by an anger and fear I couldn't let him see.

With watering eyes and a man-sized lump in his throat, John said, "Dad, did you hear what Stan said?"

And we had the conversation I had waited too long to have.

Reflections 3. . .

It's Not Easy Being Green

It's not that easy being green;
Having to spend each day the color of the leaves.
When I think it could be nicer being red, or yellow or gold . . .
or something much more colorful like that.

It's not easy being green.
It seems you blend in with so many other ord'nary things.
And people tend to pass you over 'cause you're
not standing out like flashy sparkles in the water
or stars in the sky.

But green's the color of Spring.
And green can be cool and friendly-like.

And green can be big like an ocean, or important like a mountain,
or tall like a tree.

When green is all there is to be
it could make you wonder why, but why wonder why?
Wonder, I am green and it'll do fine, it's beautiful!
And I think it's what I want to be.

~ *Kermit the Frog*
"Bein' Green"

In earlier drafts of this manuscript I included a chapter entitled, "HAVE YOU EVER DRESSED SPAGHETTI?" It was intended to address times of frustration, embarrassment, multiple levels of pain and regret, and be filled with chronicles and anecdotes about the day-to-day realities of caring for a boy with progressively deteriorating muscles.

~ There was the memory of John falling and getting up, and falling again, and getting up again, each time smiling like it was a game, each time oblivious to the reason for his stumbling. As he and his kindergarten friends frolicked around the Maypole, Cathy and I stood among picture taking-parents fighting back tears.

~ There was the story from the early days of leg braces and stretching exercises when I extended John's heel cord too aggressively to the sound of tissue ripping in his ankle and excruciating pain overwhelming his face. How would I ever forgive myself?

~ There were the countless trips to the MDA Clinic at the UC Med Center in Davis where John would be exposed to interns learning their trade at the expense of his dignity; and where grim agony awaited at the other end of yet another artery tap.

~ There were tales of endless and agonizing efforts to create seating systems for John's ever deforming torso in increasingly complex wheelchairs; accounts of living among the chimes and whirrs of myriad life-sustaining equipment that had turned John's bedroom into a sophisticated ICU.

~ Volumes could be filled with what became normal in our home as John's bedroom became mission central where life was lived for so many years. An adolescent boy, a maturing teenager, a young man in his twenty's with absolutely no privacy; taken buck naked to the toilet, held in balance by his mother or father until his body's waste uncomfortably found its way through a displaced digestive system. Injecting stomach pegs for feeding and suctioning cannulas for breathing. The inability to turn a page, or wipe his own sweat, or scratch his own nose; at first awkward, then increasingly difficult, ultimately unachievable . . . for twenty years.

Of course, when you start telling such stories, when do you stop? Now would be a good time. I think Kermit the Frog, simply and succinctly, got it right: "It's not easy being green."

Greeness

John knew something about being green; indeed, it is not easy.

In *Eden's* chapter *Purgatory*, John wrote some about the pain of cruelty and rejection. He wrote about it much more gently than he lived it. John was deeply wounded by the rejection he suffered. His greenness was always with him, never to be avoided. How does someone live a life so alone while being ever visible and conspicuous?

My capacity for compassion was sorely tested the night of John's high school graduation. He wrote about the standing ovation he received as he crossed the stage with his diploma gently nestled in Friedman's soft mouth. John was honored; I'm glad. I, however, was seething. It's been said that character is who you are when nobody's looking. It was *cool* to give John a standing-O under the footfall lights at Paradise High. But where were these students when John needed a friend to talk with, or a classmate to study with, or a bully to stop teasing Friedman? Where had they been when including him at their lunch table would have meant the world? Indeed, where had they been—for years?! And where were their parents who were now so proudly joining in the ovation? Sounds bitter, I know. Truth is, while my anger has significantly waned (patience please, sanctification is a life-long process), it remains valid to ask such questions. Among the most hurtful cruelties are those intentionally masked as if not to exist. A moment in time does not overcome years of exclusion.

Perhaps the most insidious rejection, that which is capable of inflicting the deepest wounds, is that which is born out of insensitivity rather than maliciousness from those one would expect to be the most caring.

I only saw John cry twice—on two occasions several years apart—because of his condition. Over the years we would occasionally visit a home that housed boys with whom John desperately sought friendship. It was always a bit awkward getting John and Friedman and his wheelchair through front door thresholds. But on the inside of *this* threshold were boys who would greet John warmly, his face beaming every time! Before long they would naturally engage him in simple conversation, maybe even begin a board game in which he could participate. But after a short time they would invariably disappear into the neighborhood streets to play basketball or ride skateboards . . . for hours. I'd wheel John out to the street where he could sit in invisible silence and watch these boys do what he could only dream about, his desperate attempt to belong left unnoticed. John was dismissed, excluded, and abandoned by those whose friendship he craved . . . time after time, year after year. I cried too.

We can dwell on greenness, I suppose . . . the word for that is *self-pity*. Certainly I'm not immune. It occurs to me, however, that there is a better way to live; and better options to consider. Certainly greenness is real for most of us now and then. Perhaps there is an antidote.

HESED

Near the end of John's life we developed a long distance relationship with John Ortberg who then served as a Teaching Pastor at Willow Creek Community Church near Chicago, a long way from Paradise. I'll refer to him as "Ortberg" in an effort to avoid confusion with our John.

In the last eight-plus months of John's life, he was simply too sick and too weak to attend church services on Sunday morning. So, he and I would stay home and listen to Ortberg's taped messages from the New Community services at Willow Creek. John and I came to think of him as our pastor in a unique kind of way; certainly he was our primary teacher during that season.

Each Sunday's teaching added to the sense of value I assigned to my worship time with John under Ortberg's influence. One Sunday after our time together, I felt compelled to write a note of gratitude to Ortberg, briefly explaining our isolation and expressing our appreciation for his teaching. To my surprise, he graciously responded with a hand written note that led to a correspondence in which he asked to read John's draft of *From Eden To Paradise.*

Sometime later Ortberg was preaching from Micah 6: "Do justice, love kindness, walk humbly with your God." Having read *Eden*, he chose John's basketball experience to illustrate the concept of kindness.

With permission ~

> "'Love kindness', God says. The word Micah uses is *hesed*; it's used most closely in the Old Testament associated with God's lovingkindness that flows out of and is expressed in the covenant that we've learned so much about. It's a love that *always* seeks to express itself in action; it is never confined to a feeling.
>
> In a town called Paradise, California lives a young man named John Gilbert. When John was five years old he was diagnosed with Duchenne muscular dystrophy. It is genetic, progressive, and cruel. He was told it would eventually destroy his muscle and in ten more years or so take his life. He has lived a lot longer than that, but I talked to he and his dad yesterday and he is very, very sick right now.
>
> Every year John lost something. One year it was the ability to run; he couldn't play sports with other kids. Another year he could no longer walk straight; all he could do was watch others play.
>
> He's written a manuscript of his life, it's an amazing work. And he writes that junior high was

perhaps the hardest era of his life. Junior high's difficult for almost everybody, I suppose. Tony Campolo said once that the old Roman Catholic theology is right; there really is such a thing as purgatory. It's junior high! . . . a place between heaven and hell where you're made to go suffer for your sins. But John was bullied there and humiliated 'til he was afraid to go to school.

And nobody stood up for him; maybe 'cause they were afraid.

There were other moments in his life. One year when he was a kid he was named Poster Child for the Muscular Dystrophy Association in California. He went to Sacramento and was ushered with his family into the Governor's office for a private meeting. The Governor had a big glass jar of candy on his desk and told John to 'dig in.' John looked at his mom who said it was OK to take *one* piece. But the Governor said *HE* was the Governor and John should do what *he* said . . . so John stuffed his pockets!

That night, the NFL sponsored a fund-raising dinner after a golf tournament at almost went up to John's wrist. And when the auction began, one item in particular caught John's attention. It was a basketball signed by all the members of the Sacramento Kings, the NBA team. John got a little carried away 'cause when the ball was being bid he raised his hand. And as soon as it went up his mom flagged it down. John said, 'astronauts never felt as many G's as my wrist did that night.'

The bidding for that basketball went on . . . and it kept going up. It rose to an astronomical amount . . . more than anything else even though it would appear it was not a particularly valuable item in that auction. And eventually one guy named a figure that *stunned the room*! Nobody else could match that! And he went to the front to collect that prize that had cost him so much.

But instead or returning to his seat, the man walked across the room . . . and placed the basketball in the thin, small hands of a boy who admired it so intently. He put the ball in hands that would never dribble it down a court, never throw it to a teammate on a fast break, never fire it from three point range . . .

Have you bought a basketball for anybody lately? God says . . . this is about kindness.

Do good things for the people that are around you. We make it so complicated and it's really not . . . it's really not.

Have you bought a basketball for anybody lately? Have you just gone out of your way to serve somebody for no reason at all? God says this is about kindness."[1]

§

Hesed is among those Hebrew words that no single English word adequately defines. We find it in the Old Testament again and again as God defines himself (i.e., Exodus. 20:6, 34:6-7; Numbers 14:18-19; Deuteronomy 5:10). Among the best attempts to translate the untranslatable is this: "When the person from whom I have a right to expect nothing gives me everything."[2] When the concept of *hesed* is found in the New Testament it is usually understood to be "mercy" or "grace."

Ortberg told John's basketball story—a story of kindness—beautifully, and with a sensitivity that captured the power and compassion of the moment. To this day "The Ball" is proudly and prominently displayed in our home as a testimony to something good that is within us. However, while Ortberg's account of the story was accurate, it was, through no fault of his own, incomplete.

The man who paid the unreasonable price for the basketball and put it in John's hands was a political lobbyist by the name of Dennis Valentine. His business card noted that he was in the business of "consulting" and "government relations." The buzz in the room that night, however, was that Mr. Valentine was a high powered lobbyist and considered among the most influential and ruthless players in Sacramento politics. Not your typical Teddy-bear kind of guy.

And yet, to the surprise of many at that dinner who knew him from smoked filled rooms, he was touched *beyond* the point of compassion to the point of action . . . *hesed*. And perhaps for the first time in his life, this man experienced that indescribable joy that comes from giving rather than receiving—rather than winning. And I confess I thought to myself, "Where's the church—where's *my* church—when it comes to kindness?" If a man like this, who cuts people off at the knees for the sake of political gain, can be moved to spontaneously demonstrate such kindness, such generosity, then what would be reasonable to expect from the church of Christ for the cause of Christ?

From Russia With Love

Our good friend Karynn Law was the first one to reach us in the hospital after John's failed back surgery. She was serving as a missionary in Russia when John graduated from high school. She missed the standing ovation, but offered her own by choosing to honor John from a distance with the following *hesed*-laden letter.[3]

John ~

Since I cannot greet you face to face in honor of you finishing "underling" school and being plunged into the "real world", I get to put my thoughts on paper. I wanted to write something for you that was witty and clever. A beautiful piece of literary wonder that would bring laughs, a few tears and even some appropriately timed nods and sighs. But these endeavors began two weeks and four attempts ago and I soon realized my efforts were self-centered . . . so I try again.

I redirected my thoughts toward you . . . after all, this is in honor of your graduation, your amazing achievements over the past four years of high school. You not only proved to be proficient in your course of study, but excelled at all the "extras" you added to your agenda. Not an easy task, even in the most basic form. And yet, I was surprised to discover that even you, as the focal point, are still not the most accurate perspective of all that has been accomplished.

After all, isn't it our Father, yours and mine, who gave you these abilities? And isn't it He who is glorified in your faith and trust? And isn't it He who helped you endure when times were unbearable? And isn't it

He who stood by you during those lonely moments? And isn't it He who smiled and shared your joy when you thought you would burst? And isn't it He who delights in seeing His children honored for using the skills and talents He bestows? Uh-huh!

I took a look back in my memory and recalled instances forever burned there; images of you in different circumstances over the past few years.

I have watched you ~ at an earlier graduation, an esteemed student, successful in early aspirations.

I have watched you ~ at sporting events, a restrained encourager, firm and assured in your brother's accomplishments.

I have watched you ~ during television broadcasting, a graciously humbled promoter, spotlighted for a medical cause.

I have watched you ~ at home, a devoted care-giver and friend to ever-watchful, ever-loyal Friedman.

I have watched you ~ in speaking to your peers, a yielded representative of those who have decided to stand apart for Christ.

In all this remembering, I wondered, who is it I was seeing? John Gilbert or Christ? In a moment, the answer was clear . . . I was seeing *you*.

You, encouraging others.
You, supporting a need.
You, displaying kindness.
You, standing strong in your faith.

Unmistakably you . . . living in the image of your Lord. For one is like the other. There in your eye is the reflection of Christ, in whose image you were made and in whose steps you follow. You shine as a reflection in His eye as well. The Father and child are so much alike, it is impossible to see one without the other.

Like Him, you are an artist, a poet, a brother and friend.

Like Him, you thirst for knowledge and dig for answers, content only with the truth.

Like Him, you watch, you listen, you drink in life.

Like Him, your heart is tender, yet boundless wisdom grows there.

He too was bound by physical limitations, yet created unspeakable beauty.

He was a quiet man . . . strong and gentle
in His silence.
He was a calm man . . . wise and
discerning in His peace.

I see these qualities in you.

Love, Karynn

JUST A WORD ON FRIEDMAN

The average dog is a nicer person than the average person.

~ Andrew A. Rooney

Heaven goes by favour.
If it went by merit, you would stay out
and your dog would go in.

~ Mark Twain

I wonder if you've ever had a best friend. It's dangerous, isn't it, to call someone your *best* friend? *Best* is singular;

superior. Everyone else is relegated to something less than best. *Best* sets the bar awfully high. It's tough to sustain *bestness*.

I've had three or four best friends in my six decades and counting. To be a best friend is always a reciprocal kind of relationship—you both know. Those kinds of friendships usually don't revolve around fun and good times, although happiness and adventure are certainly a valued part of the experience. "Best friend" kinds of bonds tend to revolve around a season of life that is of mutual and rich significance . . . often involving transition and dependence; often, I think, involving loss; certainly some form of growth and/or suffering. Sometimes these highly valued relationships dissipate naturally as life plays itself out. Too often and sadly our depravity finds its way to the surface of these friendships, and as the years unfold they can become flawed, perhaps destroyed.

§

John wrote rather extensively about Friedman in Chapter Eight of *Eden*. I won't prolong the tale (pun intended) except to say this . . .

Children in wheelchairs seldom know friendship. They know acquaintance. They know pity. They know condescension. But they seldom know the kind of "best friend" that is born out of mutual respect, reciprocal deference, and the simple joy of being in one another's presence. Aloneness is a big part of being sick.

Such was John's life . . . until Friedman.

Friedman was a magnificent Golden Retriever who diligently earned and proudly wore the blue and gold backpack of Canine Companions for Independence. At two years old he had been trained to respond to seemingly countless commands that had prepared him to meet the practical needs of a disabled person. That Friedman would provide John with treasured companionship was a windfall.

You've seen the bumper stickers,
"Lord, help me to become the person my dog believes me to be."

You've heard the punch lines,
Dogs humbly submit, "You must be king!"
Cats authoritatively proclaim, "I must be king!"

CCI's motto: "Help is a four-legged word."
Friedman's mission in life was clear: to serve his king.

~ A Unique Privilege

There's a story told of an intern spending time with Mother Teresa in Calcutta. Upon his arrival he was repelled by the stench of disease. He was particularly repulsed by one poor soul being consumed by leprosy. Mother Teresa is said to have put her arm around the young volunteer with this admonition: "Take good care of him. That's Jesus in disguise."

Each night Friedman slept at the side of John's bed, never off-duty; disciples never are. As the years went on John could not voluntarily move his muscles. That is, his body could not naturally adjust itself throughout the night. He could not roll onto his side; he could not raise his arms above his head or tuck them under his pillow; he could not shed a sheet in the heat of summer or cuddle a wool blanket under his chin in the chill of winter. He could not visit the bathroom. Mostly he just needed his hips moved an inch or so to lessen the pressure on his bowing spine. Someone else needed to do those things. Me.

Several times each night, night after night, year after year, Friedman would dependably respond to John's soft, almost whispered command: "Friedman, go get Dad." And this best friend would faithfully trot into our room to my side of the bed. Sometimes his stare would be enough. Often his cold nose on my cheek would be required. Side by side we would return to John's room down the hall . . . serving him together.

As the years wore on, I'm embarrassed to confess that service would occasionally become obligation; sleep deprivation has consequences. In the middle of one night, years into this routine, Friedman's cold nose once again sought my attention. I threw back my sheets in exhausted frustration and angrily huffed and puffed, stomping toward John's room. In the hallway, feeling very sorry for myself, I was confronted by God . . . really. I know, I get spooked by that kind of language too. But I was convinced then, and am now, that God's Spirit was speaking to my spirit . . . and to my selfishness with the same clarity and firmness with which he addressed Israel through the prophets.

"Bruce, don't you know that it is *ME* calling for help in your son's room?!"

And the words I had read countless times in Matthew's Gospel came immediately and shamefully to my mind . . .

> I was sick, and you looked after me . . . .
>
> Truly I tell you, whatever you did for one of the least of these brothers and sisters of mine, you did for me.
>
> ~ Jesus
> Matthew 25:36b, 40

I dropped to my knees and cried in humiliation. It wasn't long before Friedman was enthusiastically licking my face, I thought with the kind of intuitive compassion such dogs are known for. Wiping his slobber from my forehead it occurred to me, however, that this was not compassion, but the service dog telling the father, "Get up Dad—you've got work to do!"

That was our son John, *one of the least of these*; a brother of Jesus. I've learned that to be given the high privilege of serving Jesus in disguise—most especially when it is inconvenient—is an extraordinary privilege.

Reflections 4 . . .

"It's Just A Bad Disease, John"

"It can never be God's will that I should be sick." Really?

If it was God's will to bruise His own Son, why should He not bruise you? The thing that tells for God is not your relevant consistency to an idea of what a saint should be, but your real vital relation to Jesus Christ, and your abandonment to Him whether you are well or ill.

~ Oswald Chambers

I tried to make John laugh in doctor's offices, clinic visits, and hospitals (except ICU's . . . nothing's funny there.) I'd look for ways to be silly, like pretending to be a walrus with two foot long Q-tips hanging out of my nostrils (or ears . . . or both). Alan thought it was hilarious. John, and need I say his mother, found my timing wanting.

So, Patch Adams does it and they make a movie of his life. I do it and get cold shoulders and rolling eyes. Go figure.

The truth is, of course, there is nothing humorous about Duchenne muscular dystrophy. It destroys, it humiliates, it kills.

Seven Hours Into Surgery ...

At sixteen, a late but rapid onset of scoliosis was promising to seriously undermine John's remaining quality of life, such as it was. John required surgery.

I don't know what you know about orthopedic surgeons. It's been said they are a special breed. The word is - and our experiences support the notion - that many orthopedic surgeons are among the very brightest, most medically assertive, and most conspicuously self-assured professionals in the medical community (I think I said that nicely). The best among these in our part of the world was Dr. Daniel Benson at UC Davis Medical Center in Sacramento. Dr. Benson was among an elite fraternity who wrote the books and gave the lectures so that others might learn.

Our appointment with Dr. Benson was brief. UC Davis was a teaching hospital for tomorrow's physicians; there was never a shortage of eager underlings following Dr. Benson, although it seemed always at a safe distance. Among his resident students was Eric Heiden of Olympic speed skating fame who only a few short years earlier was carrying the weight of five gold medals around his neck to the adulation of an admiring world. But not today. Today Dr. Heiden (who, by the way, belies the professional stereotype) was quite comfortable being inconspicuous in the back of the pack.

I held John in a position that allowed the young doctors to inspect his deformed back. They were curiously attentive and intellectually engaged as they interacted with one another as to surgical options. Until, that is, Dr. Benson entered the room. Conversation stopped. Respectful young doctors deferred to the master as if parting a sea so that the maestro could make *his* evaluation. Barely through the door Professor Benson looked at John's body lying naked across the room and said matter-of-factly and rather disinterestedly . . . "I can do that." He never saw John's face.

Despite Dr. Benson's confidence, we had been warned that because of John's general weakness and physical vulnerabilities this would be a very high-risk procedure. Relying on the experts, an appointment was made for Harrington Rod surgery. John's back would be filleted from the nape of his neck to the base of his tailbone. Two stainless steel rods would be attached to his curved vertebral column. A ratcheting mechanism would straighten his spine to its maximum tolerance where the rods would be permanently secured allowing internal organs to better function as designed. It was anticipated to be between a ten and twelve hour procedure.

§

I did not want to admit John to the hospital that night. Before a golfer attempts a difficult play you can often hear the caddy encourage his player, "Commit to the shot."

I was not committed to this shot.
I was terribly afraid.

I slept on the floor next to his hospital bed that night. It was tortuous. They had given John a sedative to reduce his anxiety—could I have some? Cathy and Alan joined us early the next morning when surgical nurses came to get John for pre-op. Cathy was optimistic and encouraging. Alan was quiet and respectful of his environment. John was afraid, but trusting and resigned. I'm sure I did my best to convey courage and optimism; I'm pretty sure I didn't pull it off.

With John disappearing on a gurney behind large swinging doors, perhaps we could now exhale. It would be many hours before we'd be informed that he had a new back and had come through the ordeal unscathed. He would, of course . . . be okay, that is. After all, John was in the highly skilled hands of among the very best orthopedic surgeons in the entire world.

Seven hours into surgery John's heart failed.

An effort to arrest his scoliosis was abandoned in favor of saving his life. Bracing was urgently removed from his spine as he was flipped over, accessing his chest/heart; the gaping wound of a back now lying unprotected on a bacteria laden operating table. Cathy was alone in the waiting area when a grim-faced surgeon appeared to report on John's status. It was a short visit; he was needed back at Dr. Benson's side.

Alan and I had been outside tossing a football . . . trying to stay occupied and diverted. We returned to several compassionate strangers consoling Cathy who was overwhelmed at the news. We thought we were prepared for the worst; we were not. Initially we huddled together frightened, weeping and overcome with shock. At some point we each began to process John's reality in our own way. Cathy and Alan found themselves interacting with a physician who had lost *his* brother at a young age. They remained together as I returned to the lobby; my job was to wait for the physician's next report. Would it be life . . . or death?

I was consumed with prayer—"Have mercy on us, Lord." I'd love to report a resolute confidence; but I was not confident. I was fearful that John would die that day. At some point in my anguish I realized I was sitting alone—it was as if others in the waiting area had intentionally given me space. I had wrapped my arms around myself, rocking rhythmically back and forth as I stared without seeing. This may have lasted an hour. I was alone and fear had overcome me when God sent me a gift in the person of Karynn who wrote the letter in *Reflections 3*. This will sound "too cute," but when I saw her, it was as if I'd seen my first angel. No words were spoken; Karynn simply *joined me*. To not be alone was a treasure beyond words.

A couple of hours later, Cathy and Alan having returned from the ER, the surgeon returned to say that John would soon be in recovery but that his condition was very, very serious. We were summoned to the recovery room with hopes that hearing Mom and Dad's voices might somehow enhance John's subconscious will to live. To be told of John's condition was one thing; however we could not have been prepared for what we found. The attending nurses were grim; to see John's ravaged body lying helplessly in pools of more blood than the white sheets beneath him could absorb led to a gravity I had not known.

> So . . . what must it have been like for the Father when *his* Son suffered? What must it have been like for the disciple whom Jesus loved and our Lord's mother as they stood at the foot of *his* cross, watching him suffer; watching him ridiculed; watching him die; powerless to effect change?

I suppose it was my job to be the strong one.

But the bravado to which my culture calls me is simply not who I am; nor is an attitude of machismo consistent with Jesus' model and teaching on how to live well in his kingdom. I am not called to be the kind of invincible hero who pounds his chest and taunts his defeated adversaries with arrogant bluster and manufactured manliness. I *am called* to be courageous, but through a confidence born of humility and dependence before God . . . "Apart from me you can do nothing!" (John 15:5).

Machines kept John alive for the next many days. Abundant meds made the process marginally tolerable (thank you, Lord, for morphine!). About three days after surgery John's ventilator was removed. This was a critical step in his recovery. He had to breathe on his own in order to survive. We were with him every moment and within a few short hours of his vent being removed, it became obvious that he could not breathe adequately without it. As they intubated him a second time I wept in an outer room. My tears that day in the ICU were not the tears of defeat, but of dependence.

> It was about three in the morning on the first night in a dark, quiet, and ominous ICU. I was quietly in prayer at John's bedside when the shadowy silhouette of a large man tentatively entered John's room. It was Dr. Benson. The aura of impregnable confidence he'd displayed earlier was gone now. We learned later that he had never had a failed surgery. No one had ever died under Dr. Benson's care. And now, in the middle of the night, the master was not there to evaluate a patient's progress or give direction to the nursing staff. No, this doctor's world had been shaken; he was vulnerable after all. Though the room was dimly lit, I saw it clearly in his eyes and on his somber face while the strong and steady hand that had earlier held the scalpel now tenderly and gently touched the hair on John's head. He cared. He had been touched, maybe broken. And the good doctor found his way to John's room every

> night thereafter, always in the wee hours of the morning, always without a word, until he was certain that John would indeed survive.

Post-op visits with staff and surgeons were required in the wake of John's failed procedure. And while we would not again see Dr. Benson's face, we would meet with several of his most competent and esteemed colleagues. It was near Thanksgiving when John, Cathy and I sat in the office of Dr. Fry, who had assisted Dr. Benson that day. I'm not sure who asked the question, but we all wanted to know: "What happened? What was it that caused John's heart to stop in the middle of surgery?"

Dr. Fry, who could easily have dazzled us with medical lingo and physiological detail chose rather to lean forward on his stool and look sympathetically but honestly into the eyes of a disappointed boy. "It's just a bad disease, John."

SORROW

It was Father's Day a few years back; Cathy and I had joined friends at the beautiful home of Jon and Sue Sites. And while the conversation was good, the kids were enjoying being kids, and the backyard pool beckoned on this warm June day in Chico, I nevertheless found myself feeling disengaged as I allowed for the inner melancholy that is never far away.

Sue, who often notices, took me by the arm to a patio lounger away from the crowd, and read to me from a book she'd retrieved from the house . . . *Alexander and the Terrible, Horrible, No Good, Very Bad Day.*

Do you know this children's book?

It's a series of events in Alexander's young life . . . all bad. On the last page Alexander sums up his day:

> "When I went to bed Nick took back the pillow he said I could keep and the Mickey Mouse night light burned out and I bit my tongue. The cat wants to sleep with Anthony, not with me. It has been a terrible, horrible, no good, very bad day. My mom says some days are like that."[1]

Sorrow. We misunderstand it sometimes, thinking it self-pity or defeatism, and have little tolerance for it. And of course we distance ourselves from those who know it—who wants to hang out with Job? And after all, didn't Jesus say he came so that we might have *abundant* life?

I would suggest that to deny legitimate sorrow (or distress, or mourning, or burden, or disappointment...) is to discount much of Scripture and deny the *imago Dei*.[2] What do we do with David and the Psalms if distress is inappropriate? What do we do with Jeremiah if weeping is out of bounds? What do we do with frustration and anger if we are to believe the prophets really did speak for God? Biblical faith is a comprehensive view of reality. We have not been touched to our depths if we have neglected the Bible's teaching on lament.

In *The Hidden Face of God*, Michael Card speaks to lament, that biblical practice that allows for the uninhibited expression of our suffering to God in the face of his seeming absence. The inevitable consequences of Genesis 3 regularly play themselves out in our lives, at times brutally. When they do is not the time to "man up." When they do is not the time to get emotionally lost in what we've come to accept as worship. And when they do . . .

> This is not the time to try harder. This is not the moment to strain to manufacture more faith. It is the occasion to cry louder to the One, who though He may seem asleep, is most significantly still present

> with us in the boat. He is there to be awakened by our cries. He is moved to act by our tears. If you think about it, this is the very first lesson we learned as infants – a persistent cry will bring help.[3]

I like that *Alexander* doesn't have a happy ending. This is not heaven. We are not promised a good life; we are promised a good God.

> All his years of ministry have taught Paul that the path to knowing Christ and His resurrection power is the path of lament: "the fellowship of sharing in his sufferings" (Philippians 3:10). If you could ask the apostle what lament is all about, he would simply answer, "It's about knowing Christ." That is everything. Nothing else matters, whether you are facing execution or just the prospect of another meaningless day – only the knowledge of Jesus Christ, gained through redemptively entering into His sufferings, can give perspective and meaning to life. "To live is Christ," Paul said to the Philippians (1:21).[4]

In the wake of a failed back surgery that nearly took his life, a tracheotomy that did take his voice, and trapped in a body devastated by the consequences of dystrophy, John describes his yet again disrupted life as, "living this way can be frustrating at times" (see *Eden 12*). John avoids his father's language—"devastated, overwhelmed, ruinous." He chose rather to consider his reality as "frustrating at times." Paul taught the Corinthians that "No temptation has overtaken you except what is common to us all. And God is faithful," Paul said, ". . . he will not let you be tempted beyond what you can bear. But when you are tempted, he will also provide a way out so that you can endure it" (1 Corinthians 10:13). I am persuaded that the "way out" is seldom removal from the crisis at hand, but almost always perspective within it.

And while sorrow is a necessary place to visit when appropriate, it is not a place to reside. I will come back to it at the proper time, but to linger there beyond its usefulness corrupts perspective. While lament is an important ingredient in the recipe of Christian maturity, we are not ultimately called to wallow, but to overcome. Perspective matters.

PERSPECTIVE INDEED

Standing vigilant over his frail and ravaged sixteen-year-old body several days into an increasingly doubtful recovery, Cathy and I became aware that John, having been fully aware that he may well not return home from this surgery, had secretly written of his great hope. Alan, home with friends by now, located John's thoughts and faxed them to our attention.

"Please see to it that these papers
get to Bruce Gilbert . . . Room 716"

We awaited their arrival like it was the Holy Grail itself. It read in part . . .

> And finally, as I face this great obstacle before me, it is this that I would shout to the whole world if I had the voice:
>
> Behold, you who see me as the least among you! Death has no victory in my life! Disease may have taken my body now or later but my soul is secure with God. I have suffered in pain and humiliation but I have overcome these things. Jesus has saved me and made His victory mine. I am not perfect; I have

done and said things I regret. But by His sacrifice I am made perfect in the eyes of God. As I look back on my life I see God's blessings as bright lights illuminating the "valley of the shadow of death." Don't cry for me, because all I have suffered is immeasurably small compared to the glories I will soon see. Once I could barely sing but I will praise the Living God with an angelic thunder-voice. Once I could not walk but I will soar like the eagles above. I will surf the edges of nebulae and fly through the unknown beauties of the heavens. All this a free gift from the only One worthy to be praised.

There is a great story called *Les Miserables* that has reflected in some ways the struggle of my life. In it an ex-con named Jean Valjean lives a life of freedom in the midst of bondage. This is how I have lived my life and how anyone can choose to live if they let Jesus into their life. The final song* in the musical version of *Les Miserables* nearly says it all.

John Gilbert

* Les Mis

From the heart of a dying Jean Valjean, alone in the shadows with a bare wooden cross for his company, soon to be joined by Eponine and the spirit of Fantine.

God on high, hear my prayer
Take me now, to thy care
Where You are, let me be
Take me now, take me there
Bring me home, bring me home

Come with me where chains will never bind you
All your grief, at last, at last behind you.
Lord in Heaven, look down on him in mercy.

Forgive me all my trespasses and take me to your glory.

Take my hand, and lead me to salvation
Take my love, for love is everlasting
And remember, the truth that once was spoken:

To love another person is to see the face of God!

And then a final plea ~ a call to celebrate the rubble of the barricade; victory over sin and the promise of a glorious forever.

Do you hear the people sing?
Singing a song of angry men?
It is the music of a people who will not be slaves again!

When the beating of your heart echoes the beating of the drums
There is a life about to start . . .
When tomorrow comes! [5]

Reflections 5. . .

What If It's Not *About* John?

Yet when I hoped for good, evil came;
when I looked for light, then came darkness.
The churning inside me never stops;
days of suffering confront me..
I go about blackened, but not by the sun;
I stand up in the assembly and cry for help.
I have become a brother of jackals,
a companion of owls.
My skin grows black and peels;
my body burns with fever.
My lyre is turned to mourning,
and my pipe to the sound of wailing.

~ Job
Job 30:26-31

What if all this has not really been about John?

What if all the tears and surgeries and loneliness and very real pain have not been *primarily* about a young boy with dystrophy? What if it's all been about something else? What if John's realities were but reflections of our human condition and that in them our Creator has lessons for us to learn? Let's imagine . . .

WHAT IF JOHN'S LIFE WAS REALLY ABOUT JOY?

The wisdom of Oswald Chambers defines joy as "the perfect fulfillment of that for which I was created and regenerated, not the successful doing of a thing."[1] I love that phrase; have quoted it often. But how does it compliment the realities of John's life? Did God create John to be alone, suffer, and die? It helps, I think, if we're careful not to confuse joy with happiness.

> Happiness is the anticipation of, or response to, positive events.
>
> Joy is the consequence of willful surrender.
>
> Happiness is closer to excitement and celebration.
>
> Joy is closer to contentment.

What if John's life was an opportunity to know joy?

WHAT IF JOHN'S LIFE WAS REALLY ABOUT SURRENDER?

> God discovers Himself to 'babes' and hides Himself in thick darkness from the wise and the prudent. We must simplify our approach to Him. We must strip down to essentials and they will be found to be blessedly few.[2]
>
> ~ A.W. Tozer

Surrender, of course, requires tremendous courage. And in its purest form it *is* clearly *surrender*. But when it's less than pure . . . is it surrender then? And if it's not, is it fraud, or simply a surrender that has yet to mature?

Two wonderful movies may offer some insight.

In *Remains of the Day*, Anthony Hopkins plays Stevens, the perfect 1930's era English butler, an ideal carried by him to fanatical lengths as he serves his master, Lord Darlington. Nothing could tempt him from his life's mission. Not love, not the death of his father, not even his master's dubious alliances. Stevens is fully devoted; a purist, his obedience was real. He dedicated his life to the service of his master altogether surrendered to his master's authority.

In *Mary Poppins*, Julie Andrews plays Mary. Also a servant, Perfectly Proper Mary is a spirited nanny who floats out of the London sky and into the lives of two playfully mischievous children. She makes every chore a game and every day a "Jolly Holiday." The children's father, George Banks is quite different: precise, prim, and proper. It will take more than a "Spoonful of Sugar" to cheer him up!

Mary the nanny is attractive and charming, and takes her role as nanny quite seriously. Stevens the butler is less attractive and not particularly charming at all, but he takes his responsibilities as lead butler at Darlington Manor also quite seriously.

Two servants seemingly equally committed to their mission. On closer look, however, there is a difference. While Stevens lives to serve unhesitatingly within the boundaries established by his employer, the charming and attractive Mary has an edge about her. Within her role as nanny, and beneath her seeming obedience, she *really does know better* than her employer, the children's father. She usually does as he requires—*except* regarding those issues for which she knows herself to be better qualified.

Now, this metaphor may well break down on a number of levels (neither of the two movie "masters" have much in common with God!), but is it possible that many of us live our lives like Mary when it comes to surrender? We do our best to be "good Christians" (whatever in the world that means) and often lead morally decent lives. But truth be told, we think we *really do know better* than the Father.

What if John's life was about volitional submission to benevolent authority?

What If John's Life Was Really About Perspective?

Jan Doney, wife, mother and grandmother, musician and artist, teacher and servant, was fifty-seven years old when she shared the following perspective, shortly before a rare and rapid cancer took her life. God's principle of inversion found in Scripture (the first will be last, the weak will be strong) plays itself out in the everyday lives of authentic people who innocently and genuinely trust. Jan's life gave testimony to another inversion: the frightened will be brave. John and Jan had trust and courage in common; remarkably so. They also shared a common faith; not a faith born of opinion, or emotion, or blind commitment, but a faith born of *knowing*. As her days here wound down, Jan knew the kind of peace that Scripture refers to as being "beyond human understanding."

Wonder Valley[3]
Posted Dec 21, 2009 7:06pm

For all of you faithful prayer warriors, I have news. We are no longer praying for surgery for Christmas. The scans showed no shrinkage of any of the cancer after all the chemo. After a long talk with the doc about options, I have decided to live out my remaining days (and that could be a short time or a long time) as fully as possible and be completely present with those I love so much. It's not a defeat. It is a different reality than I was hoping for, but I am completely at peace. I would like to share a story that taught me volumes about the difference between what I want and what I need.

When we were in our early 30s, an opportunity presented itself that we just knew was tailor made for our family. A house had been put on the market that we could afford and was so much more than just a house. It was in Wonder Valley, a place as wonderful as it sounds. The house sat in the midst of a beautiful little valley with a creek running through it. The entire area was open range, no fences, and for every acre someone owned, a horse or cow could be kept. Every year there was a neighborhood round-up. Everything was set. We wrote the check and took it to the realtor, and he said, "Oh, bad news folks. Just today the owner went into bankruptcy and thus needs to liquidate his assets. Now the entire price of the house is required in cash." We left brokenhearted - it may as well have been millions in our situation. Our dreams were dashed, as well as those of our children who had been promised a horse by some dear friends, and the prayer we had prayed seemed to have fallen on deaf ears.

A year or two later we learned that Wonder Valley had flooded, taking most of the homes. People lost their life savings, their homes, and a beautiful way of life. Since the valley lay in a flood plain, no insurance paid out. We just looked at each other and said "Thank God we were denied our earnest request." We were so sure!

On that day, I learned a deep and enduring lesson. I cannot see what lies down the road. But God can, and since He loves me so much (why?), He sometimes has to move in ways we misunderstand as flat denial or downright orneriness! I now have a mental file titled "Wonder Valley." When I don't understand the denial of a seemingly good, positive request, it goes in the file. I'll look again later when hindsight kicks in! So, my friends and dear ones, this last request concerning surgery is now filed under "Wonder Valley." I am at peace because God has such a great track record. I have only to be still and try to honor Him with all my days.

Jan

§

While undergoing chemotherapy a friend asked, "So, Jan, how you doin' with all this?" Her response:

"If a man had given you a hundred dollar bill every day for fifty seven years—and then, for whatever reason, stopped—would you be angry, or would you be thankful for a lifetime of generosity? I am thankful for his generosity and can trust him when he chooses another course."

What if John's life was much like Jan's . . . a lesson in perception?

What If John's Life Was Really About Character?

As the years wore on, John spent more and more time in his room . . . reading, writing, thinking, praying. And as the years wore on, he was able to spend less and less time in his wheelchair which proved to be quite uncomfortable for a progressively deforming body. Lying prone on his bed, pillows tucked here and there for support, provided some relief. It was there that he could escape reality for a while. And the word for that is television!

Now in his twenties, John had his own television set with its own cable package. He could watch whatever he chose: history, public affairs, science fiction, news . . . and of course, comedy. He thoroughly enjoyed *Barney Miller*, *Home Improvement*, and *Murphy Brown*. And he also enjoyed shows that had a bit more of an edge, like *Seinfeld*, *Cheers*, and *Frazier*. John loved the unique characters, the clever writing—his whole body would often jiggle when he laughed.

I learned *much* about character observing
John watch television.

As much as John enjoyed the clever humor of a show like Seinfeld, he quickly learned when it was about to cross a line. There was language and a certain crassness he occasionally found distasteful. Sometimes he'd "hang around" if he sensed it would go away soon. But when it came to sexual impurity, whether it was subtle or brazen, John had no tolerance. Lying with the remote control positioned in his right hand and resting on his chest, John would react with lightning speed at the first hint of danger—an inappropriate word, a provocatively dressed woman, an impure innuendo—*click!* The channel was changed or the TV was off.

At first I thought it was embarrassment with Mom and Dad in the room. It's like watching something funny but questionable with your pastor. Are you supposed to laugh? But it wasn't that. It was something much more informed; much more deliberate.

While John's muscles were vulnerable to dystrophy, his developing hormones were not. He still went through puberty and as a teenager and young adult he certainly had normal and appropriate interests and desires. Two things he did not have was (1) a life that allowed him to pursue his interests, even in healthy ways, and (2) a confidant to talk with about what is for every young person a confusing time. Simply put, John was trapped in a body that wouldn't work and alone with no one to discuss his most intimate feelings (this is best friend territory, not Mom and Dad territory).

When does a dying boy with a bending body become aware that he will never have a girlfriend? When does it dawn on him that he will never have a physical relationship with a wife he will never marry? How does an adolescent grow into a young man dealing with the increasing realities of his limitations? But John did. And important to that process was the immediate removal from sexual temptation. What psychological torment he endured in the quietness of the night I'll never know. But to the extent that he had control—with the remote in his hand—he simply would not submit himself to the anguish of sexual fantasy.

What if John's life was a lesson in discipline . . . and dying to self?

What If John's Life Was Really About Influence?

Why did John's life touch so many other lives? Why did people listen when he spoke? Could it be that in a world consumed by competition and instant gratification and Facebook dribble, there is a discernible absence of grace? It been said of my generation that we've forgotten how to blush. Humility and integrity are no longer prevalent as cultural values; celebration of self has overcome unity as team; and wisdom long ago gave way to intellect. But Cathy and I have been privileged to witness the vanishing qualities of nobler generations up close in the deformed, deteriorating body of our son, John. To look at his body was to cringe at its disease; to look in his eyes was to see eager hope. Others saw it too.

In November 2001, John began a long series of progressively difficult pneumonias that various meds could not overcome. John was dying. When the word got out that the end was nearing, good people from the past looked for ways to express themselves. Representative is this note[4] from a childhood friend:

To My Friend, John ~

Flashback, say 12-15 years
Picture us at the cabin, lots of snow, big hill, sleds, nerf football, bad outfits, a crowded cabin, decent cooking, laughter. Memories fill my mind and my heart. I remember the ping pong, the snow ball fights, the coupons to Jack in the Box (man, those were the best). I also remember your smile, contagious, long lasting and full of energy. I remember thinking, man, this is one happy kid . . . .

Flashback, say 10-15 years
Wait a second, John Gilbert drew that, that beautiful picture of the lion (oh shoot, maybe it was a tiger?); all I remember was that it was nice, actually

better than nice. Mom stuck it on the frig for at least a year and then she moved it to the family room. People commented on it, lots of people. Everyone said, "Who did that?" We all bragged, "Our friend John". . . .

Flashback, say 5-8 years:
Kellogg's house, some event (they all run together these days, can't keep track), and I see your mom, and you, and your smile. The same smile I saw so many years before was still there, still contagious, still long lasting and still something I will never forget. I remember our conversation; you were going to school, studying hard, still steadfast, still determined, still happy . . . .

Flashback Today:
Lump in my throat, eyes about to burst from tears (I must hold back, I am at work), feeling guilty for the times I have taken life for granted, friends I haven't appreciated, phone calls I haven't made, hugs I haven't given, I love you's I haven't said. I feel a sense of emptiness in the life I sometimes lead, successful for the world, not so successful in the mind of my Savior . . . the lack of prayer, the lack of Bible reading, the lack of giving of myself to others . . . I must work on these things as they are what matter, what make a difference, and what life is all about. So, as I ramble on, from a reflection of life, I will conclude with this. . .

My friend, I do know this, I will forever cherish you, your smile, your quick wit, your intelligence, your heart, your character. I constantly try to take qualities from people I admire, and I try to incorporate them

> into my personality. So, I take these things from you. I wish you the best, the very best.
>
> Lots of love and admiration.
> Your friend from long ago . . . Aaron Cain

Or maybe . . . what if John's life was really about *faith* and *forgiveness*, *confidence* and *hope*, *grace* and *trust*? Certainly it was! But . . .

What If John's Life Was Really About Suffering?

Ahh . . . now we're getting to it!

If suffering is the soul's response to experiencing evil,[5] how do we then not talk about John's life in the context of suffering? And isn't suffering at the heart of the most basic questions of Christian faith? Indeed, how can an allegedly loving God allow bad things to happen to good and innocent people; why is there so much suffering in the world?

Perhaps it was Saint Clive who asked some of the most insightful questions and offered some of the most profound perceptions and observations regarding this complex topic.

> Suffering . . . why? If you love someone you don't want them to suffer. You can't bear it! You want to take their suffering on to yourself. Even I feel like that. Why doesn't God!?[6]
>
> Isn't God supposed to be good? Isn't God supposed to love us? And does God want us to suffer? What if the answer to that question is yes? 'Cause I'm not sure that God particularly wants us to be

> happy. I think he wants us to be able to love and be loved. He wants us to grow up. I suggest to you that it is because God loves us that he makes us the gift of suffering.[7]

Many fine thinkers have contributed their insights to the questions of suffering:

Oswald Chambers: "To choose to suffer means that there is something wrong; to choose God's will even if it means suffering is a very different thing. No healthy saint ever chooses suffering; he chooses God's will, as Jesus did, whether it means suffering or not."[8]

Shadowlands, the story of C.S. Lewis's late-in-life marriage to Joy Davidman, includes a telling scene in which Lewis is sitting among several of his students at Oxford when he refers to a piece of poetry that mentions the image of a perfect rosebud. Lewis asks what the image of the bud represents. One of the students responds, "Love?" The professor penetrates deeper, looking for more.

> "What kind of love?" says Lewis impatiently.
>
> "Untouched," says a student.
>
> "Unopened, like a bud?" says another student.
>
> "Yes, more?"
>
> Another student says anxiously, "Perfect love."
>
> "What makes it perfect?" says Lewis, "Come on, wake up." The students are quiet. They don't know the answer. So Lewis answers his own question:

> "Unattainability. The most intense joy lies not in the having, but in the desiring. The delight that never fades. Bliss that is eternal is only yours when what you most desire is just out of reach."[9]

But is that true; was Lewis right? Perhaps it is so within the boundaries of human relationships; that is, human to human. But not, I'd suggest, within the parameters spiritual relationships; that is, humans with their Creator . . . for it is within that reality that the free gift of forgiveness is offered by the God of grace. And *that* desire, *that* bliss, is never out of reach. It is forever readily accessible.

Larry Crabb refers to the reality of suffering in the language of shattered dreams.

> Shattered dreams open the door to better dreams, dreams that we do not properly value until the dreams that we improperly value are destroyed. Shattered dreams destroy false expectations, such as the "victorious" Christian life with no real struggle or failure. They help us discover true hope. We need the help of shattered dreams to put us in touch with what we most long for, to create a felt appetite for better dreams. And living for the better dreams generates a new, unfamiliar feeling that we eventually recognize as joy.[10]

Theresa of Avila was a sixteenth-century Carmelite nun and author of *The Interior* Castle who suffered from paralyzing illnesses. She wrote, "For his Majesty can do nothing greater for us than grant us a life which is an imitation of that lived by his beloved Son. I feel certain, therefore, that these favors [sufferings] are given us to strengthen our weakness."[11]

John of the Cross, persecuted and thrown into prison, authored his classic *The Dark Night of the Soul*. "O you souls who wish to go on with so much safety and consolation," John wrote. "If you knew how pleasing to God is suffering and how much it helps in acquiring other good things, you would never seek consolation in anything, but you would rather look upon it as a great happiness to bear the Cross of the Lord."[12]

These giants of our faith from earlier traditions tell us that faith becomes strongest when we forfeit comfort, walking into the darkness of this fallen world with complete abandon. Faith is not really faith if we *require* God constantly holding our hand and cheering us on. True faith, that which is not blind but confident, echoes the heart of Jesus in Gethsemane, "My Father, if it is possible, may this cup be taken from me. Yet, not as I will, but as you will" (Matthew 26:39). True faith says, "Let this be done, Lord, according to your will" – even if I don't know what "this" is.

And what of Isaiah's prophecy of the Suffering Servant some seven hundred years before the birth of Christ? The life Jesus lived would serve the Father's purposes, even though it brought the Son intense and unprecedented suffering. If ever suffering gave birth to good, it was so in the death of Jesus.

> He was despised and rejected by others,
> a man of suffering, and familiar with pain.
> Like one from whom people hide their faces
> he was despised, and we held him in low esteem.
> Surely he took up our pain
> and bore our suffering,
> yet we considered him punished by God,
> stricken by him, and afflicted.

> But he was pierced for our transgressions,
> he was crushed for our iniquities;
> the punishment that brought us peace was on him,
> and by his wounds we are healed.
> We all, like sheep, have gone astray,
> each of us has turned to our own way;
> and the LORD has laid on him
> the iniquity of us all.
>
> ~ God, through the Prophet
> Isaiah 53:3-6

And, of course, at the core of the gospel is the incarnation . . . that God himself came near in the person of Jesus who emptied himself of his divine privilege—the *kenosis*—experiencing human life on this side of Genesis 3, yet without sin. And then he died. Clearly God himself suffered. And dare I suggest that the prophets' description of the Suffering Servant seems almost understated when we look retrospectively at the cross; that when you add up the physical, mental, and emotional pressures Jesus endured in the hours leading to the cross, it was all as if nothing compared to the incomparable desolation of spirit he experienced when the Father turned his back on the Son who had become sin for you and me.

§

It seems to me that Philip Yancey asks some of today's best questions regarding Christian faith. In his predictably challenging book, *Disappointment With God*, Yancey asks three questions no one asks aloud: Is God unfair? Is God silent? Is God hidden? It is the first question, the question of fairness, which seems particularly aligned with the question of suffering. How *could* a fair God possibly allow suffering in this world? Yancey relays a story told by Henri Nouwen of a family Nouwen knew in Paraguay.

> The father, a doctor, spoke out against the military regime there and its human rights abuses. Local police took their revenge on him by arresting his teenage son and torturing him to death. Enraged townsfolk wanted to turn the boy's funeral into a huge protest march, but the doctor chose another means of protest. At the funeral, the father displayed his son's body as he had found it in the jail – naked, scarred from the electric shocks and cigarette burns and beatings. All the villagers filed past the corpse, which lay not in a coffin but on the blood-soaked mattress from the prison. It was the strongest protest imaginable, for it put injustice on grotesque display.[13]

Yancey then asks . . .

> Isn't that what God did at Calvary? "It's God who ought to suffer, not you and me," say those who bear a grudge against God for the unfairness of life. The curse word expresses it well: God be damned. And on that day, God was damned. The cross that held Jesus' body, naked and marked with scars, exposed all the violence and injustice of this world. At once, the Cross revealed what kind of world we have and what kind of God we have: a world of gross unfairness, a God of sacrificial love.[14]

It occurs to me in reading Nouwen's account of the tragedy in Paraguay that stories like that are played out countless times every day in our world. The doctor's son had been savagely ravaged by evil men. And in the middle of the night on June 3, 2002, John's body was also naked; it also had been marked with scars—on his back, on his heels, in his chest, and a hole in his throat where a trache would no longer give him breath. This twenty-five year old man being rolled out of our home in a body bag weighed but fifty pounds; a body broken and twisted not by evil men, but by evil nevertheless.

Yancey again:

> The question that obsesses modern thinkers, "Why do bad things happen?" gets little systematic treatment in the Bible because Bible writers believed *they knew* why bad things happen: we live on a planet ruled by powers intent on blocking and perverting the will of God. . . . Of course bad things happen! On a planet ruled by the Evil One we should expect to see violence, deception, disease, and all manner of opposition to the reign of God.[15]

Here's what I think: Scripture is thoroughly realistic about the role of suffering, both physical and emotional, in a predictably troubled world (John 16:33). In the lives of believers suffering exists to punish sins, to test us, to teach us God's will, to teach us patience, to humble us, to discipline us in love, to drive us to repentance, to get us to rely on his grace, to purify us, to promote his glory, and to further the gospel. To become a Christian is not to escape suffering, but to be able to bear suffering with dignity and hope.

When John was diagnosed I determined that I would not allow my life to be consumed with "why." Double standards are always selfishly motivated. I can't ask God "why" now in the face of crisis when I didn't think to ask him "why" when John and Alan were born, or on my wedding day. I didn't ask him "why" as my career unfolded nicely or when we sold homes at a profit. Certainly I didn't ask him "why" when I accepted his saving grace. How dare I challenge him now? I'm still looking for the star athlete who points to the heavens when he misses a tackle that costs the game. Anybody can be pious in the end zone.

§

Every day of my life since John's diagnosis in August of 1981 has been influenced profoundly by the reality of my son's disease and consequent death; influenced, I trust, primarily in healthy ways, in perspective-giving ways, in transforming ways. And yet, I've come to realize that while his life will always be precious in my heart and mind, those last twenty years were not really *about* John. And even those considerations above—joy, surrender, perspective, discipline, affecting others, and even suffering—each true, each integral, somehow come up just short of the mark.

Goodness

So how do we talk about suffering, and surrender, and perspective without talking about Job? And what if the story of Job is not really about Job and his suffering; what if it's a story of God's goodness? And what if John's story is not really about John and his suffering, but about God's goodness? What does it say that John's life and death brought both John and others (certainly me) to a new depth of surrender and consequent joy we likely would have never known had John not suffered?

David Needham is a Distinguished Professor Emeritus of Bible at Multnomah University where I was privileged to sit under his wisdom in a class on the Psalms—his last at Multnomah after a forty-three year career influencing young and occasionally more seasoned minds. I was writing in the library one morning when he dropped by my table. I was struggling with how to best tell John's story and asked for his counsel; perhaps he could help me organize my thoughts in a way that would make sense to future readers. In front of me was the text of John's thoughts regarding "How I Face The Future" (*Eden* 13) which Professor Needham asked to read. He was moved by John's words, and upon completing them he said,

> "You know Bruce, John did not know joy in the face of tragedy because he worked at it. John knew joy in the face of tragedy because God is good."

That's it, isn't it? God is good.

In his classic, *A Long Obedience in the Same Direction*, Eugene Peterson contends that the basic conviction of a Christian is that God intends good for us and that he will get his way in us. When we cry out to God for mercy, our prayer is not an effort to entice God to do what he is otherwise unwilling to do, but rather align ourselves with what he has every intention of doing.[16]

We live in a fallen world marked by sin, yet God remains eternally *good*. We cheat and steal, lie and murder; we suffer the realities of natural disasters and genetic disease; yet God is good. He is loving, immutable, faithful, compassionate, just... *and*, his goodness was perfectly and thoroughly expressed on a Roman cross where his Son died—satisfying the Father's wrath, the understandable consequence of disobedience (sin)—so that you and I might spend forever in his presence if we so choose. That's it!

But there is a curiosity (some would say cynicism) in me, and I find myself thinking ~

When we hear that God is good, it seems that an honest if unspoken response might well be, "So what?" When we're told that God loves us . . . so what? When we're told that God does not change, that he is faithful, that he is just, and compassionate, and sovereign, that he is *this*, that he is *that*

. . . so what? When I'm told that Jesus died for my sin . . . *so what?*

Well . . . if the character of God as described in the Bible is true, what implications does that have for my life? What would be a reasonable response?

My good friend Kim Jim Seok lives in Songtan, Republic of Korea. When he came to Christ a few years ago, he gave himself the name "Stone." His thinking was that if Peter was the Rock on which Jesus would build his Church, to be a part of that Church, even if only a *stone*, would be a magnificent way to live. Stone taught me that Westerners are often satisfied with simple answers to difficult questions; face value is satisfactory. But not Asians. In Stone's culture, the simple answer is always inadequate. Not because it is wrong, but because it is not enough.

What if Professor Needham is right and God is always and wholly good . . . so what?

When Charles Colson learned that his son Wendell was diagnosed with bone cancer, he asked,

> "But what happens when you have relied on an intimate relationship with Jesus and the day comes when God seems distant? What happens in the dark night of the soul? The operation to remove a malignant tumor took 10 hours – the longest day of my life."[17]

Sometime later, in the wake of this struggle and others, Colson found himself moved at the glory of God's creation, this time manifest in a stunning view of the Smoky Mountains. He came to realize, "It's impossible not to know God as the Creator . . . for there is no other rational explanation for reality. God cannot not be." He goes on ~

> "It struck me that I don't have to make sense
> of the agonies I bear or hear a clear answer.

> God is not a creature of my emotions or senses. God is God, the one who created me and takes responsibility for my children's destiny and mine. I can only cling to the certainty that he is and that he has spoken."[18]

If it's true that God is ultimately *good*, and I "get that" at a level deeper than cerebral ascent, then it seems to me that the reasonable response would be to position myself under his authority. If God is unquestionably good, why would I choose not to accept his invitation to live in this kingdom that has come—in the *goodness* that has come near in the person of Jesus (Mark 1:15)?

Stone would suggest that a life well lived, as was John's, seeks more than simple answers. It even seeks more than truth, for truth *alone* lives in the academy, and truth *untried* resides with the scholar. But truth *applied, appropriated, lived, owned* . . . that kind of Truth ultimately trumps the inevitable disappointments and losses of life. That kind of Truth resides first in the heart, and then in the relationship, and then in the ICU, and finally in the cemetery standing over your child's grave. And then, Truth owned can find a home in the telling of stories that matter; stories that at their core tell of a *good God*, who at his core wants nothing more than to be in oneness with you and me.

> My prayer is not for them [Christ's disciples then] alone. I pray also for those who will believe in me [Christ's disciples now] through their message [their stories] that all of them may be one, Father, just as you are in me and I am in you. May they also be in us so that the world may believe that you have sent me.
>
> ~ Jesus
> John 17: 20-21
> (clarifications added)

And there will come a prearranged instant, *a moment of something stronger than time*, when the door will be opened to unimaginable oneness, and goodness will be manifest like never before. Dallas Willard offers encouraging assurance:

> Indeed, the very creation itself is groaning under the strain of the process through which humanity will step into its destined role in the cosmos, into "the coming glory to be revealed in us" (Romans 8:18-23). But in the Prophecies the way of God simply must succeed, because God *is* God. "I am the Lord," he says, "who exercises lovingkindness, justice and righteousness in the earth; for I delight in these things" (Jeremiah 9:24). These things must, then, prevail. It cannot be otherwise.[19]

Reflections 6. . .

The Wounded Innocent

> Going on from there, he saw two other brothers, James son of Zebedee and his brother John. They were in a boat with their father Zebedee, preparing their nets. Jesus called them, and immediately they left the boat and their father and followed him.
>
> ~ Matthew
> Matthew 4:21-22

When you first meet the disciple John, you barely do meet John. First you meet James—and then you meet John. James is always put first. You read about James & John. You never read about John & James. James was likely older. Certainly he was more impressive.

If you were having a dinner party and were sending out invitations, you'd invite James and say, "you can bring John along if you have to."

So John kind of lived in the shadow of his brother James; he's the little brother who never quite got the attention he deserved.

Maybe you know someone like that?

~ Ken Needham

ALAN

Our dear son Alan, now thirty-two years old, has never known not having a brother who was either dying or dead.[1]

Alan called. I *love* to hear his voice! He'd roll his eyes and think I was terribly *sappy*, but there are times when the words "Hi, Dad" make my heart race and my eyes moisten.

Alan and his bride Paige had purchased their first house and he was calling to say he was on his way to pick up the keys. Exciting! We crave roots, don't we? We need to belong. We were made to be part of something—a family, a community, an identity. Alan's unfolding life reminds me that the pain of aloneness is always trumped by the joy of oneness. Alan's life is of immense value to Cathy, to me, and most certainly to our God who loves each of us enough to not only nurture us, but to prune us and shape us with the simple intent of using us for his purposes in the kingdom that has come near in the person of Jesus.

And now as John's writing comes available, Alan and Paige have welcomed Sydney Elizabeth Gilbert into their lives. Life continues and joy mounts. Uncle John would have been thrilled!

§

The military calls it collateral damage; uninvolved civilians caught in the wake of aggression. Sometimes blameless combatants are wounded, sometimes killed, by friendly fire. Certainly it was unintended. The victim was minding his own business, doing his own job. He's one of the good guys; he's on *our side* for goodness sake! But in this fallen world the innocent sometimes suffer; often suffer. Sin plays itself out in insidious ways.

Alan.
The forgotten griever; the wounded innocent.

His name means "harmony," but he found himself born into a family where learning to live up to the spirit of that name would not come easily. And while John's disease brought pragmatic realities that required attention, they never brought preference. Nevertheless, the boy in the wheelchair with the charming spirit, beautiful service dog, and sterling report card was the conspicuous center of *all* of our lives through no fault or desire of his own. As parents we thought we did balance pretty well; but how can a younger brother with legitimate needs of his own understand it all? Indeed, life is not fair, and Alan intuitively knew it. The last twenty years of John's life that consumed our family coincided with the twenty most formidable years of Alan's life. These are the years during which character is formed, values are imprinted, and self-image is established. The ground is level at the foot of the cross; but the ground on which Alan stood during those critical years was too often riddled with potholes and seemingly tilted in his brother's direction.

"*My* name's not John!"

> How many times did Alan have to say that;
> want to say that?

Many, *many,* over the years did their very best to include, recognize, and celebrate Alan and his personhood, his uniqueness; certainly those in the MDA and telethon families included and encouraged him. I remain grateful for their sensitivity.

Others . . . perhaps not so much.

There were the teachers who remembered having John, a model student, in their classes three years earlier. Would Alan "meet the standard" his brother had established? *Could* he, in their eyes, "measure up"? Would he be allowed to be the best "me" he could be, or would there always be, even if subtle, that *other* expectation?

Alan would come to include his mom and dad in the category of those who too often lacked sensitivity. How many times over the years did John's stretching and breathing exercises trump Alan's desire to get help with his homework, or learn how to fish? How many times did he hear from behind the desk in my home office, "Sorry, Alan. Can't play catch right now. Got work to do." Certainly we loved Alan. Certainly countless hours were happily invested in him—his many years in competitive gymnastics, his music lessons and marching bands, coaching his Little League Teams, the list goes on. But . . . .

We'd like to think that our *desire to love* is necessarily understood as *loving well.* But as with all communication, the value is not in what is presented but in how it is perceived. I'm pretty sure that seeing ourselves as not having been loved *well enough* humanly often marks us in ways that only supernatural grace can overcome.

DISMISSED

Alan must have been about twelve, John about fifteen. We were spending a few days visiting Ted and Margaret Faris, good friends who lived in a beautiful tri-level home overlooking Escondido's picturesque San Pasqual valley. John's wheelchair did not, of course, navigate their home well, so, as had long ago become the norm, John was picked up and transported whenever and wherever so that he might be a part of things.

At bedtime, Cathy picked John up out of his chair to take him to his bedroom, a journey that required descending two short flights of stairs, while Alan and I remained visiting with our hosts upstairs.

Moments later we heard the unmistakable and thunderous sound of trouble; thuds against a stairwell, cries of alarm and pain. On the second flight of stairs, Cathy had lost her footing. She went down with John in her arms, landing in the hallway crumpled, intermingled . . . injured?

I flew to their side, ignorant of the reaction of others. John dazed and bent, Cathy moaning, still clinging to her son; I stood over them for an instant to take inventory. As I kneeled down to unravel their bodies without causing more harm, Alan—just seconds behind me— rushed excitedly to the scene, wanting to help, wanting to rescue (I now know rescuing is intuitive for him. . .that's how he's made!). Blindly focused on John and Cathy, I only subconsciously sensed him at my side.

Adrenaline rushing, concerned that necks had been broken, I instinctively and forcefully thrust my arms open to full extension in an unconscious effort to "clear the area." My forearm caught Alan flush in his face, knocking him backwards, knocking him down. He was humiliated; I was oblivious.

~ ~ ~

Turns out, John was fine. Cathy, however, suffered a fractured arm that she had instinctively positioned between John's head and the wall as they fell. While our host took Cathy to the hospital, I continued with the time-consuming routine of putting John to bed.

Now a good forty-five minutes after the fall. . .where's Alan?

Oh, my gosh! Where's Alan!? As I went to look for him, my mind rehearsed the scene at the bottom of the stairs where I had knocked him away, discounting him, crushing his spirit, humiliating this fine young man for coming to the rescue of those he *also* loved; devaluing him, marking him, perhaps beyond repair.

I found him upstairs, huddled alone in a dark corner . . . sullen, angry, tense, withdrawn, and *deeply wounded*. I apologized sincerely, but my apology included a defense. Can you believe it? I defended myself! Surely he could understand the heat of the moment. Surely he could understand a father's instincts. Oh, by the way, Alan . . . are you OK?

But Alan wanted nothing to do with my concern or explanations.

He'd been *dismissed* and *devalued* . . . by his *father*!

Those words don't belong in the same sentence together.

How I would give anything to have those moments back; to do them over, to live them better . . .

~ At the bottom of the stairs where I would welcome his help and value his contribution!

~ Or late that night in the dark corner with a wounded boy. I would offer no defense for a defenseless act; but would simply hold him, and cry with him.

Parenting In The Rear View Mirror

Regretful empty nesters are often encouraged that "we did the best we could with what we knew and what we had."

I suppose that's true; I trust that's true for Cathy and me. Often, however, it feels terribly inadequate. It feels too much like making excuses in dark corners. I understand that inappropriate regret is a powerful weapon in Satan's toolbox, and that it is only trumped by an accurate understanding of our identity in Christ. I do hope, however, that any comfort taken in "doing the best we could" does not become a flippant dismissal of responsibility . . . *"whatever"* . . . but rather a healthy awareness and appreciation that we are divinely loved, under grace, in spite of—indeed, *because of* our depravity.

§

In *Apprenticeship With Jesus,* Gary Moon writes insightfully of the redeemed life made accessible through a living, interactive relationship with Jesus Christ. Among his stories is that of his daughter Jenna coming to a point during her college years when she began to question the divinity of Jesus. Dr. Moon and his wife had vowed to raise their two daughters in the faith; family devotions each night, mission trips with the youth of their church, daily prayer offered "*in Jesus' name.*" How could there be any question of his divinity? Moon writes,

> And then it hit me. Despite all the Jesus talk, Jenna had seen few, if any, examples of people who had apprenticed themselves to Jesus and experienced real alchemy of soul. Most every representative of Christ in her life had shown her more of the result of non-transformation than transformation. In her eighteen years of life she had heard sermons from a parade of pastors who were more CEOs than shepherds, witnessed a church split so ugly that Jerry Springer should have sent a camera crew, and she

> had been crushingly and repeatedly betrayed by a potpourri of "good Christian" friends.
>
> My daughter had heard TV evangelists pronounce hurricanes to be God's judgment and wrath for promiscuity. She had seen the vivid horror of the World Trade Center imploding and later stared down into the crater where the towers had stood. And she had watched peers join the military and go off to fight in Iraq — in what they perceived in some measure to be a religious war between Christians and Muslims. And then, only a few months ago, she wept at the funeral of one of her best friends who died there.
>
> But perhaps most confusing of all, she grew up in a home where both of her parents made their living from counseling, teaching, and writing about transformation, while often looking a whole lot more like creatures of dust than light. While she was still on the road back to the university, I felt like more than a jaded observer, I felt like the chief among charlatans.[2]

Alan's youth was not dissimilar. I, too, have often felt like the chief among charlatans.

There was that time when Alan attended the local auto races with his church's youth group. At thirteen, his growth spurt hadn't kicked in yet and Alan was small for his age. At the ticket booth he was encouraged by his Youth Pastor to lie about his age—after all, two dollars could be saved if Alan would say he was under twelve. Of course, it wasn't really a lie, just a little fib. And besides, everybody does it . . . *whatever*.

And where were Alan's parents when the story found our ears? Consumed by life . . . easier to let it go; easier to avoid confrontation with both our son and our church. "Gosh!

We're trying to hold this family together with a dying child in the next room. Cut us some slack. . . .!"

But avoiding conflict and discipline were only part of the problem. Perhaps more significant was the model Cathy and I too often gave our boys. As an apprentice of Jesus, my call in life is to live my life as Jesus would live it were he me.

But like Dr. Moon, Cathy and I too often looked a whole lot more like creatures of dust than light. As all children do, Alan observed intently as his parents—certainly from his perspective—"performed" one way on Sunday morning and quite another Monday through Saturday. Were we conspicuously evil; manipulative and deceitful? Probably not. But quick to voice an opinion that was too often critical, too often condemning, too often less than loving? Sure . . . often.

In a young boy's mind, that must be how life's lived.

Gary Moon wrote of his imperfect parenting in the wake of his daughter's revelation. And while I found comfort in being reminded that my inadequacies are not unique, I was very much challenged, yet again, to love well now.

Semper Fi

Alan had long dreamed of becoming a Marine. Cathy and I were not enthused. Cathy did not like the idea of her son at war. For me, the Marines in my past had almost always been brash, arrogant, and very full of themselves. I didn't want Alan in an environment that would fuel *machismo*. He sat on our bed one night maturely stating his position (I hate it when he does that!). As I confidently pled my case against the arrogant bravado and selfish pride engrained in those who chose to be part of the Marine community, Alan responded with, "Oh, you mean like Chuck Swindoll?"[3]

He enlisted the next day.

John's words from *Eden* . . .

> I was honestly excited to be going to Alan's graduation. I gained so much respect for my brother and what he had done. Some of the ideals of the Marine Corps, which were introduced to family in the two or three days prior to the graduation, were very noble. I also admit that the military pomp and circumstance, which is not without meaning, was thrilling to me. But most importantly I was deeply proud of my brother.

The good news, of course—the *really* good news—is that impressionable young boys become seasoned young men. Unfairness in life need not necessarily cause irreparable damage. Rather, it can shape, it can educate, and it can foster growth. Wounds can heal and scars can fade. And in spite of life's inevitable pitfalls, the wounded innocent have every reason for hope.

Now, years later, the rescuer that I snuffed at the bottom of the staircase has grown into a courageous and respected contributor on the front lines of his community. After graduating from the Fire Academy, Alan spent several years engaging uncontained forest fires, running back into flame-engulfed homes to retrieve wedding pictures for the woman whose priceless memories were being reduced to ashes, and offering the tender and secure comfort of his arms to the dying infant who had been beaten with a table leg by his drugged mother because he wouldn't stop crying. The teenager I attempted to discourage from becoming a Marine would grow into a proud and dedicated Devil Dog who served the Corps honorably for six years. And out of a youth continuously exposed to the injustice of disease and the cruelty it wrought came an *adult rescuer* who, having proudly graduated with honors from his Police Academy, now serves with honor as a sworn Police Officer.

> Start children off on the way they should go, and even when they are old they will not turn from it.
>
> ~ Solomon
> Proverbs 22:6

"The way they should go" is the way of wisdom that always trumps both knowledge and experience; a wisdom that includes the living of a life consistent with how God created that life to be lived.

Well done, Alan.

BROTHER TO BROTHER

In our world, the best intentions, the deepest thoughts, the heartfelt expressions of gratitude too often go unsaid.

> Why does it take courage to offer grace?
> Why so many self-imposed boundaries?

In any case, his body now devastated by a relentless enemy, John wrote the following to his brother just two months before he would fly. It was to be read . . . later.

April 2002

Dear Alan,

I can picture so many times when you came into my room to show me some new thing, share something fun like a movie, or even just to tease me. I guess you see that uncontrollable smile that comes across my face no matter how much I try to hide it. I always fail. The reason is that you simply make me happy when you are around. I also miss you terribly when you are gone, even if it is for just a week. A few friends have come and gone, but you are the only person who ever lit up my heart just because you entered the room. That is the absolute truth. Even when you make me want to tear my hair out, (as all brothers do to each other!) you have always been my favorite person in the world. I ask forgiveness from you and often from my Lord if I ever gave you the idea otherwise.

I think you should know that I worry over you more than anyone else, especially at this time in my life. It is not because of anything you have done wrong or any danger I think you are in. It isn't mainly that kind of worry. Let me try to explain the best that I can. I worry because I know how much you hate what I'm going through and how desperately you wish you could fix it. It brings tears to my eyes to see you struggle and be in so much pain because of this stupid disease. I wish so much that I could just say the magic words and make it go away, not even mostly for my own sake, but for yours. I really wish everything had been different.

But I know that this time isn't the end of our relationship. I still think of you often even though it is from very far. Aaron Cain recently wrote to me and expressed regret that he didn't spend more time getting to know me. I told him that there is a lot more time ahead than behind. What I meant was that we'll have so much time in heaven to "catch up" that any missed opportunities in this life won't matter anymore. For you I would say the same thing but for a slightly different reason. All our regrets over everything that seemed to go wrong would pale in comparison to what we will someday share. I use these thoughts to encourage myself and I hope they encourage you.

Love always,

John

Reflections 7. . .

"Now John Knows"

To suggest that, "Oh, he/she is in a better place now"
is simplistically inadequate
and a naïve understanding of eternity.

This is the end . . . For me the beginning of life.

No one has yet believed in God and the kingdom of God, no one has yet heard about the realm of the resurrected, and not been homesick from that hour, waiting and looking forward joyfully to being released from bodily existence . . . . Death is hell and night and cold, if it is not transformed by our faith. But that is just what is so marvelous, that we can transform death.

~ Dietrich Bonhoeffer

These kinds of stories are supposed to have happy endings. Lassie always rescued Timmy. The Babe always hit the home run promised to the sick little boy in the hospital. One minute finds our loved one warmly sharing his final good-byes with expressions of gratitude and love; and in the next moment he has seamlessly slipped into eternity future with a smile on his face and a hymn on his lips. But not always . . .

April 25, 2002

Dear Friends,

John is tired. Recent years and recent months have not been kind. He has fought his fight and run his race in ways that humble us. He has now decided that the finish line needs to be close. He has chosen to discontinue those medications that are designed to prolong his life.

Two nights ago Dick Thorp, our friend and family physician, spent 90 minutes with us in John's room to discuss the management of that process. The three of us ended our time surrounding John in prayer. Dick mustered the courage to tearfully affirm John, and tell John of his impact on his life. He offered words of life to our son and through honesty and transparency, prayer and affirmation, a conversation dreaded for twenty years turned into a holy moment. We are such a fearful people, and yet when dreams are shattered, God faithfully and predictably comes near.

Dick could not predict the timing of John's death. People are unique and variables are unforeseen. His best guess . . . a few weeks. These days will see many tears. Love and patience will be at a premium. But while this time is sobering and void of frivolity, there is nevertheless an almost uncanny peace in this home. We believe it to be a consequence of our belief that Jesus is indeed who he said he was. As you think of John and care for us all through this brief season now upon us, we have great hope that you will come to share our peace.

With love . . . Bruce, Cathy, & Alan

Noble on one side; grotesque on the other . . .

Representative of the love and support we received in the wake of John's decision was this expression of friendship from Ken Needham[1] . . .

Dear Bruce & Cathy ~
Just got your message; thank you for telling us, and for honouring us with John's recent thoughts. I do not know what it cost him to put them into his computer . . . still less do I know what it cost him to arrive at those conclusions . . . less again what it has cost you two to come to this point. Any comment of mine would only trivialize a situation that is noble on the one side, and grotesque on the other. . . just like the Lord on the Cross.

In the love that goes with faith and hope,
and outlasts all this temporary planet has to offer ~ Ken.

§

Shadowlands again ~ the intimate story of C.S. Lewis (Jack) and his bride Joy as they together face her inevitable death resulting from cancer. Against a rail fence in the valley of his boyhood dreams, they find themselves engaged in this powerful exchange of a husband's love and a wife's wisdom.

Jack: "You know, I don't want to be somewhere else anymore. Not wanting for anything new to happen. Not looking 'round the next corner. No next hill. Here and now. That's enough."

Joy: "That's your kind of happy, isn't it?"
After a pause, "It's not going to last, Jack."

Jack: "Let's not spoil the time we have left."

Joy: "It doesn't spoil it. It makes it real. I'm going to die. And I want to be with you *then*, too. The only way I can do that is if I'm able to talk to you about it *now*."

Jack: "I'll manage when the time comes."

Joy: "It can be better than that. *It can be better than just managing*. What I'm trying to say is that the pain *then* is part of the happiness *now*. That's the deal."[2]

That's the deal indeed.

Still questioning after all these years, still sorting through what's real and what isn't about God and heaven and death, it was at Joy's death bed Lewis thought, "When it gets close, you find out if you really believe it or not."[3]

At John's bedside during his final hours, I scribbled this note:

> This is the moment, isn't it? All my faith, all I have believed in culminates here; now. How could I be tested further? What greater loss could I experience? To come out the on other side of this—whole—still in love with Jesus, will be a testimony to *his* strength, not my own; to *his* faithfulness, not my own—a testimony to the fact that he really, truly, is enough.

The old hymn says "trust and obey." We don't sing songs like that much anymore. But its message is resolute. Christ is enough; Jesus is sufficient, not because I need him to be, but because he is.

In his timeless classic, *The Weight of Glory*, C.S. Lewis declares,

> If we consider the unblushing promises of rewards promised in the gospels, it would seem that our Lord considers our desires not too strong but too weak. We are far too easily pleased. Like an ignorant child who goes on making mud pies in a slum because he cannot imagine what is meant by an offer of a holiday at the sea.[4]

Scripture paints a picture of a glorious "holiday at the sea," a very real heaven in which we will experience magnificent, even unimaginable blessing: perfect oneness, perfect community forever embraced in the presence of God.

Just before he died, Jesus prayed, "Father, may they be one, even as you and I are one" (John 17). *Oneness*—perfect community—the prominent theme from Genesis to Revelation will be the prominent theme in a heaven where believers will know deep, open, intimate, joy-producing, trusting relationships that never end. You don't have to fear rejection or even carefully pick your friends—everybody is somebody you want to be with.

> Then I heard a voice from heaven say, "Write: Blessed are the dead who die in the Lord from now on."
>
> ~ John on Patmos
> Revelation 14:13

When the Christian dies, Jesus says he/she is "blessed." Not distraught, not alone, not forsaken; but happy, fortunate, privileged. At that moment when our faith indeed becomes sight we will be more alive than ever before or ever imagined!

The Apostle tells us heaven is like a city with streets made of gold and extremely expensive gemstones around every corner. Maybe he means that we should expect to see curbs and gutters and diamond studded billboards directing us to a celestial Rodeo Drive where everything's free? Maybe he's saying that in heaven we will have finally caught up with the Joneses? But what if he's not painting a detailed picture of a specific place? What if he's doing his best within the boundaries of human language to express the inexpressible—to describe the unimaginable essence, the flavor, the uninterrupted existence of an eternal certainty in the presence of YAHWEH? Could it be that he's just trying to tell us we will finally be home . . . that we will finally live in perfect oneness? No more fences. No more anger. No more broken homes. No more alienation.

No more *greenness*.

DEATH IS A PARADOX

I could write forever about the last days of John's life and their influence on my own. But it is the *moment* of his death that has marked me so profoundly. After weeks of bedside vigilance, Cathy and I were on either side of John when he took his last breath. Death is not always conspicuous; often we appear to simply *slip* away. Nevertheless, we knew. And in that moment that lasted seemingly forever, a lifetime of emotion came gushing out of us. Our grief and wailing was intense beyond our capacity to console one another. It was raw, much like the moments we embraced for hours in the irreversible reality of John's diagnosis twenty years earlier. Now it was over.

I am incapable of adequately expressing the raw and conflicted emotions that fought for my attention and were simultaneously overwhelming.

- In that moment, loss that seemed ruinous somehow coexisted with a union with God I had not yet experienced.
- In that moment, I *lost* that which had been so precious—my firstborn son, while the Father *received* that which is priceless—yet another fully redeemed life.
- In that moment was a clear awareness of what was so noble on the one side, and yet so grotesque on the other . . . yes, just like the Lord on the Cross.

For the believer in Jesus that's the great hope, isn't it? It's that moment in time we long for—to somehow, mysteriously, see God. Of course, no one is exempt from that moment; receiver and rejecter alike will know truth like never before. The day is coming when our faith—or lack of faith—will indeed become sight.

Now John Knows

The morning after John died we began the process of informing those who would want to know of his passing. Love was warmly expressed and genuine condolences were offered. Each expression of love and compassion was truly appreciated and valued . . . really.

One response, however, provided a unique and insightful perspective. John Ortberg had graciously invested in our clan in the months that led up to John's death. Certainly he would want to know of John's passing.

"John, this is Bruce Gilbert in Paradise. John died last night and I wanted you to be among the first to know." His response was calm and certain:

"Oh . . . now John knows."

Simple—Wise—Profound—True

Indeed, John *does* now know.

> No more worry; no more speculation.
> No more fear, or aloneness, or artery taps, or ICU's.
> No more doctrine; no more theology.
> All that *stuff* had, in an instant, fallen into the category of "old news."

And while those kinds of issues consume long hours of debate deep into the night of seminary dorm rooms, I have increasingly less confidence that they are of any practical import or eternal value. At one end of the Church are those with no intellectual curiosity, content to sway back and forth to the music and nod affirmingly at every unchallenged word from the pulpit, while for too many others the objective appears to be arguing excruciatingly fine points of doctrine, finding satisfaction only in the debate itself. Would it not be of imminently greater value were we to become intentional about engaging in the process of developing the character of Jesus, for the cause of Christ; not the defining of the kingdom, but the living in it, the embracing of it? Would our lives not be better lived, and would we not better serve our God, were we to finally understand that Jesus is fully sufficient, and as a result, "all these things [are] given to you as well" (Matthew 6:33b).

The Apostle Paul was caught up into the third heaven (2 Corinthians 12:2); that is, not to the immediate heaven of the earth's atmosphere, nor to what we've come to know as outer space, but into that realm generally understood as "heaven" where one finds the presence of God himself. Because of his remarkable experience, Paul has a certain and consequent credibility, and is therefore eminently qualified to proclaim the great hope that to be absent from the body is to be home with the Lord (2 Corinthians 5:8).

There will be a time when our faith becomes sight; when our belief in Jesus leads to our presence with Jesus. I believe it will happen in a seemingly uninterrupted instant—in that moment of time just beyond our final human breath.

Moses knows; and so does Isaiah.
Barnabas knows, and so does Dorcas.
Harry knows; and so does Maude.

And now, John knows too.

On an early June morning at a quarter past midnight, this precious, redeemed, eternal soul said goodbye to an earthly vehicle that was simply out of gas. And very alive, quite alert, and thoroughly undefeated, John's spirit, John's soul—the *who he really is*—entered the presence of God in the perfect fulfillment of that for which he was created.

Now John knows . . .

And there will come a moment of *something stronger than time* when you and I will know as well.

What Does John Now Know?

It has been true for centuries and remains so today that that the word "Christian" is understood quite differently from culture to culture and tradition to tradition. Often these understandings (or misunderstandings) are political in nature. Perhaps other language, then, is helpful in better identifying the follower of Christ. Dallas Willard has brought attention to a scriptural perspective almost too conspicuous to be noticed. That is, the word "disciple" is found on the pages of the New Testament 269 times while the word "Christian" is found there only three times. The New Testament is a book about disciples, by disciples, and for disciples of Jesus Christ.[5] Dallas has further introduced this generation to the concept of *apprenticeship* to Jesus in an effort to bring fresh appreciation for biblical *discipleship*, a term that in its misuse has become fuzzy in recent decades.

What does it mean to be a biblical Christian; a follower, an apprentice of Jesus? Clarity can be found throughout Scripture, to include these simple and unambiguous words of the Apostle John found in the fourth Gospel:

> Yet to all who did receive him [*Jesus*](*and to those who receive him still!*), to those who believed in his name, he gave the right to become children of God

- children born not of natural descent, nor of human decision or a husband's will, but born of God.

~ John
John 1:12,
(additions mine)

§

So, what is it exactly that John Gilbert—child of God, receiver, believer, Christian—now knows? What does the Christian have reason to expect in the passing from this life to the next? What is the magnificent and ultimate hope we have been promised?

I believe, *in a moment of something stronger than time*, we will pass from this world into what theologians rightly understand as the *intermediate heaven*, perhaps best understood as *paradise*—that same paradise Jesus referenced on the cross when acknowledging the faith of the criminal at his side (Luke 23:39-43). We could say that paradise is that *place* Paul alluded to when he described life immediately after death as being "with Christ, which is better by far" (Philippians 1:23) . . . and that would be true.

If you drove east on the Skyway from the valley floor into the Sierra foothills you would come to our hometown. Welcoming you at our town limits would be a sign that reads:

You Are Now Ascending Into Paradise
May It Be All Its Name Implies

Admittedly it is not . . . all its name implies, that is. However, our greeting begs the question: What *does* the word *paradise* imply? Our thinking regarding such a "heavenly" existence finds quite diverse understandings, with the respected Randy Alcorn representing one school of thought while the notable N.T. Wright holds firm to a quite different position. My own best understanding—one among many I hold rather loosely—is comfortably aligned with the late Ray Stedman who suggested that to think of paradise—the intermediate heaven—as a physical place, a tangible destination, is to reveal both an interpretive predisposition and a fundamental misunderstanding.[6] Too often we think in terms of space: earth is "down here" while heaven is "up there"... somewhere. Russian hero Valery Bykovsky told newsmen in 1963 that no Soviet cosmonaut believed in God, and none of them had seen anything to change their minds during their space flights.[7] They could not find heaven; there was no sign of it "up there." Their conclusion was that such a place does not exist; and indeed, such a *place* does not.

Paradise is much like God himself: *wholly other*. Heaven, or in Matthew's language "*the heavens,*" is best understood not as a physical destination (think St. Louis, or Munich), but as the reality of God's *presence*. This understanding helps us appreciate why the word "heaven" is not capitalized in the biblical text. It is a realm well beyond our experiences in the commonplace world which is visible to our senses and shapes our perspectives. Admittedly there is mystery here; perhaps we would do well to become more comfortable with mystery. While God, through his creation, his Son, and his inspired Word, has revealed to us what he's chosen to make known, certainly he has not yet revealed *all there is* to know. My best understanding is that paradise is not the final destiny for the submitted follower of Christ, but rather an intermediate *place* of rest, refreshment, and bliss. Paradise is that state in which the believing dead are held firmly within the intensely tangible love of God, and the conscious presence of Jesus Christ, while awaiting the definitive fulfillment of our destiny and the perfect finale to God's redemptive plan. The ultimate victory and predictable consequence of Christ's work on the cross is sin's last breath. And the *final* destiny for the believer in Jesus Christ is found in our hope of the resurrection of our bodies and the continuation of eternal life in the presence of God on a redeemed earth positioned among new heavens.[8]

> Then I saw 'a new heaven and a new earth,' for the first heaven and the first earth had passed away.
>
> ~ John
> Rev. 21:1

One evening after having decided to discontinue those extra-ordinary efforts keeping him alive and pondering what his soon to be new reality would be, John said . . .

Sometimes I think the moment I enter heaven,
my first thought will be,
"Oh John, silly boy! Why were you so afraid?"

How often have we mused, "When I get to heaven, I'm going to ask Jesus about . . . *this or that*." I've come to a place where I'm uncomfortable with such impertinence. Such questions will simply be of no consequence, even less importance, and trivialize the magnitude of our then current reality. Imagine being sin-forgiven and debt-free in the very presence of the Triune God commencing a timeless journey of worship, community, joy, responsibility ("You have been faithful with a few things; I will put you in charge of many things" [Matt. 25:23]), creativity, productivity, and reunion—whether in a transitional paradise or ultimately within the limitless boundaries of a new heaven and a new earth—while somehow being concerned with whether Calvin or Wesley had the predestination thing right, or whether two moths actually rode on the ark or if they, in fact, hovered over it. Really? We may now find such things worthy of our interest; they will not be one day.

I suppose among the most difficult things for anyone to believe, those within the Church not exempt, is the infinite value and worth God assigns to the individual person. Recent years have seen a popular perspective that says, "It's not about me." And while I appreciate and support the intended notion—that we are created to bring God glory, not vice versa—the cross at Golgotha would suggest that apparently *something* is about us. We are not *nobody's* among a faceless mass. St. Clive offers his classic perspective:

> There are no *ordinary* people. You have never talked to a mere mortal. Nations, cultures, arts, civilizations—these are mortal, and their life is to ours as the life of a gnat. But it is immortals whom we joke with, work with, marry, snub, and exploit—immortal horrors or everlasting splendours.[9]

Nor are Christians simply sinners saved by grace. My friend Stone would correctly argue that while that's true, it is not complete. Such a simplistic perspective robs us of what Scripture informs us is the true *identity* in Christ for those who have "*believed in his name,*" and frees those professing believers from assuming responsibility for the pursuit of those distinctives incumbent in that identity[10] . . . they're a gift!

I am loved by God. (John 3:16)
I am Jesus' friend. (John 15:15)
I am a joint heir with Christ, sharing in his inheritance. (Romans 8:17)
I am a new creation. (2 Corinthians 5:17)
I am a saint. (Ephesians 1:1/)
I am a son [daughter] of light and not of darkness. (1 Thessalonians 5:5)

I am seated with Christ in the heavenly realms. (Ephesians 2:6)
I am born of God, and the evil one, the devil, cannot harm me. (1 John 5:18)
I am a child of God and I will resemble Christ when he returns. (1 John 3:1-2)

Merely saved, simply forgiven . . . is that who we are?

Or is it God's purpose to pluck out of human history an eternal community of those who were once thought to be just *ordinary* human beings? I believe that just such a people, each one a believer in God, will one day "pervade the entire created realm and share in the government of it. God's precreation intention to have that community as a special dwelling place or home will be realized. He will be its prime sustainer and most glorious inhabitant."[11]

We will *know* . . . for the first time. And, we will *be known*, consumed in unimagined intimacy; certainly by YAHWEH—Father, Son, and Counselor—but also by countless angels and the joyful welcoming spirits of those who have gone before us.

> But you have come to Mount Zion, to the city of the living God, the heavenly Jerusalem. You have come to thousands upon thousands of angels in joyful assembly, to the church of the firstborn, whose names are written in heaven. You have come to God, the Judge of all, to the spirits of the righteous made perfect, to Jesus the mediator of the new covenant . . . .
>
> Hebrews 12:22-23

What a Day It Will Be[12]

What a day it's gonna be
When at last your captive heart beats free
And all that's within you sings
In heaven's own harmony
Sweet release from all your darkest fears
The sound of laughter that's been lost for years
You'll never cry another lonely tear
As your sad heart finally
Finally sings

Hallelujah
What a day it will be
Hallelujah
What a day it will be.

~ ~ ~

Note:

May I encourage you to read John Ortberg's *Everybody's Normal Till You Get To Know Them.*[13] In particular, chapter twelve, entitled *Normal At Last: Heaven*, offers a biblical, insightful, and even humorous peek into eternity future. You will be treated to a fresh glimpse of forever; highly recommended!

May I further encourage the reading of Arthur Roberts' *Exploring Heaven: What Great Christian Thinkers Tell Us About Our Afterlife with* God[14] for an eternal perspective grounded in scholarship, Christian orthodoxy, and good sense.

Reflections 8. . .

A Mother's Farewell

Cathy, My Bride

When mothers talk about the depression of the empty nest, they're not mourning the passing of all those wet towels on the floor, or the music that numbs your teeth, or even the bottle of capless shampoo dribbling down the shower drain. They're upset because they've gone from supervisor of a child's life to a spectator. It's like being the Vice President of the United States.

~ Erma Bombeck

ight months after John died, my bride wrote her son a letter.

It was a confession she felt compelled to express for the sanity of her soul. Cathy had been my hero during the twenty years of John's illness. Her incredible gift/skill at care-giving, her relentless courage, stamina and work ethic, her stubborn persistence that each of her boys would lead the best life possible, and thousands of dark early mornings in prayer for her family . . . somehow, it all came up short in her own eyes. She could have done better and cared more; could have been distracted less and loved better. And she needed to say it "out loud."

Deep down, while her letter was addressed to John, it was meant for her heavenly Father. I read it only years later with her permission. It may well be the most beautifully transparent expression of love and self I have ever read! It was insightfully honest, emotionally naked, and attractively vulnerable. It was cleansing . . . for Cathy to have written it, and for me to have read it.

There is great value in introspection. Personal awareness and honesty is a required prerequisite to healthy relationship; with others, with self . . . certainly with God. Primarily, however, Cathy's letter marked me because of the courage it took to confess so openly and completely. To agree with God in the ownership of our sin must please him immensely.

To lay ourselves bare before God in the humility of our flaws may well be worship in its purest form.

Cathy's letter modeled for me the power of living a "palms up" kind of life and a fresh dependence on God's consistent flow of grace.

In the last crucial years of John's life, the pain of having endured abuse as a young girl surfaced to the extent that it could no longer be suppressed. An effort to confront and reconcile with her abuser after decades of silence resulted instead in a decade of reciprocal bitterness that spawned guilt-ridden memories of related bad choices that made caring for her son selflessly more difficult, perhaps beyond reasonable. And for dessert, Cathy's aging mother suffered a stroke that landed her in a local convalescent hospital where it fell on Cathy to be her legal and medical advocate, her champion, her attentive and faithful daughter. With John and Friedman so often in tow, Cathy was an almost daily visitor to a mother who in the anger of her declining health was often relentlessly difficult, demanding, and even cruel to the only one showing up day after day. My bride's wheelbarrow was full to overflowing.

Very few knew the full brunt of Cathy's responsibilities or emotional load. Her integrity saw to that.

Some were not kind.

An acquaintance, Morris (not his real name), had casually observed our lives from a safe distance during the last few years of John's life. Sometime after John died, Morris and I had lunch. The conversation was pleasant enough—until he flippantly commented on what he perceived to be Cathy's oft-exhibited martyr complex. His comments concluded with words somewhat less crass than this, but his message was unmistakable:

> "Nobody's suggesting that losing a child is easy.
> But, *come on* . . . it's been awhile now!"

It is tragic that some so readily create acceptable boundaries for the grieving process of others. I tried to hide how offensive I found Morris' condescending comments, but I've seldom managed my face well. And though his verbal candor was insensitive, his sentiment was not without company. There were others in the cheap seats.

I wish I had defended my bride better in those days. I wish I had responded to Morris and those whose perceptions he shared with a firm grace. I wish I had been her champion . . . then. I know of no one who would voluntarily sign up for the life Cathy lived, day and night, for the *twenty years* she served as John's primary care-giver. And I know of precious few who could have lived it with the dignity and resolve routinely exhibited by this woman of immense character.

Irma Bombeck's quote above makes us laugh.

But Cathy did not go from supervisor to spectator. After twenty five years of not only loving and nourishing like any mother would, Cathy had invested *every ounce* of who she was into serving in the most earnest, intimate, emotionally invested and physically demanding ways imaginable in her dying son. And when John died . . . she was left with a seemingly irreparable hole in her heart. She had not only lost her firstborn son; Cathy had lost her identity.

In a search for sanity, catharsis, and some degree of closure (whatever that means?), Cathy wrote a final love letter to her son. She never expected anyone else would see it. It is offered here with her humble, if somewhat reluctant consent.

THE COURAGE TO CONFESS

Dear John,

I don't know what to say to you now. There are so many regrets, so many memories, so much pride in who you were. God has arranged for me to do this work on your computer, our main method of communication for so many years.

It's now eight months that you've been gone. I know you'd want me to go on with life but I don't know how. *You were my life*. Normally in a family a child grows up with the family's faith and at some point breaks away and develops his own faith. As with so many other things, our family was unique. I'm beginning to think that your faith was the family's faith and now it's time for us to develop our own. Your example of courage and strength was the most amazing thing I have ever seen. No matter what dirty trick was thrown at you, you used it to become better, not bitter. I miss your model to follow. Your insight and application of God's word was beyond your years. Your smile and joy was beyond human understanding. So many people wanted to be close to you but it never went to your head. You knew it was Jesus they wanted, not you. Even in your last hours your only concern was for someone. Oh, how I wish I knew who you were speaking to but we just couldn't understand the name you said. I look forward to the time that I will see those sparkling blue eyes of joy again. When I will see your smile. When I will see your healed body. This last weekend I had the opportunity to experience in part what you experience in full, moment by moment . . . the joy of worshiping God. I want to stand with you and sing to the Lord. John, I want your example of courage and faith back in my life!

I deeply regret the last two or three years of your life. I was burnt out taking care of you and Grandma. I was emotionally stressed trying to finally deal with my past. I was not good to live with. Please forgive me! I will never be able to regain those years. You give me far too much credit for how you were. God gave you His Spirit and you chose to glorify Him in your life. You had all the reasons in the world to resent me, my demands on you, and you, of all people, saw my flaws up close and personal. But you loved me. And now that your love is gone I struggle to find my value. I regret that I did not have a servant's heart toward the end and became concerned about my needs and myself. I am so sorry my life interfered with our last days! Dad tells me that I've been hard to live with since I've been dealing with my past. I know it's true. I should have trusted you enough to share the truth of what I was going through — I'm concerned you thought my problems had to do with my care of you rather than the pain my family caused.

Do you remember the fun we had when you were a child? How you ran into your bed every night and Dad would be waiting to tuck you in. You were so filled with life, so happy, so inquisitive about your life and the world around you. As your disease got worse and Dad and I hurt for what you were experiencing then and for what we knew you would experience later, you sat back and truly enjoyed the life others were having.

You will never kiss a girl or go out on a date.
You will never marry and have children.
You will not experience the fear of Alan going off to war.
You will not be there for his wedding or know his children.
And you will be missed each and every step of the way.

Today is Valentine's Day. You never had someone care enough about you to be your valentine. Their loss!
You'll never again express yourself in a drawing.
You'll never again experience pain and rejection.
You'll never again be bullied, ignored, mistreated or threatened.
You'll never again be lonely or afraid.
You'll never again write your words of wisdom and strength and appreciation for what God has given you over what had been taken away.

John, I miss your bear hugs; they have been gone for so long. The tubes and machines along with the lack of muscle took that from us long before your life was over. I do regret I didn't hold you in my arms one more time before they took you away. I was afraid. I remember the first telethon after your birth . . . being awake at night nursing you, holding you, rejoicing over the beautiful and perfect child in my arms. I never dreamed that MDA would be a part of our lives. I want that little boy back in my arms again.

I prayed that God would let your heart stop. You made your wish so clear . . . you didn't want to be kept alive with machines any longer. Your systems stopped. Your kidney's failed. We couldn't feed you. You were always hungry because nothing stayed in your stomach. You stopped breathing on your own. The only breaths you took were from the vent. I don't know if you were aware of what was happening or not. I hope you felt our presence. We never left. We never left! I hope and pray you felt the love around you in those last days and hours. Oh John, I want to watch you and Alan enjoy each other. Oh, how I want that!

I want to know what Alan said to you that allowed you to tell me not to worry about him. I want to watch Star Trek with you and imagine what the future could really hold. I want you to explain Lord of the Rings to me. I want to read Plato and Socrates with you. I want to discuss the liberal nonsense of your professor's lectures.

A part of my heart is dead and I can't imagine it ever being revived on this side of eternity. That healing will need to wait until we see each other again. I'm so glad God's word says we will know each other again. I wish you could tell me if Pop Pop, Grandma and Grandpa are with you. I wish I knew if Friedman and you were together. What a joy that would be.

John, I don't want you forgotten. When people ask me about how many children I have I haven't known how to respond. I have two sons but now only one son. I get the feeling that I'm supposed to let go of you. I don't even want to finish this letter . . . it's as if I have to say good-bye to you again. How do I let go of the wonder of having you grow inside me when I wasn't even supposed to have a child? How do I let go of the years we spent together? How do I let go of the miracle God gave us? How do I let go when all I really want to do is hold you in my arms again?

You are now safe in your Holy Perfect Father's arms where the world and its people can no longer cause you pain. Someday we'll be together again. I look forward to that time more than I can express. But for now I'm going to try to find God's purpose for keeping me here.

Please, John, forgive all the pain I've caused you. I love you more than words will ever be able to express.

Until we meet again!

Mom

Here's what I think ~

In his wisdom, Solomon rightly notes in Proverbs 12:4 . . .

> A wife of noble character is her husband's crown.

Of course he has it exactly right. And if I may say, a *mother* of noble character is her *children's* crown as well. Allow me to take some liberty with the words, though not the spirit, of Proverbs 31 where the author observes that a noble woman, a woman like Cathy, is. . .

> Worth far more than rubies.
> Her husband and her children have full confidence in her;
> they lack nothing of value.
> She brings them good and not harm
> all the days of her life.
> She selects wool and flax
> and works with eager hands.
> She is like the merchant ships,
> bringing her food from afar.
> She gets up while it is still night;
> she provides food for her family . . . .
>
> She considers a field and buys it;
> out of her earnings she plants a vineyard.
> She sets about her work vigorously;
> her arms are strong for her tasks.
> She sees that her trading is profitable,
> and her lamp does not go out at night.
> In her hand she holds the distaff
> and grasps the spindle with her fingers.
> She opens her arms to the poor
> and extends her hands to the needy . . . .
>
> She is clothed with strength and dignity;
> she can laugh at the days to come.
> She speaks with wisdom,

> and faithful instruction is on her tongue.
> She watches over the affairs of her household
> and does not eat the bread of idleness.
> Her children arise and call her blessed;
> her husband also, and he praises her.
> "Many women do noble things,
> but you surpass them all."
> Charm is deceptive, and beauty is fleeting;
> but a woman who fears the LORD is to be praised.
> Honor her for all that her hands have done,
> and let her works bring her praise at the city gate.
>
> ~ King Lemuel
> Proverbs 31

Cathy . . . God is well pleased with you!

You have paid a great price—more profound than most were privileged to observe. A sacrifice of love and obedience, never of obligation.

> Love is patient, love is kind. It does not envy, it does not boast, it is not proud. It does not dishonor others, it is not self-seeking, it is not easily angered, it keeps no record of wrongs. Love does not delight in evil but rejoices with the truth. It always protects, always hopes, always perseveres. Love never fails . . . .
>
> ~ Paul
> 1 Corinthians 13:4-8a

And your love, Cathy, never failed John.

I would often leave our home very early in the morning. On such a morning there was a violent storm; it was raining hard, the wind was severe, and it was very dark. As I pulled away from our home I looked back through the downpour, and at 5 AM saw the lone light in the neighborhood coming from our small living room. I knew you were under that light, wrapped in your afghan, reading your Bible, praying for your sons, and so many others as you have done every day for decades. And as tears came to my eyes, I thought to myself, "could it be, at this very moment from God's perspective, that that little light might just be the brightest light in the universe?"

Cathy, you are my bride and my sister. Before all who read these words, I want to thank you and applaud you for your selflessness. You have been wife, mother, and obedient saint. You have run this long leg of your race with excellence and a great dignity. You are deeply loved.

§

You'll find nothing theologically sound about the following poem, but the author's charming imagination provides for a noble consideration nevertheless. Bombeck's verse might well have been written with my bride specifically in mind. Cathy ~ equally comfortable in the elegance of a European castle as in the rugged demands of a nineteenth century wagon train. Grace and toughness . . . buy one, get one free.

The Special Mother[1]
by Erma Bombeck

Most women become mothers by accident, some by choice, a few by social pressure and a couple by habit. This year nearly 100,000 women will become mothers of handicapped children. Did you ever wonder how these mothers are chosen? Somehow I visualize God hovering over Earth selecting his instruments for propagation with great care and deliberation. As he observes, he instructs his angels to take notes in a giant ledger.

"Armstrong, Beth; son. Patron Saint, Matthew."

"Forrest, Marjorie; daughter. Patron Saint, Cecelia."

"Rutledge, Carrie; twins. Patron Saint... give her Gerard. He's used to profanity."

Finally he passes a name to an angel and smiles. "Give her a handicapped child."

The angel is curious. "Why this one, God? She's so happy."

"Exactly," smiles God. "Could I give a handicapped child a mother who knows no laughter? That would be cruel."

"But does she have the patience?" asks the angel.

"I don't want her to have too much patience, or she'll drown in a sea of self-pity and despair. Once the shock and resentment wear off, she'll handle it."

"I watched her today. She has that sense of self and independence so rare and so necessary in a mother. You see, the child I'm going to give her has a world of its own. She has to make it live in her world, and that's not going to be easy."

"But Lord, I don't think she even believes in you."

God smiles. "No matter, I can fix that. This one is perfect. She has just enough selfishness."

The angel gasps, "Selfishness? Is that a virtue?"

God nods. "If she can't separate herself from the child occasionally, she will never survive. Yes, here is a woman whom I will bless with a child less than perfect. She doesn't know it yet, but she is to be envied. She will never take for granted a spoken word. She will never consider a step ordinary. When her child says Momma for the first time, she will be witness to a miracle, and will know it.

I will permit her to see clearly the things I see—ignorance, cruelty, prejudice—and allow her to rise above them. She will never be alone. I will be at her side every minute of every day of her life because she is doing my work as surely as she is here by my side."

"And what about her Patron Saint?" asks the angel, his pen poised in the air.

God smiles. "A mirror will suffice."

~ Love Expressed To Mom ~

John saw his mother for the faithful, godly woman she is, and made efforts to tell her so through carefully considered gifts. The following are representative poems and notes given to Cathy for special occasions throughout the years; tokens of the deep, mutual love shared between mother and son.

What Is A Mother?

Maker of the finest home,
she forms an abode

out of treasured things
that comfort and give strength
to all who enter and dwell.

Overseer of Godliness,
she teaches the love of
the Lord, and shows that
solutions to every need are
revealed in His inspired Word.

Motivator of offspring,
she molds her sons
with wisdom and truth
to nurture and protect them from
those things that would do them harm.

And you, Mom, are the best of them all.

~ ~ ~

One year, John gave Cathy a beautiful plant as a Christmas gift. It was accompanied by this poem ~

Mom,

This simple gift is meant to be a symbol
of things which go too long unsaid.
From its beginning as a tiny seedling, this
plant was cared for by loving and knowl-
edgeable hands.
Its caretaker fed it with the elements of the earth
so that it would grow into the beautiful
and unique life that it is today.
As we enjoy watching this plant grow,

we feel that it is much more than the sum
of its parts because of the one who gave
up so much of herself to give it that special quality.
And while the plant still needs care and attention,
it is a testament to its sower's greatness.
Someday this plant will only be a memory,
and there will never be another exactly
like it.
But it is the order of nature as God ordained it
that life of old bears fruit which
brings forth life anew so that life's fullness is breathed into our happy memories.
Because of your love I can be like that plant,
and you are its faithful keeper.
Whenever you water it or care for it in some
other way,
remember how much I appreciate the
wonderful mother that you are.

Love, John
December 1995

~ ~ ~

In recognition of Cathy's 50th birthday ~

Dear Mom,

The Proverbs say:
"Listen to your father who begot you.
And do not despise your mother when
she is old."

I thought about stopping with that but I realized the depth of your sense of humor might be hard to gauge on this occasion. So . . . the writer continues:

"Buy truth, and do not sell it—
Get wisdom and instruction and understanding . . .
Let your father and your mother be glad,
and let her rejoice
who gave birth to you."

Proverbs 23:22-23 & 25

I hope those words hold truth in your eyes because they do in mine. I think wise old Solomon was telling the sons in the world that their mothers are a source of "wisdom and instruction and understanding." I know that has been my experience. He instructs us that the things we learn from our mothers are so valuable that we should hoard them and never let them go. I have always believed that if I ever had a question or problem from the spiritual to the temporal, you would be a great source for finding the solution. And although we may not agree all the time, you have always been a trustworthy oracle of wisdom. I hope you take the time to think about that and accept the truth of it. A mother who loves me has set me on the right path.

Have a happy 50th birthday.
Love, John

~ ~ ~

For what he knew would be his final Mother's Day, John sent me on an errand to find a ring for his mom. Not just any ring, mind you. It was to be a pearl ring. The pearl was to be as flawless and as simple as possible. No extra gold or silver to muddy the waters, just a pure pearl in its natural beauty. A month before he died I escorted Cathy into John's room where he presented his mother with his selfless gift. It was accompanied by this note:

Dearest Mother,

No gift that I could give you could ever compare to all the gifts you have given me during the last twenty years.

Nor could any trinket ever express the full value of how thankful I am for the love you have given me.

This small attempt is intended to demonstrate my gratitude in a temporal way.

An oyster had to work very hard for a very long time to create the beauty of this pearl. In the same way, you had to work with equal devotion to help me live a life that, in hindsight, was more beautiful than I could have asked for.

I hope you cherish this ring and are reminded every day that I have become the person I am largely through your efforts. And the person I am is someone who learned to love the Lord, and will stand in His presence more beautiful than any jewel on earth.

Love, John
Mother's Day, 2002

Reflections 9. . .

"Good Night, Gracie"

A Father's Farewell

Don't cry because it's over, smile because it happened.

~ Anonymous Proverb

"ood night, Gracie"[1]

These were my last words to John every night for twenty-five years. He'd almost always grin; eyes almost always twinkle with that look that says, "I know. I love you too." I so deeply miss those moments.

When John died, many gathered to honor him and celebrate his life. From among my reflections offered that day are these thoughts, offered now as a final tribute to our son.

Thoughts On John

In an envelope plainly marked for its intended purpose, John left a clear message as to what he wanted today to be about.

From the private graveside service to this larger gathering, John's hope was that we would leave here refreshed rather than depressed, and that we'd not only know where he is, but why. It's my intent to honor his request.

When Jim Elliott preached at the funeral of his own son, he said, "God is not populating heaven just with old men." Certainly, that's true.

It's been said that "when words are most empty, tears are most apt." Many tears are being shed in sorrow; certainly that's been true for me. And while I have not been exempt from tears of loss, there are many joyful tears shed in recognition of God's sovereignty and faithfulness. He is a magnificent God, true to his Word in the finest detail. John is free.

~ ~ ~

And now, we need to understand an important truth!

Today as we mourn, John is in the presence of God! We say things like that at times like these; perhaps to deter the hurt. But on *this* day, to say that John is with God is not flippant pain relief. This is no philosophic concept; no religious tradition. This is revealed Truth.

Years ago, John asked for and received the only gift worth having.

John asked—and while his body remained vulnerable to the consequences of a fallen world, his soul became "off limits." John's affliction was overruled by the saving of his soul. Paul said, "To be absent from the body is to be present with the Lord." John is with God!

There's a scene in the movie *Apollo 13*. After a failed moon mission, the astronauts are about to try re-entry. It's extraordinarily tense at Mission Control when authoritative government officials enter the room and make their presence known. Defeated, and with his voice reflecting the fear and embarrassment of a botched mission, one official softly pronounces to no one in particular, "With the eyes of the world on us, we're about to experience America's greatest tragedy."

But the Flight Director—remember the guy in the white vest?—he overhears the language of defeat. Turning quickly, indignant and defiant, his eyes connect with those of the dignitary. "Excuse me, sir. We will *not* experience America's greatest tragedy. I believe we are about to experience America's greatest triumph!"

~ ~ ~

John has experienced his greatest triumph . . . through no fault of his own!

We often envision things—imaginary things—that make our sufferings and losses more tolerable. I believe—based not on comforting fantasy but on biblical teaching—that in those last several hours as John's body was struggling to let go on this side of eternity, that just on the other side—*in a moment of something stronger than time*—countless angels had gathered at some point of entry preparing for a joyful and enthusiastic celebration of arrival (see Hebrews 12:22-23), perhaps led by the Father himself, rising from his throne, standing enthusiastically; maybe cheering John on as a father would celebrate a child's victory at the finish line. "You can do it, John. Way to go, son! Well done, John!"

Of course, God is Spirit. He does not have a body with which to stand, and thrones are the language of metaphor. But the imagery is not without value, is it? Certainly the Creator and sustainer of life was intimately involved in the process of John's passing from one existence to another; certainly Jesus himself was there to greet John.

~ ~ ~

Today as we gather to celebrate John's life, in some supernatural and mysterious way that I cannot yet fully grasp, John—the *who* he really is—can see God. They have spiritually embraced, and John has been welcomed home.

Imagine yourself, the "Who" you really are, face to face with God: the Creator of the universe; the God who "knit you in your mother's womb;" the God who sent Jesus Christ to die on a cross for your sin. Imagine all barriers removed between you and him; unfettered love and delight in his heart for you, and in your heart for him. The Bible says that you will experience, in that moment, a wonder and awe and joy like you cannot express or imagine. And in an attempt to express the inexpressible, the writers of Scripture say this:

> You will go out in joy,
> 	and be led forth with peace;
> the mountains and hills
> 	will burst into song before you,
> and all the trees of the field
> 	will clap their hands.
>
> ~ God, through the Prophet
> Isaiah 55:12

All of creation will rejoice together in unimaginable glory and splendor. And within a not yet fully revealed forever, you will see God.[2] And as the tears come down our cheeks, that's John's reality—at the head of the parade—because of a simple but life-changing decision he made. And it was his greatest hope, and it is my greatest hope, that you will know this reality, too.

~ ~ ~

But for now, we remain here. And after we mourn for a while, we'll begin a new season with fond, priceless memories of yesterday, and life will go on abundantly. You see, this really isn't about John; it's never been about John. It's about the gift John received and held on to so tightly. It's about the precious, living God; about voluntary and intentional surrender and obedience to him. John isn't the story. John was a beautiful, captivating, precious *chapter* . . . in *God's* story.

And what a chapter he was.

I have composed my final thoughts about John innumerable times—mowing lawns, driving long, boring stretches of highway into the wee hours of the morning, in endless waiting rooms and too many ICU's, and standing at his bedside *in the middle of a thousand nights*. My every thought, fear, hope and prayer for both our boys would fill libraries.

But it was within the boundaries of simple truth that John's life was lived. And so now, at the end, it is simple truth that is required.

> Cathy, Alan, John and I have been on an exhilarating and blustery adventure.
>
> The highest highs and the lowest lows.
>
> And I wouldn't trade a moment; not a single moment.
>
> I have been taught the difference between happiness and joy.
>
> John brought me joy.

~ ~ ~

It was important to me that John not leave this world without clearly knowing my heart. These words were my gift to him on his twenty-fourth birthday:

> "John, in years gone past, you have penned words that have blessed us by expressing your love for us in creative and unique ways. Without the creative flare,

I'd like to mark the occasion of your twenty-fourth birthday by expressing my love for you.

Twenty-four years ago today I experienced joy beyond my wildest dreams. From my youth, I wanted to be someone's Dad. And there you were— taking your first breath before my eyes. Joy is about the perfect fulfillment of that for which we were created (OC). The day you were born defined joy for me.

John . . . a common name. Most dad's hope their sons will become great. Perhaps a great athlete? Maybe even a great doctor or lawyer? Well, maybe not a lawyer. But you were named remembering John the Baptist. My only dream, my earnest prayer, was that my son would grow to love Jesus—and that he might stand tall in *his* wilderness, bold in his faith, and pronounce Truth during his lifetime. My dream came true, my prayer was answered. Little did I know.

You have suffered greatly, unreasonably.
  Without hesitation, I would have traded places with you were that possible.
I am sad that you have had to bear this burden.
  I am privileged that my Father would see my son as worthy to carry such a cross.
It humbles me that you bear it with such grace and dignity.
  You understand grace . . . and surrender.
  I see Jesus every time I look into your eyes.
Fathers should teach sons. But you have taught me about Godly character.
  You have taught me about patience and perspective and inconceivable courage.

For you, life is simple . . . it's Jesus plus nothing.
Some know about God . . . you know God.
Some seek success . . . you seek the Father.
Some see you as among "the least of these."
You'll spend eternity among the first of these.

It is my great honor to be your father.

Love, Dad

~ ~ ~

Some would look at John's life and be sad at what was missed:
There would be no Bavarian castles,
His many gifts and talents would not translate into a career of significance.
No first kiss; no fatherhood.
He was asked to replace the love of a woman with the companionship of a dog.

Yet he knew no bitterness, no envy . . .
John chose wisdom before intellect,
Character before pride,
Learning before grades, and
Others before self.
His message was never about the burden of dystrophy,
It was always about the gift of grace.

Knowing him, we have been given something priceless; we have been blessed beyond reason.

And as we mourn . . . John is having the time
of his life!

~ ~ ~

I'll close with two thoughts:

When John was diagnosed twenty years ago, the doctors got a few things wrong. They told us Alan had dystrophy—until the lab called several days later to say they had confused Alan's blood with John's. They said John would live to be about sixteen years old. He lived to be twenty-five. I asked if dystrophy was painful. They said no, but John suffered beyond reason. And they told us that the highest divorce rate in our culture was among parents of terminally ill kids. They warned us, almost predicting a failed marriage. They were wrong.

But they got some things right. In the wake of John's failed back surgery nine years ago, Dr. Fry tearfully summarized the reality of Duchenne Dystrophy: "It's just a bad disease, John." This "bad disease" can make a young boy's body deformed and grotesque. It robbed John of his childhood, and just past midnight last Sunday morning, it ultimately took his life. Dystrophy is cruel.

But you should know that dystrophy is limited: There are things it cannot do:

It cannot cripple love
It cannot shatter hope
It cannot tarnish faith
It cannot atrophy peace
It cannot destroy confidence
It cannot kill friendship

It cannot erase memories
It cannot silence courage
It cannot invade the soul
It cannot abolish eternal life
It cannot quench the Spirit of God

And it cannot lessen the power and the truth of the resurrection of Jesus Christ!

And finally:

Bruce Medes writes, "Tammy Kramer was chief at the outpatient AIDS clinic at Los Angeles County Hospital. She was watching a young man who had come in one morning for his regular dose of medicine. He sat in tired silence on a high clinic stool while a new doctor at the clinic poked a needle into his arm, and without looking up at his face said, 'You're aware, aren't you, that you are not long for this world–a year at most?'

The patient stopped at Tammy's desk on his way out, his face twisted with pain and hissed, 'That *&%#@* took away my hope.'

Tammy Kramer said, 'I guess he did. Maybe it's time to find another one. Maybe it's time to find another hope.'"[3]

That's the question, isn't it? Is there another hope?

> I asked John what he wanted his memorial service to be about. He said, "Dad, that will be my last chance to tell them about the hope I have in Jesus. Tell them about my hope!"

Nearing the end of his life, John struggled with a decision only he could make. "When is enough, enough? When do I let go? When is it time to go home? What would please my Father?" Ultimately resolving his conflict he penned these words that so well describe the hope he wanted shared this day.

[These words of John's appear elsewhere in this effort. They bear repeating]

The image of letting go of something solid is just an illusion. As soon as I feel myself letting go of something solid for something ethereal, I will realize the exact opposite is the case. Reality will be unveiled; as the feeling of losing something transitory will be replaced by the firm embrace of Another. In a moment of something stronger than time I will stand with immeasurable humility and awe in the presence of the King of the universe. As His attention suddenly turns to me and just before I realize that the burden of that interest is more than I can bear, His Son will stand beside me and claim me as His own.

"And what joy will fill my heart . . ." as I finally understand that I simply had *no idea,* and could never have found the words to explain how wonderful it would be. All my cares and worries will be wiped away—like so many tears on the fingers of the scarred hand of a carpenter.

I will stand there before Him in complete comfort like I've never known and He will be the first one I will embrace with strong new arms. Or perhaps better yet, I will kneel at His feet and unload all the troubles I've carried once and for all. Others who got there ahead of me, some who knew me and some, who from afar, could not wait to meet me, will welcome me. We will join the chorus to praise the One who reunited us all with each other and Himself. And I hope, before I even know it, what we once called time will have passed on Earth, and you will join us there.

Now Many Years Later . . .

Considerable time has passed since I shared those thoughts with those who assembled to say goodbye to our boy. Other thoughts have now joined them.

I hope I will never forget that moment in time when John took his last breath. Cathy and I wept uncontrollably, unashamedly for what seemed like forever. It was more devastating than I had imagined. Yet it was cleansing, even purifying; somehow holy. How can that be?

I hope I will never forget those last few days of his life, when our faith was tested, and we found it—through no fault of our own—to be real.

I hope I will never forget John's last year. Always close, our souls meshed like never before. Maybe it was all those Sunday mornings worshiping/learning, "having church" together in his bedroom? We could express volumes with a soundless glance. How I miss that.

I hope I will never forget the sound of John's voice, or the silence of his last years. His voice was traded for the capacity to breath—his "trache" allowed air to escape the stoma in his throat before it reached a tongue anxious to express every thought; every dream, every fear and hope. We'd never again know the nuanced depths of his heart and mind, excruciatingly and unsatisfactorily "resolved" with feeble attempts to read his lips. How could we then have known that his lost voice would give birth to his written word . . . a precious and timeless gift?

I hope I will never forget his submissive courage, the capacity for wisdom beyond his years, and an innocence that never left.

I hope I will never forget his smile.

I hope I will never forget how John's life has shaped us in ways that will continue to surface throughout our days. Cathy, Alan and I were for so long the mother, the bother, and the father of the dying boy in the red wheelchair. And then he was gone.

I hope I'll never forget the observations made and the lessons learned about relationships that were so vividly influenced by the inclusion in our family of a terminally ill child. They were often beautiful; they were sometimes repulsive. We were deeply wounded and unreasonably blessed.

I hope I'll never forget how God used the bodily ruin of our first born son to better expose his own Son in so many lives; mine perhaps foremost.

> God is the eternal, independent, and self-existent Being; the Being whose purposes and actions spring from Himself, without foreign motive or influence; He who is absolute in dominion; the most pure, the most simple, the most spiritual of all essences; infinitely

> perfect; and eternally self-sufficient, needing nothing that He has made; without limit in His immensity, inconceivable in His mode of existence, and indescribable in His essence; known fully only by Himself, because an infinite mind can only be fully comprehended by itself. In a word, a Being who, from His infinite wisdom, cannot err or be deceived, and from His infinite goodness, can do nothing but what is eternally just, and right, and kind.[4]
>
> ~ Adam Clarke
> 1762-1832

Good night, Gracie

~ Love Expressed To Dad ~

My Blooming Apple Tree

My blooming apple
Tree shades me from the
Bright sun rays as
They peek through the
Tiny white flowers.

With ocean colored
Eyes, and the smile
Of a giant Blue Whale
He swims through my
Thoughts. Like a humorous
Otter, he's as funny as
Can be.

My understanding
Redwood Tree stands, straight and tall.

§

There once was an Elephant lost in the jungles deep in the land. He cried out for help and the great Lion, the King of the jungle, heard him. As He had for many others, the Lion sought out the young Elephant to point him in the direction of His inner kingdom where He lived with others who once were lost. When the Lion found the Elephant he was so happy to have been found by such a magnificent creature, beautiful even with the obvious scars on His paws.

The Elephant followed the Lion and though there were dangers along the way, he reached the Lion's sanctuary. He learned wisdom, strength, and the mysteries of the Lion as he grew in His fold. The Elephant grew so wise that others in the fold came to him for advice and learned about the Lion through him. And the Elephant had children and he led them to wisdom too. He led them by the trunk to the wonderful riches of the Lion, and they loved him for it, very much.

Happy Father's Day!
Love, John
1997

A Final Muse . . . Or Two

I have often thought the best sermons
were the ones the preacher knew he needed to hear.

Life can only be understood backwards;
but it must be lived forwards.

~ Søren Kierkegaard

We found John's final words to us in a three page letter nestled in an appropriately marked envelope. Among his thoughts were these:

> The only thing I really think about right now is my book. It is out of my hands now. But whatever you do, please remember I don't think God burdened me to write it so that it would gather dust. Even if it is never published, one way or another I meant it to be read by whoever can get their hands on it. I'll trust you to use your best judgment.

I introduced this effort with a confession that I had for a decade failed to honor John's request. I have done so now. Allow me to conclude with some miscellaneous observations.

As I consider Kierkegaard's words and reflect on the life of our boy, I've come to better grasp that John's life was principally that of a disciple, although likely not in the way we have come to understand the word. We modern evangelicals have an interesting way of thinking about discipleship. Among our readily available phrases is, "I was discipled by. . *so and so*." I've never quite known what that means. I suspect for many it says that they've attended a series of classes that taught Christian doctrine; or, maybe they learned about atonement and eternal security in a coffee shop, one-on-one; that would be good. But biblical discipleship—*apprenticeship to Jesus* as Willard has helped us better understand it—has never been about accumulation of information or adherence to standards.

The story is told that on the way out of church the pastor asked Abe Lincoln how he liked the sermon, to which Mr. Lincoln responded, "You didn't ask me to be more than I am."[1] It seems to me that the spirit of his comment should be at the heart of Christian discipleship.

Discipling done well is the life-long process of building authentic relationships with the intention of influencing people to follow Jesus. It is a dynamic process that is always changing and evolving. It is a messy, time consuming, and mysterious process that offers no guarantees.[2] In the eighteenth century John Wesley offered this observation: "It was a common saying among the Christians of the primitive church, 'The soul and the body make a man; the spirit and discipline make a Christian.'"[3] That biblical discipleship requires our sustained participation in the process is not a new thought.

§

Michael Card's life has been forever marked by his professor, mentor, and treasured friend Dr. William Lane. In *The Walk: The Life-Changing Journey Of Two Friends,* Card tells the story of how Bill invested in him as he faced the challenges of life, learning and growing in due course as the recipient of Bill's knowledge, wisdom, and capacity to care. Over time, this rich and deepening friendship shaped *both* men's lives. Perhaps that is among the essentials of true discipleship—when the student *and teacher too* are mutually open to the kind of grace manifest only in the person and life of Jesus. We will do well when we add to the concept of educational discipleship where doctrine is taught, the notion of discipling relationships where character is caught.

When Bill Lane was diagnosed with terminal cancer, he told his friend Michael, "I want to show you how a Christian man dies."[4] How much he must have loved the protégé who had become a brother. Finishing the race with integrity is something I aspire to. Michael Card had Bill Lane to model that. I had John.

§

Years ago I gave a copy of John's original *Eden* manuscript to a friend. Finished reading, my friend dared to ask the awkward. "Bruce," he said, "I couldn't help but notice that John didn't have much to say about *you* in his book."

Fathers are not supposed to learn from their children. But learn I did, and learning I am, from a Forgiver and Leader who transformed the life of a dying boy who in turn altered my heart and shapes my life still. The Sunday mornings worshipping, praying, and learning with John in the cloister of his bedroom during his final year of life fostered and culminated the kind of kinship I believe Michael and Bill enjoyed;

the kind that speaks the same language . . . the kind where no words are required.

§

John died in 2002. We sold our business in 2004, our home in 2006. In January of 2009, after too many years of growing disproportionately older and grumpier, I was most fortunate to find myself enrolled in Portland's Multnomah Biblical Seminary at age sixty . . . an experience rich beyond words. Thank you, Tom!

One rainy Sunday morning at the Pearl Church, Cathy and I sat down near Ben and Rachael, a couple of very bright Multnomah students whom I greeted as "scholars." They deflected the intended compliment, and looking at the evidence of our advancing years, noted that they'd prefer to have our wisdom than their scholarship. "Well," I said, "you know what wisdom is: Wisdom is simply living long enough to cross off all the stupid choices you've made. 'Ooops, don't do that again.'"

My life has been filled with "Ooops."
    My pride has not served me well.
    It has kept me from loving fully.
My fear has not served me well.
    It has kept me from appropriating the kind of
    joy I might have otherwise known.

Oswald Chambers wrote of joy being the perfect fulfillment of that for which we have been created. Happiness is good. Surely God himself is a happy person; how could he not be? But joy is something different. Joy in the life of the believer is deep and rich, and necessitates sacrifice, and suffering, and service, and deference to others. And when such a life is lived well, you wouldn't trade it for anything!

§

Some have asked what I learned at Multnomah. I tell them I learned a lot about "*ologies*:" theology, phenomenology, eschatology, soteriology, ecclesiology, and bibliology; but that the "ologies" were not to be outdone by the "*isms*:" universalism, pantheism, modalism, tri-theism, and gnosticsm among others. My favorites may well have been supralapsarianism and infralapsarianism—my favorites not because I adequately understood the concepts, but because being able to pronounce them seemed to justify my tuition.

At Multnomah, I learned the importance of context. In hermeneutics class, Dr. Robertson informed us that if we didn't know an answer on one of his tests, we'd do well to write down either "Jesus" or "context" and the chances were 50/50 we'd get it right. It was Dr. Davis who I first heard refer to "IBS" in his lectures. It took me awhile to figure out that he was talking about Inductive Bible Study and not Irritable Bowel Syndrome. I was, after all, sitting in a seminary classroom. Context is everything. And while it annoyed me at the time (a little hokey, I thought, for graduate school), I came to greatly appreciate Dr. Weck's relentless and demanding challenge: "What *does* the text say?!" That he would open the door to his classroom and have us yell the question at the top of our lungs so that everyone in the seminary building would know ~ something? ~ always seemed a bit sophomoric. However, as I have since matured as both a student and a teacher of the text, that query has become an important consideration now engrained in my thinking.

This was a treasured time in the wake of John's passing, the conclusion of a thirty year business career, and saying goodbye to our home that had seen so much laughter and too much death. And yet, as valued as my time at Multnomah was, the richness comes not from Multnomah as an institution, nor from having attended seminary in general.

The richness comes from having made an exclusive investment in exposure to God's Word among God's people for an extended and dedicated period of time. I am so grateful for this opportunity. In the process . . .

I have learned that God is infinitely greater than my capacity to define him.

I have learned that living in apprenticeship to Christ is never simply a matter of personal preference, but always the recognition of irrefutable truth.

I have learned that some very bright people have honest disagreement about important things, and that despite our differences it is highly likely that John Calvin and John Wesley currently co-exist quite nicely.

I have been reminded that I am entitled to one thing only: a Christless eternity. Everything else is grace.

I have learned that the temptation of relevance is always overwhelmed by the practice of prayer[5], and that spiritual maturity is almost never about being "right;" that it is almost always about the willingness to be led where I would rather not go.

I have learned yet again that the way of Christian maturity is not the way of upward mobility in which our world has invested so much, but rather the way of downward mobility—always reflected in selflessness; always ending on a cross.

I am learning that the Christian life is rooted in humility and inconspicuous service; never in prominence, never in celebrity, and that issues of purity and truthfulness are central to a life well-lived.

As one who has too often allowed reasonable judgment to morph into forbidden condemnation, I am learning that . . .

> Justice never does justice to justice; only love does justice to justice.
> Justice never does forgiveness; only love does forgiveness.[6]

I am learning again and again in fresh ways that Jesus is not a subject to be studied.

> He is not a philosophy to which we ascribe;
> Rather, he is the God to whom we surrender.
> Anything less simply misses the mark.

I am learning that Christlikeness is not about what I *don't* believe, or *won't* do, but rather about who I am, and who I am becoming. It is therefore about what I *do* believe and what I *will* do.

I have come to learn that the essential questions worth considering have little to do with theology proper, or exegesis, or world religions, or Greek grammar, or eschatology. These are wonderful, even fundamental topics to study, and I fully endorse their pursuit. However, I can be thoroughly familiar with their content . . . and not know God. There are better pursuits. They have to do with hope, and they come in the form of questions. Two come to mind:

What is the Christian gospel?

I think Jesus himself answers this best in the Gospel of Mark 1:14-15 (PAR[7]):

Jesus then came into Galilee announcing the good news from God.
"All the preliminaries have been taken care of," he said,
"and the rule of God is now accessible to everyone.
Review your plans for living
and base your life on this remarkable new opportunity."

Jesus is saying:

The kingdom of God is here—right now!
Change your ways—choices matter!
And you can be a part of it if you want to!

So, is that true? *Is it?*

Did the kingdom of God come near to very real human beings in the person of Jesus, the carpenter from Nazareth? And if it did, and if he is who he said he was, what implications does that have for my life?

Isaiah John was a nine-year-old Philipino boy who lived a few doors down from Cathy and me on the Multnomah campus. I.J. and I became friends. Saturday mornings often heard a soft knock on our apartment door. It was I.J. "Can Bruce come out and play?" I almost always did.

Whenever I'd see I.J., I'd ask him how he was doing. He would always say, "I'm nice." He was not "fine." He was never "doin' good." He was "nice." I liked his answer; I.J. *was* nice. I liked him very much. At nine years old, he had a certain sparkle in his eye, a certain contentment with his life. It was nice.

One October I found out that I.J. had never carved a jack-o'-lantern. So, with his mom's permission, I invited him to our apartment and surprised him with his very own pumpkin and the tools to carve it. I offered some guidance, but I.J. (who was "nice") was also stubborn. He decided he would carve his pumpkin his way. But he'd never carved a pumpkin before, and both his design and method had flaws. I knew that if he followed his plan, his pumpkin would look very different from what he had imagined. But I.J. could not be deterred, so he carved his pumpkin his way. And the word for that is *independence*.

So . . . what is the Christian gospel? Does it allow for independence, or does it require dependence . . . and submission to authority? Does it primarily have to do with the saying of a prayer? Or, is the gospel, and therefore the path to salvation as Christians understand it, something else? Is it possible for people to intellectually acknowledge Jesus Christ as their Lord only to be denied eternity in his presence? Is it possible for people to identify themselves with Christ, only to *trample him under foot*, *insult him*, and *treat his as unholy* (Hebrews 10:26-29) by virtue of the choices they make in the living of their lives? Is it possible that the gospel we've come to take comfort in has more depth, and requires more of us, than a simple bridge illustration would suggest?[8] And then . . .

What kind of person do I want to be?

Or maybe we could ask, "Who would I be if Jesus were living his life through me?" Our sermons tell us how to have better marriages, be better parents, and successfully manage our resources. Biblically based, certainly those issues are of value. But what question are they answering? It seems to me that answering the "Who would I be if . . ." question necessarily lends itself to issues of marriage, and parenting, and stewardship, and a whole array of issues found under the umbrella of living life well. What kind of person do I want to be? One who carves his own pumpkin, or one who joyfully submits to the model and authority of the Master pumpkin carver?

John Gilbert answered one question in light of the other.

Duchenne muscular dystrophy and all that comes with it proved no hill for this young climber. For twenty-five years we lived life deeply together. As his body failed and his faith grew, John modeled for all who would take notice the richness of abiding in Jesus (John 15), through whom all things were made (John 1:3). Though he lived every day seemingly in the darkest valley (Psalm 23:4), John regarded his disease as a light and momentary affliction (2 Corinthians 4:17) in light of the easy yoke (Matthew 11:30) that had been made available in the kingdom that had come near him (Luke 10:9).

It has come near to us as well.

John's story, *From Eden to Paradise*, is very human and all too common. While John's body readily testified to its disease, our maladies are less conspicuous, although no less devastating. "Noble on the one side, grotesque on the other," John's reality knew courage and brokenness, belly laughs and weeping, and an abundance of grace pointing faithfully to our hope in the resurrection.

Included in John's final letter to us were the following thoughts. They were meant for our eyes ~ Cathy's, Alan's, and mine. However, if you are weary and burdened, and are looking for a way to lay it all down, we are pleased to share John's expressions of love and encouragement with you, who like us, and in spite of our wealth and seeming abundance, truly are in need of great hope.

> I have thought often about this time for you. It has left me going to sleep with a few tears many nights. A part of me just wished I could fix everything you feel right now, but I know nothing I can say will do that. All I know is that even though none of us is in control, God is. I hope before too long you can gain some good perspective on what

has finally happened for me. Maybe a trip to Israel would help; you can be where Jesus was while I am where Jesus is! It isn't just a quaint saying; I really am better off now. I hope someday instead of getting angry about that you can celebrate it. I hope you can picture me not the way I left but as what I've become. Whenever you see a movie about Jesus healing a lame man, try to realize that is exactly what has happened to me in every way. This old world isn't going to have Gilbert to kick around anymore! I know you would like very much to see for yourself that this has been given to me. Someday (and I hope it is very far in the future with lots of happy healthy new family to enjoy the meantime with) you will see me, and receive it all yourself; so just be a little patient.

I love you each very much.

John.

A Word on Grief

No one ever told me that grief felt so like fear.
I am not afraid, but the sensation is like being afraid.
The same fluttering in the stomach, the same restlessness, the
yawning. I keep on swallowing.

§

Talk to me about the truth of religion and I'll listen gladly.
Talk to me about the duty of religion
and I'll listen submissively.
But don't come talking to me
about the consolations of religion
Or I shall suspect that you don't understand.

§

It is hard to have patience with people who say,
'There is no death' or 'Death doesn't matter.'
There is death!
And whatever is matters.
And whatever happens has consequences,
and it and they are irrevocable and irreversible!

~ C.S. Lewis

Good grief!
Does such a thing exist?

In the ten years John has been gone, three people have approached me with an expression of thoughtful concern regarding the death of our son. Three people have taken the initiative to say something like, "Bruce, would you like to talk about John? I'd love to listen," or "Bruce, it's been a few years now since John has passed. How you doin' with that?" Three.

I confess that this has been a sensitivity for me.

Is it true that time really does fix such things as the death of a child, and that over time expressions of interest, compassion, care and support are therefore unnecessary? No . . . that's a myth of convenience. Time can dull memories and mask realities. Time can even provide justification for being less than we might otherwise be. But time alone has no capacity to resolve or to heal.

Could it be that people simply do not care? Is their silence a message to get over it and move on? Or, is there something more fundamental at play? Could it be that such reticence to engage the wounded speaks primarily to our dulled unwillingness (perhaps to our capacity?) as a culture—and as a Church—to express our hearts? I think so. Certainly there are welcomed exceptions. But many of us, I think, have not learned to serve one another well through the process of grieving. I don't believe this is because we don't care (our hearts have not yet become *that* hard), nor do I believe it is an attempt to consciously offend. I suspect it is primarily because we are afraid.

We are quite capable of helping in a practical and immediate sense; and, we do well from the safety of distance. We are comfortable and most generous supporting unfamiliar people overwhelmed by hurricanes, and tsunamis, and famines. Good for us! And we often help from closer in . . . providing meals for families whose lives are disrupted for any number of reasons from births to deaths. Many are gifted at consoling the aged widower who has just lost the bride of his youth, or crying with the freshly abandoned young wife who didn't see it coming. But our compassion is so often limited to the moment . . . when wounds are fresh. We are less likely to invest in those whose emotional wounds are now well established. First inning empathy is a welcome gift; grieving, however, is an extra-inning ballgame. "So, how are you doing . . . really?" That is a life-giving question that brings *tremendous* comfort when spoken by a true friend long after, even years after, the crowds have disappeared. It opens the door to process—to release and relief. Such a question expressed from a sincere heart speaks volumes about living out the theme of genuine community found from Genesis to Revelation.

"*To know and be known; to understand and to be understood....*" Now well into my sixth decade, I confess to finding an increasing sense of contentment as I read and re-read the eloquent words of Dr. Gilbert Bilezikian, who expresses the deepest longings of my soul with a moving clarity I've seldom found elsewhere:

> Each one of us hides an awful secret. Buried deep within every human soul throbs a muted pain that never goes away. It is a lifelong yearning for that one love that will never be found, the languishing in our inner selves for an all-consuming intensity of intimacy that we know will never be fulfilled, a heart-need to surrender all that we are to a bond that will never fail.
>
> The silent churning at the core of our being is the tormenting need to know and to be known, to

understand and to be understood, to possess and to be possessed, to belong unconditionally and forever without fear of loss, betrayal, or rejection. It is the nostalgia for our primal oneness, the silent sorrowing for paradise lost, the age-long pursuit after the encompassing embrace for which we know we were created. It is the search, however wanton and sullied, for the pristine grace of holding and being held, for the freedom to be who we really are without shame or pretense, for release and repose in the womb-like safety of unalterable acceptance and of overarching love.

When we take time to become silent and to listen, we may hear the scream from the depths of our being, the clamor to bare our souls and to reveal the mystery of our true selves. Just listen, listen closely. . . . It is the distant echo of the wail in the garden at the loss of innocence, of the grieving after a remembrance of shared freedom, of the release of body and soul to the embrace of absolute oneness.

Our mourning is for the closeness that was ours by right of creation. Our grief is for the gift lost in the turmoil of rebellion. And now, whenever there is hope, our hope is for paradise regained, for human destiny remade in the redemptive restoration of community, the only certainty of oneness for here and for eternity.[1]

§

May I commend three excellent books on grief: one on the process of dealing with grief and two works by men who have lost their children to sudden death. These writings are of value both to those who find themselves mourning as well as to those who desire to better understand how to provide comfort—"So how are you doing . . . really?"

The Grief Recovery Handbook[2] is authored by John James and Russell Friedman, both of whom write from the experience of loss. Their effort is light on philosophy and long on awareness and applicable process. It has been said that while grace is opposed to merit—you can't earn it—it is not opposed to effort.[3] I think it equally wise to acknowledge that while mourning and grief are perfectly normal and natural reactions to loss, recovery through and from grief is also not opposed to effort. In fact, effort is required.

If you were to Google "grieving gorilla," you would find the story of Gana, a then eleven year old female gorilla at Muenster Zoo in northern Germany. The gallery of photos records Gana mourning the loss of her three-month old son Claudio as she holds tightly to his limp dead body. Look in her eyes. You will see profound grief and a determination to protect, even though her son is gone. The baby's body can only be recovered by zoo attendants when the mother leaves it behind. Gana must be allowed to *process this loss on her own terms and in her own time* . . . and so must we.

§

Retired Yale professor Nicholas Wolterstorff is among our nation's foremost philosophers and a committed Christian. He lost his twenty-five year old son Eric to an Austrian mountain climbing accident. In the wake of his tragedy he responded with *lament* flowing out of the overwhelming grief for a deceased child. Twelve years after Eric's death, Dr. Wolterstorff decided to voice his grief. He has written *Lament for a Son*, "in the hope that some of those who sit beside us on the mourning bench for children would find my words giving voice to their own honoring and grieving."[4]

Henri Nouwen said of Dr. Wolterstorff's writing,

> *Lament for a Son* is a simple, honest, and poignant expression of one man's grief, but it is more. By sharing the depths of his grief, not in trite phrases but honestly, Nicholas Wolterstorff helps open the flood-gates for those who cannot articulate their pain. . . . This little book is a true gift to those who grieve and those who, in love, reach out to comfort. Wolterstorff's words are, indeed, 'salve on our wounds.' Thank God he did not remain silent.[5]

I so resonate with the writing of Dr. Wolterstorff. Though his intellect is immeasurably beyond my own, his grief is not. In *Lament* he wrote . . .

> Death is the great leveler, so our writers have always told us. Of course they are right. But they have neglected to mention the uniqueness of each death—and the solitude of suffering which accompanies that uniqueness. We say, "I know how you are feeling." But we don't.[6]

§

John Terveen, professor of Greek and New Testament studies at Multnomah Biblical Seminary, lost his fourteen-year-old daughter Rachel, who died from a fatal heart attack during a late-afternoon track practice at her middle school. In the wake of this horrific tragedy this father has responded with *hope* stemming from the comfort and wise counsel of Scripture. He has written *Hope For The Brokenhearted*[7], a moving effort that reveals how only God can truly heal us in the wake of such a devastating loss. Dr. Terveen offers a careful biblical analysis of such topics as heaven, guilt, doubt, and anger by asking difficult questions and probing the responses only a compassionate Lord can provide.

In *Hope* Dr. Terveen relays a tender story that says much about being emotionally near and personally accessible.

> Recently our pastor told the story of a little boy who had a wonderful relationship with an old grandfatherly neighbor. The two became good friends. One day the old man's wife passed away, and the little boy told his father that he was going over to see his elderly friend, so he did. Later, upon returning from his visit, his father asked the little boy what he had said to the old man. The little boy quietly replied, "Oh, I didn't say anything. I just helped him cry."
>
> What a beautiful picture of love—being emotionally present and personally available.[8]

Drs. Wolterstorff and Terveen ~

In reply to the enemy death, one man responds with *lament* but not without hope, while another with *hope* but not without lament.

To know and be known, to understand and to be understood... indeed.

Noticing

God weeps with us
so that we may one day laugh with him.[9]

~ Jürgen Moltmann

A significant component of grief is the overwhelming sense of being alone—knowing that no one else can appreciate my circumstances, nor do they care about them. Perhaps an expression of love in the form of *noticing* offers some degree of support and comfort. And while such solace may well be only temporary, it can offer a muster seed of hope, a cherished treasure to the grieving.

The Lady in Safeway . . .

Sometime after John died I was in a local grocery store waiting patiently in line with my few items, doing my best to look somewhere other than the magazine rack to my left. I couldn't help but notice a woman entering the store just in front of the checkout booths where I was standing. With one hand she was pushing a wheelchair, with the other pulling a grocery basket - all the while wrestling with an automatic door that sequentially wanted to close first on the chair, then her, then the cart. The grocery cart was as yet empty. The wheelchair was not, accommodating a teenage boy, presumably her son.

Over the years I've become more and more aware of, and sensitive to, what I believe to be promptings from the Holy Spirit. Such was the case in the checkout line. Upon seeing the woman and her son awkwardly negotiating the uncooperative door, I felt immediately compelled to connect with her.

Paying for my milk and bread I made a U-turn back into the store, searching for her, first one isle, then another. What would I say when I found her? I had no idea, but the draw was tangible.

And then, there she was—in front of the canned fruit, still awkwardly managing both her son and a now half full cart.

"Excuse me," I said. "You look like you've got your hands full. Would you like some help?"

Now I was closer than before. Now I could see in her eyes and posture that life had been hard. Her son was probably about sixteen and clearly very sick. Without looking up and going about her business this burdened forty-something woman muttered, "Nope. Been doin' this a long time."

"I'd really like to help," I said. "Any chance you'd trust me to hang out with your son in the front of the store while you finished up?"

Her silence suggested I should go away. But for whatever reason, I did not. I stood quietly nearby for a few uncomfortable moments. And then she looked up at me, her protective detachment now sensing connection and daring hope. With a gently affirming nod of her head and a new calmness in her voice, she confirmed to herself, "You know, don't you."

"Yes," I responded as tenderly as I knew how. "I know."

And now her countenance began to soften. It was as if she began to morph into the someone she had once been, where laughter lived and hope was fresh. The furrowed brow released its stress; the hunched shoulders relaxed and stood a bit taller; the sense of burden and anger began to dissipate—at least a little bit.

Without warning she said, "Your son is dead, isn't he."

"Yes, he is," I said. "And it would give me great pleasure to sit awhile with your son while you finished up your shopping."

And then with a presence and demeanor that clearly reflected someone who was no longer alone, she said this remarkable thing:

"No, thank you, really. It's enough just that you noticed."

I'm not sure what to think about "kindred spirits." I don't know much about how one person connects with another through nothing more sophisticated than a glance. But apparently that is adequate. Apparently, for those of us deeply wounded and feeling very much alone, someone *simply noticing*—though it may well offer no lasting resolution—can be enough, at least in the moment.

Chico State's Flag

A short time after John died we received a notice from the administration of Chico State University where John had attended, with excellence I might add. They had become aware of John's passing and wanted to honor his memory by flying the American flag at half-mast. How thoughtful; very nice, indeed.

Chico State enjoys a stunningly beautiful campus. Old brick buildings are buffered by manicured lawns, colorful gardens, and quaint bridges crossing Little Chico Creek babbling through the university grounds. And of course there are the trees—stately elm, majestic redwood, American chestnut, California sycamore—many well over a century old.

It was in the midst of those trees that I planted myself at about dawn on the appointed day. Equipped with only lawn chair and Bible I planned to spend the day, and so I did.

I first noticed it within just an hour or so of the flag having been raised to its appropriate height. Students, staff, and administrators all arriving to begin their days, many walking within feet of the dominant flag pole; but no one was looking up. No one seemed to notice that the flag was at haft-mast.

The day wore on and what I thought curious and temporary earlier in the morning had now become conspicuous. Although a memo had been sent to faculty and staff, and students had seen notices on corkboards throughout campus explaining the reason for the flag's status, no one of the thousands passing by bothered to look up. No on stopped to contemplate John's life. No one shed a tear in his memory. I felt alone and hurt. Something of great value to me was being ignored.

"Why am I the only one here?"
"Don't they know how special he was!?"
"Why doesn't anyone care about my son!?"

In the early evening a couple from the neighborhood, likely in their fifties, was enjoying a nice summer's eve stroll through campus. From where I had been since sunup, I couldn't help but overhear the woman say,

"Oh look, the flag's at half-mast. I wonder who died?"

"Oh, yeah," her husband replied. "I didn't see anything on the news. It must not have been anyone important."

I was crushed.

But . . . not unlike so much of what disappoints us in this life, the man's comment, his honest observation, was not without value.

It almost immediately occurred to me that while I was deeply cut by what the man had said, I was not the first to have been wounded by indifference. God the Father had also lost a Son—a sacrifice of monumental significance—and for two thousand years and counting too few notice. Jesus is everywhere conspicuous, just like the dominant but all too familiar flag pole positioned in a high traffic area *for the expressed purpose* of being noticed; yet all too few look up. Though, as that memorable day wore on with an excruciating sluggishness, I was hurt that busy lives could not pause for even a moment of reflection, how much greater must the Father grieve at the reality that for so many of us, *his* Son is not worthy, not simply to be noticed, but to be worshipped?

EMBRACING GRIEF

I suppose grief is the emotion that derails us like no other. It is the dream turned tragedy; the sucker punch we do not see coming. Grief is more than sobering; it is sapping, debilitating, and in its midst it undermines hope. It's easy to get lost here.

Dave and Bonnie Lambert serve with Cadence International, having dedicated themselves to sharing the gospel and their lives with the military community. Death is no stranger when you serve the military. But this phone call brought its horror closer than most.. . .

> "My heart aches tonight in ways it never was created to ache. We received word that our good friend's only child was killed fighting as a Marine in Afghanistan. He was due home in three short weeks and I was going to have the honor of officiating his and Britney's wedding in July.
>
> We have many questions but have to rest in the fact that he had a relationship with the Lord and is in Eternity with his Savior. We are so proud of you Keaton. Thank you for laying down your life so that we can live free."[10]

Later, Dave would say that he could hardly catch his breath through the tears he shared with Bonnie and their daughter Katie.

A Marine dog handler always leads the way. It was their task, Keaton and his exceptional K-9 Denny, to detect IED's, those wicked instruments of death, thereby protecting those troops in their wake. It was in that service to his country that Keaton had taken a sniper's bullet just days before returning home to marry his sweetheart. Dave was to have performed the ceremony; now he would be officiating at Keaton's memorial service.

§

What is real when someone dies? What does reality come to look like for the deceased, and for those of us who remain and ache like Dave and Bonnie? I never knew Keaton, but I know the Lambert's grief. I've never met Grant and Inger, Keaton's parents, but I know their horror. Because of Christ's work on the cross, death is a defeated enemy. And yet, in our humanness, death retains its ability to haunt us like little else.

When I first heard Dave's initial expression of grief, "*My heart aches tonight in ways it never was created to ache,*" I thought I fully understood the cry of his heart. There are times we experience a woundedness we never thought possible. Later, however, I found myself wondering if what he said was really true—that our hearts were not created to ache *like this*.

And I thought, what if our hearts were designed to ache *exactly like this*! I wondered if it's not these seasons of overwhelming grief and mourning when we best understand and are most perfectly aligned with *God's heart*... the Father who sent and sacrificed *his* son in response to *his* aching. I wondered if it's at times like this when we are most conspicuously in his image, and therefore most alive? Could it be that at times like this our very best option is to embrace the anguish that has its talons embedded so deeply in our souls? Could it be true that without this embrace, without this kind of ownership in the *imago Dei*, that our capacity for compassion and urgency for the gospel is diminished? Could it be that embracing the agony of devastating personal loss is, perhaps, our best chance for wholeness to be like our Creator?

After Keaton's memorial service, Dave helped me to better understand his initial reaction to his friend's death. On hearing the news that night, Dave's heart ached "*in ways it never was created to ache,*" not because it was never designed to hurt, but because it was never conceived to say goodbye! What a beautiful thought! How wise! While I was sensitive to what God must have experienced as he turned his back on the Son who had become sin for you and me, Dave was sensitive to God's heart in eternity past. *In the beginning* when YAHWEH created men and women in his image, the jewel of his creative energies, it was for the purpose of uninterrupted community, the kind of *oneness* Gilbert Bilezikian writes of so majestically above. We were never designed to say goodbye. Thanks, Dave.

§

"Come to me," Jesus pled, "and I will give you rest for your souls." Could it be that this kind of peace, that which is found only in Jesus' arms, is found best in the process of grieving well? What if the best response to grief and mourning is more readily available than we think? What if emotional wellbeing, spiritual health, and hope in the midst of a broken heart revolves not around the managing of grief, but in the embracing of it?

Easy Yoke . . . Really?

And if there is comfort to be found in the embrace of grief, exactly how does one go about actually finding it?

A young man I care about was recently given some advice by a Christian leader. The topic was "living the Christian life," and the advisor said:

"If it's easy, you're probably not doing it right."

And I thought to myself, "That's exactly wrong!"

I understand that we've come to think that way, to live that way. But if the advisor's statement is true, what do we do with the apostle's teaching when he says, "In fact, *this* is love for God: to keep his commands. *And his commands are not burdensome*, for everyone born of God overcomes the world" (1 John 5:3-4, emphasis mine). And what do we do with the words of Jesus himself found in Mathew's Gospel (11:28-30) where the Lord calls out, seemingly to anyone who will listen,

> Come to me, all you who are weary and burdened, and I will give you rest. Take my yoke upon you and learn from me, for I am gentle and humble in heart, and you will find rest for your souls. For my yoke is easy and my burden is light.

Jesus is imploring. There is a *pleading* in his voice.

"*Come to me!*"

So in light of this plea, this invitation to come and drink from apparently readily available and abundant streams of living water, are we right to understand the Christian life as a perpetual up-hill climb? It's been said that "spirituality wrongly pursued or understood is a major source of human misery and rebellion against God."[11] Could it be that, "If it's *easy*, you're probably not doing it right," is spiritually wrongly pursued?

"Come to me . . ."

This is the tender call to intimacy with the Son of God for all of us who are just exhausted by the living of life, and all of us who are overwhelmed with unbearably heavy loads we don't know how or where to put down. This is an invitation to not just know *about Jesus*, but to become his apprentice, his friend, his brother, his child—and to find a rest in him that can be found nowhere else.

"Take my yoke . . ."

This yoke was not the wooden harness that joined two oxen so that they could pull weighty cargoes with more ease. Nor was it the metaphorical yoke of 1st century Judaism that referenced the Law or the crushing oppression of foreign governments.

Jesus' invitation was different. His offered yoke was a metaphor for discipleship with him, for apprenticeship under the Master Teacher of life. It remains an invitation that promises rest from weariness and burden because it is grounded in nothing less than a personal and intimate relationship with the Son of God—a relationship that both assumes and requires commitment, even covenant, on the part of the disciple.[12]

Jesus does not cause grief to disappear any more than he himself did not escape the challenges of human life. Illness, and calamity, and loss, and woundedness remain a part of this fallen world. But for those who live in the kingdom that has come near, there is a promise—not that Jesus will protect us *from* grief, but that he will sustain us *through* grief—as we receive his offered yoke.

Maybe we deem the Christian life "hard" because we've entered relationship with Jesus for the wrong reasons? Could it be that recognizing our sin, we are really more *sorry* than we are repentant? Could it be that some of us have created a *hard* yoke because we've not yet come to recognize that apprenticeship to Jesus is not essentially a religious obligation? Could it be that following Jesus is not simply *hard*, it is *impossible* (and therefore impossibly frustrating) when we attempt to do it in our own power and consistent with our own agenda?

In *The Easy Yoke*, Douglas Webster writes this:

> His [*Jesus'*] easy yoke is neither cheap nor convenient. The surprising promise of the easy yoke was meant to free us from a self-serving, meritorious, performance-based religion. It is easy in that it frees us from the burden of self-centeredness; liberates us from the load of self-righteousness; and frees us to live in the way that God intended us to live. . . . The easy yoke sounds like an oxymoron. Plowing a field or pulling a load is hard work! And nowhere does Jesus promise soft ground for tilling or level paths for bearing the load. What he does promise is a relationship with Himself. The demands are great but the relationship with Jesus makes the burden light.[13]

And then there is this wisdom from the pen of Eugene Peterson who points out that faith in God invariably encounters difficult challenge—even harsh tribulation—throughout the pages of Scripture. Jesus was right: we will know trouble in this life (John 16:33). Children die; that *is* hard. However . . . included in Jesus' instruction regarding effective prayer is this request of the Father: "Lead us not into temptation, but deliver us from evil." It is clearly not a petition that trouble be eliminated, but that we be protected from sinful attitudes and behaviors (pride—something to prove, and fear—something to lose) as we live life in a Genesis 3 kind of world. That prayer is answered every day, Peterson notes, in the lives of those who walk by faith. He reminds us of Paul's words to the troubled and immoral Corinthian church: "No test or temptation that comes your way is beyond the course of what others have had to face. All you need to remember is that God will never let you down; he'll never let you be pushed past your limit; he'll always be there to help you come through it" (1 Corinthians 10:13, THE MESSAGE). Then with refreshingly bold exhortation, Peterson holds us to account, not as defeated sinners saved by grace but fighting a relentless up-hill battle, but as princes and princesses (with their inherent privilege *and* responsibility) in the kingdom that has come near in the person of Jesus:

> Three times in Psalm 121 God is referred to by the personal name Yahweh, translated as GOD. Eight times he is described as the *guardian*, or as the one who guards. He is not an impersonal executive giving orders from on high; he is present help every step of the way we travel. *Do you think the way to tell the story of the Christian journey is to describe its trials and tribulations? It is not. It is to name and to describe God who preserves, accompanies and rules us.*[14] (Emphasis mine)

The yoke Jesus offers *really is* easy and light. But there is a condition. His yoke does not mysteriously appear when we "say the prayer." Rather, weariness is trumped by hope and burdens lose their oppressive nature consistent with the genuineness of our submission to Christ's authority as we faithfully pursue his character—the process of a lifetime. Such character is not obtained by any means other than full immersion in kingdom living; that is, an intentional and consistent investment in not only "falling in love with Jesus," but in actually living our lives consistent with what he taught and how he modeled life to be lived. We might call this being spiritual formed in the likeness of Christ. So, the Sermon on the Mount and the Twenty-Third Psalm become not merely heart-warming but unreasonable visions; rather they become actual blueprints for living to which we become unvaryingly committed. We invest ourselves in owning passages of Scripture like Philippians 2-4, the Disciple's Prayer found in Matthew 6, Romans 8, Colossians 3, Ephesians 4-5, and similar texts for the purpose of living life as Jesus would live it were he me. And while many believe that actually becoming like Jesus in character and life belongs largely in the category of "wouldn't it be nice, but . . .," I believe that becoming like Jesus in character and the living of life as he modeled has never been an impossible dream from the perspective of Jesus himself. Speaking of Jesus, Willard notes:

> He invites us to leave our burdensome ways of heavy labor—especially the "religious" ones—and step into the yoke of training with him. This is a way of gentleness and lowliness, a way of soul rest. It is a way of inner transformation that proves pulling his load and carrying his burden *with him* to be a life that is easy and light (Matthew 11:28-30). The perceived distance and difficulty of entering fully into the divine world and its life is due entirely to *our failure to understand that "the way in" is the way of pervasive inner transformation and to our failure to take the small steps that quietly and certainly lead to it.*[15]

I believe living in the "Way,"[16] under God's rule and reign, is the antidote to grief—and sorrow, and loneliness, and joylessness. It has always been an attainable *expectation* for those who choose to be his child. And, in the coming of the kingdom, and the inauguration of the New Covenant in the person of Jesus, God's Spirit provides the same strength to carry *our* load that Jesus himself relied on to carry *his* load—all the way to his cross.

"*Come to me, all you who are weary and burdened . . .*"

All you who are grieving loss!
All you who face life-threatening disease.
All you who have dead children.

All you who are exhausted from trying so hard to earn a living, or make someone else happy, or get religion right.

Jesus says, "*. . . I will give you rest,*"

> "Take my yoke upon you and learn from me, for I am gentle and humble in heart, and you will find rest for your souls. For my yoke is easy and my burden is light."

Our world says, "Try harder!"
Sometimes in our churches we hear, "Try harder!"

"If it's *easy*, you're probably not doing it right."

But when it comes to finding comfort in the bitter realities of grief, when it comes to living in the kingdom that has come near in the person of Jesus—in his love, under his grace, invested in those disciplines that lead to his character—perhaps the better understanding is ~

If it's *hard*, maybe we're not doing it right.

If it's *hard*, maybe we've misunderstood the gospel.

With Gratitude

I am truly grateful to Pamela Cubas, whose final and required nudge led to the fulfillment of my promise to John.

It's been said that good authors write first with their heart, and only then with their head. While John did both well in the writing of *Eden*, I required considerable help with the latter in the formulation of *Reflections*. I am especially grateful to Randy Dunn and Paige Gilbert for reading transcripts and offering guidance. I am further indebted to Jenna Christophersen, whose personal and interactive investment—and consequent ownership—in this project proved to be more than equal to her considerable editing talents. Randy, Paige, and Jenna—this effort is substantially more readable because of your generous and selfless contributions. Thank you.

~ ~ ~

This book and the lives it reflects have been marked by many wonderful people, who over the years have been our friends, touched our lives, shaped our thinking, and filled us up. To the many beyond those noted below who are highly and equally valued, and on behalf of the Gilbert family, please accept our heartfelt gratitude.

> We love Janiece Wiley; thank you, friend. Chronologically suited to be John's grandmother, spiritually suited to be his sister—like Jesus, you found John and met his deepest needs. Everyone should be loved by someone like you; you ooze everything good about being good.

We are forever grateful to Al and Elsa Gilbert, and Manny and Doris Canepa, for deeply loving us and our sons . . . gone now, never forgotten, always honored.

From among the many who have graced our lives, we are particularly appreciative of . . .

Ken and Eva Needham for more than this space can accommodate. You have been mentors, teachers, pruners, and models for much of what is important in life. Moreover, you have offered *yourselves*, even from oceans away, providing a sense of oneness, perspective and hope that has both served us well in this life and prepared us well for the next.

John and Pat Law for giving themselves to our family in extraordinary ways, and then giving more. You have loved our boys as if your own.

Kathy Machuga for modeling the gift of presence, and for being the sister Cathy always dreamed of having.

Linda Beadle for listening to John in his later years when he most needed to be heard. That he trusted you with his heart speaks volumes about who you are.

Kim Hernandez, long-time confidant who knows such loss all too well.

Tom and Jennifer Miles for a prized bond and a shared dream. Though you did not know John, you do know us.

Calvin Blom for teaching me well, slowing me down, and broadening my perspectives. You have taught and modeled the transformed life for many; many are grateful.

Dave Workman for friendship in the midst of challenge.

Dick Thorp for representing everything good about medicine.

Ted Faris, Bill Fontana, and Wes Mudge for giving me freedom to be with my wife and children in the most critical years; a generous and treasured gift indeed.

The MDA Family—Mike Crandall, Royal Courtain, Nita McCarron, Stan Atkinson, Margaret Pelly Larson, Dino Corbin, Steve Sorensen and countless medical professionals and selfless volunteers—you have mattered greatly.

And of course . . .

My love to Cathy with whom I am equally
and forever yoked to our Savior.
My love to Alan who has so often put a
smile on *all* of our faces, and to
Paige who loves him dearly.

And to Sydney—my prayer is that one day you will pick up an old dusty copy of this effort and come to know your Uncle John. More importantly, that you will one day join him.

Finally, *Reflections* are offered with gratitude to and recognition of John Ortberg and Dallas Willard whose reasoned insights I have come to so highly value over the years. Cathy and I have been richly blessed by your wisdom as we have sat invisibly at your feet. Thank you for gracefully challenging us to think.

Grateful to one and all,
and on behalf of my bride,

Bruce Gilbert

Endnotes

FRONT MATTER

1. Paul Grand, *Blessed Are The Uncool; Living Authentically in a World of Show* (Downers Grove: InterVarsity Press, 2006).

EDEN 3 ~ CHILDHOOD

1. "Old Weird Harold" is a boyhood character often referenced by Bill Cosby in his stand-up comedy routines.

EDEN 5 ~ PAST THE TIME OF INNOCENCE

1. The Book of Job, found in the Old Testament, is the story of Job, his trials at the hands of Satan, his discussions with friends regarding the origins and nature of his suffering his challenge to god, and finally a response from God.

EDEN 6 ~ "PEOPLE SAY I'M BRAVE, BUT I DON'T SEE IT THAT WAY"

1. Dean Martin and Jerry Lewis were named Muscular Dystrophy Association National Co-Chairmen in 1952, hosting several Telethons together. After a successful 1956 Telethon (Martin's last), Lewis was named the organizations National Chairman, a voluntary position he would hold for fifty-five years. Lewis continues hosting the annual MDA Labor Day Telethon to this day.
2. The Muscular Dystrophy Association (MDA) is the nonprofit health agency dedicated to curing muscular dystrophy, ALS and related diseases by funding worldwide research. The Association also provides

comprehensive health care and support services, advocacy and education.

EDEN 8 ~ RED TAILED HAWKS, DEER CREEK . . . AND FRIEDMAN

1. Canine Companions for Independence (CCI) is a non-profit organization that enhances the lives of people with disabilities by providing highly trained assistance dogs and ongoing support to ensure quality partnerships. Headquartered in Santa Rosa, CA, CCI is the largest non-profit provider of assistance dogs, and is recognized worldwide for the excellence of its dogs, and the quality and longevity of the matches it makes between dogs and people. The result is a life full of increased independence and loving companionship.

EDEN 9 ~ FUN IS GOOD

Epigraph: Dr. Seuss, *Oh, the Places You'll Go!* (New York: Random House Children's Books, 1960).

EDEN 10 ~ PURGATORY

Epigraph: John Ortberg, *Everybody's Normal Till You Get To Know Them* (Grand Rapids: Zondervan, 2003), 197.

EDEN 11 ~ DEATH IS REAL ~ DEATH IS NEAR

Epigraph: *How Firm A Foundation.* Author uncertain although some attribute to "Keen", 1787, alt. Composer: Bernhard Schumacher, 1931.

EDEN 12 ~ "WOULD YOU MIND IF I RAMBLE FOR A WHILE?"

1. A tracheotomy is a surgical procedure intended to enhance breathing. The surgeon first makes an incision in the skin of the lower part of the neck that lies over the trachea. The neck muscles are separated and the thyroid gland, which overlies the trachea, is usually cut down the middle. The surgeon identifies the rings of cartilage that make up the trachea and cuts into the tough walls. Plastic banana shaped tubing called an inner and outer cannula is then inserted through the opening. These tubes act like a windpipe and allow the person to breathe. In John's case a mechanical ventilator was then attached to the cannula to bring oxygen to the lungs. That device was often disconnected so we could remove secretions continuously building up in his lungs.

EDEN 13 ~ WHEN PEACE LIKE A RIVER

Epigraph: Dallas Willard, *The Great Omission: Reclaiming Jesus's Essential Teachings on Discipleship* (San Francisco: HarperCollins, 2006), 11.

REFLECTIONS ~ FROM MY PERSPECTIVE

Epigraph: Madelein L'Engle, *An Acceptable Time* (New York: Square Fish, 1989), 275.

1. Bill Hull, *Christlike: The Pursuit of Uncomplicated Obedience* (Colorado Springs: NavPress, 2010), 36.
2. Duchenne muscular dystrophy (DMD) is a recessive X-linked form of muscular dystrophy, resulting in muscle degeneration, difficulty walking, breathing, and ultimately death. The disorder is caused by a mutation in the dystrophin gene, located in humans on the X chromosome. Females typically carry the defective gene, males typically manifest the disease. Approximately 1 in every 3,600 boys is born with this killer. Symptoms usually appear in young boys before age five. Early signs include enlarged calf and deltoid muscles, low endurance, and difficulties in standing alone or climbing stairs. As the condition progresses, muscle tissue begins to waste away and is eventually replaced by fat and fibrotic tissue. John wore leg braces by age seven and was in his first manual wheelchair by age ten. Later symptoms typically include abnormal bone development like (the human body is not designed to grow well in the sitting position) that lead to skeletal deformities, in John's case curvature of the spine (scoliosis). Progressive muscle deterioration means loss of movement and increased dependence. Occasionally Duchenne boys suffer from some degree of intellectual impairment . . . thankfully John was spared this trial. We were told John would live to be about sixteen. The current average life expectancy for patients afflicted with DMD is around 25—exactly John's age at death.
3. C.S. Lewis, *Mere Christianity* (San Francisco: HarperCollins, 1952, Copyright renewed 1980, 2001), 196.
4. See Deuteronomy 28

REFLECTIONS 1 ~ EARLY DAYS

1. Giovanni Francesco di Pietro di Bernardone, *The Writings of St. Francis of Assisi*, trans. Paschal Robinson, [1905], at sacred-texts.com, (Accessed April 19, 2012).
2. Dietrich Bonhoeffer, *The Cost of Discipleshi*p (New York: McMillan, 1963), 88-89. Addition mine.

3. Ibid., 171.
4. President Harry S. Truman, recognizing the responsibility inherent in the presidency, was noted for saying, "The buck stops here!"
5. Creatine phosphokinase (CPK) is an enzyme found mainly in the heart, brain, and skeletal muscle. An elevated level of CPK is among the indicators of Duchenne muscular dystrophy.
6. Karl Barth quoted in Kenneth Leech, *True Prayer* (San Francisco: Harper & Row, 1980), 68.

REFLECTIONS 2 ~ A DREADED FIRST

1. Public domain.

REFLECTIONS 3 ~ IT'S NOT EASY BEING GREEN

Epigraph: *"Bein' Green"* Music and Lyrics by Joe Raposo

1. John Ortberg, "*Doing Justice*": A message on Micah 6 presented to the New Community, Willow Creek Community Church, 2002.
2. Michael Card, *Luke; The Gospel of Amazement* (Downers Grove, IL: InterVarsity Press, 2011), 29.
3. Used with the permission of Karynn Law

REFLECTIONS 4 ~ IT'S JUST A BAD DISEASE, JOHN

Epigraph: Oswald Chambers. *My Utmost for His Highest.* (Westwood, NJ: Barbour and Company, Inc., 1935), 337.

1. Judith Viorst, *Alexander and the Terrible, Horrible, No Good, Very Bad Day.* (New York: Atheneum Books for Young Readers; an imprint of Simon & Schuster Children's Publishing Division, 2003), 27.
2. Image of God, commonly referred to by the Latin phrase *imago De.*
3. Michael Card, *The Hidden Face of God; Finding the Missing Door to the Father Through Lament* (Colorado Springs: NavPress, 2007), 19.
3. Ibid., 176.
4. *Les Miserables.* The stage musical based on the novel *Les Miserables* by Victor Hugo. Music and lyrics by French composer Claude-Michel Schonberg, with English lyrics by Herbert Kretzmer.

REFLECTIONS 5 ~ WHAT IF IT'S NOT ABOUT JOHN?

1. Chambers, *My Utmost*, 65.
2. A.W. Tozer, *The Pursuit of God* (Camp Hill, PA: Christian Publications, Inc., 1982), 17-18.
3. Used with permission of Glenn Doney
4. Used with the permission of Aaron Cain.

5. Dan G. McCartney, *Why Does It Have To Hurt?* (Phillipsburg, NJ: P&R Publishing, 1998), 7.
6. *Shadowlands*. Written by William Nicholson (screenplay and play); directed by Richard Attenborough, 1993.
7. Ibid.
8. Chambers, *My Utmost*, 223.
9. *Shadowlands*.
10. Larry Crabb, *Shattered Dreams* (Colorado Springs: WaterBrook Press, 2001), 35.
11. Teresa of Avila, *The Interior Castle* (New York: Paulist, 1979).
12. Kieran Kavanaugh, ed., *John of the Cross: Selected Writings* (New York: Paulist, 1987).
13. Philip Yancey, *Disappointment With God* (New York: Walker & Company, 1988), 260-61.
14. Ibid.
15. Philip Yancey, *Prayer; Does It Make Any Difference?* (Grand Rapids: Zondervan, 2006), 117-18.
16. Eugene Peterson, *A Long Obedience in the Same Direction* (Downers Grove, IL: InterVarsity Press, 1980), 64.
17. Charles Colson, "My Soul's Dark Night," *Christianity Today*, December 2005, The Back Page.
18. Ibid.
19. Dallas Willard, *The Divine Conspiracy; Rediscovering Our Hidden Life In God* (San Francisco: Harper, 1998), 384-85.

REFLECTIONS 6 ~ THE WOUNDED INNOCENT

1. The inclusion of this chapter and its content is offered with the permission of Alan Gilbert.
2. Gary Moon. *Apprenticeship With Jesus*. (Grand Rapids: Baker Books, 2009), 95-96.
3. Charles Swindoll is a prominent evangelical Christian pastor, author, and educator.

REFLECTIONS 7 ~ "NOW JOHN KNOWS"

Epigraph 1: Bruce Gilbert

Epigraph 2: Dietrich Bonhoeffer, in a letter from Hugh Falconer to Gerhard Leibholz, October 1945, quoted in Eric Metaxas, *Bonhoeffer* (Nashville: Thomas Nelson, 2010), 517.

Epigraph 3: Dietrich Bonhoeffer, from a sermon delivered in London, November 1933, quoted in Eric Metaxas, *Bonhoeffer* (Nashville: Thomas Nelson, 2010), 517.

1. Used with the permission of Ken Needham.
2. *Shadowlands*.
3. Ibid.
4. C.S. Lewis, *The Weight of Glory* (San Francisco: Harper Collins, 1949), 1.
5. Dallas Willard, *The Spirit of the Disciplines* (San Francisco: Harper Collins, 1988), 258.
6. Ray Stedman, *Talking To My Father (*Portland, OR: Multnomah Press, 1975), 96ff.
7. *Soviet Cosmonauts,* http://www.apologeticspress.org/, 1963, p. D7. (Accessed May 7, 2012).
8. N.T. Wright, *Surprised By Hope* (New York: Harper Collins, 2008), 171ff.
9. Lewis, *Weight of Glory,* 9
10. For an insightful perspective on this subject, see David Needham's *Birthright; Christian, Do You Know Who You Are?* (Portland, OR: Multnomah Press, 1979).
11. Willard, *Divine Conspiracy*, 385-86.
12. *What A Day It Will Be*. Music and lyrics by Greg Furguson. Ever Devoted Music (ASCAP), 1996.
13. Ortberg, *Everybody's Normal*, 219-234.
14. Arthur O. Roberts, *Exploring Heaven: What Great Christian Thinkers Tell Us About Our Afterlife with God* (San Francisco: Harper Collins, 2003).

REFLECTIONS 8 ~ A MOTHER'S FAREWELL

Epigraph: Erma Bombeck. http://www.raskys.com/erma.html, Accessed 26 May, 2012.

1. Erma Bombeck, *Special Mother*, http://www.our-kids.org/archives/special_mother.html, Accessed 26 May, 2012.

REFLECTIONS 9 ~ "GOOD NIGHT, GRACIE"

Epigraph: Likely an anonymous proverb, this quote is sometimes attributed to Gabriel García Márquez, in Spanish: "No llores porque ya se terminó... sonríe, porque sucedió."

1. "Say Good Night, Gracie" The legendary closing line of George Burns to Gracie Allen, born of their vaudeville routine and carried over into both radio and television.
2. As I write these words, I know they are not my own. Through the years I have absorbed the passionate teachings of John Ortberg on such matters, and so acknowledge him here.

3. The Tammy Kramer story is attributed to Bruce Medes in a sermon entitled, "*Desperate for Ultimate Hope*" by Dr. Bruce Tippit, Pastor of First Baptist Church, Jonesboro, Arkansas on February 27, 2005.
4. Adam Clarke, *Commentary on the Whole Bible,* Vol. 1, 1810-1826 (Albany: AGES Digital Library, 1997), Accessed 28, 2012, 9.

A FINAL MUSE . . . OR TWO

Epigraph: Søren Kierkegaard in, Michael Strawser. *Both/And: Reading Kierkegaard: from Irony to Edification* (New York: Fordham University Press, 1997), 148.

Epigraph: Bruce Gilbert

1. Abraham Lincoln. http://www.brainyquote.com/quotes/authors/a/abraham_lincoln_4.html. (Accessed April 6, 2012).
2. Thank you Dr. Calvin Blom! Associate Professor of Spiritual Formation, Multnomah Biblical Seminary; Head Pastor, Battle Ground Baptist Church, Battle Ground, WA.
3. John Wesley, sermon on "Causes of the Inefficacy of Christianity," in his *Sermons on Several Occasions*, 2 vols. (New York: Waugh & Mason, 1836), 1:437.
4. Michael Card, *The Walk; The Life-Changing Journey of Two Friends* (Grand Rapids: Discovery House Publishers, 2006), 109-111.
5. Henri Nouwen. *In the Name of Jesus; Reflections On Christian Leadership* (New York: Crossroad Publishing Company), 1989, 27.
6. Dallas Willard, Ministry in Contemporary Culture Seminar at the George Fox Evangelical Seminary, September, 2008. Additional reference: *Knowing Christ Today: Why We Can Trust Spiritual Knowledge* (New York: HarperCollins, 2009), 83.
7. Willard, *Divine Conspiracy*, 15.
8. May I recommend Alan Stanley's, *Salvation Is More Complicated Than You Think* (Colorado Springs: Authentic Publishing, 2007) for an intelligent and biblically founded discussion regarding salvation: what it is, what it is not. Stanley would argue that what is being said today concerning salvation, though not wrong, is incomplete. I concur, and believe it to be the critical issue before the church today.

A WORD ON GRIEF

Epigraph 1: C.S. Lewis, *A Grief Observed* (San Francisco: HarperCollins, 1961, restored 1996, C.S. Lewis Pte. Ltd.), 3

Epigraph 2: Ibid., 25.

Epigraph 3: Ibid., 15.

1. Gilbert Bilezikian, *Community 101; Reclaiming the Local Church as Community of Oneness* (Grand Rapids: Zondervan, 1997), 15-16.
2. John W. James and Russell Friedman, *The Grief Recovery Handbook; The Action Program for Moving Beyond Death, Divorce, and Other Losses* (New York: Harper Perennial, 1998).
3. Dallas Willard, "*Live Life To The Full*" in *Christian Herald* (U.K.), April 14, 2001.
4. Nicholas Wolterstorff, *Lament For A Son* (Grand Rapids: Eerdmans, 1987), 5.
5. Henri Nouwen, in Wolterstorff's *Lament*, back cover.
6. Ibid., 25.
7. John Terveen, *Hope for the Brokenhearted* (Colorado Springs: Victor, 2006).
8. Terveen, *Hope*, 111-112.
9. Jürgen Moltmann, *God in Creation: A New Theology of Creation and the Spirit of God* (New York: Harper & Row, 1985).
10. Used by permission of Dave Lambert
11. Willard, *Spirit of the Disciplines*, 81.
12. Michael J. Wilkins, *The NIV Application Commentary: Matthew* (Grand Rapids: Zondervan, 2004), 422-24.
13. Douglas Webster, *The Easy* Yoke (Colorado Springs: NavPress, 1995), 8, 14.
14. Peterson, *A Long Obedience*, 42-43.
15. Dallas Willard, *Renovation of the Heart* (Colorado Springs: NavPress, 2002), 10.
16. The "Way" is likely the earliest term by which the followers of Jesus Christ referred to themselves. Jesus said "I am the way, the truth and the life" (John 14.6). The Apostle Paul said "I worship the God of our fathers as a follower of the Way" (Acts 24.14).

CPSIA information can be obtained at www.ICGtesting.com
Printed in the USA
LVOW08s0757061213

364065LV00001B/6/P

9 781624 192869